NIGHT KEEPING

MELISSA PEARSON

Published in Australia by
Rising House
Postal: PO Box 165 Springvale Victoria Australia 3171
Email: risinghouse@optusnet.com.au
Website: melissapearson.com.au

First published in Australia 2017
Copyright © Melissa Pearson 2017

All rights reserved. No part of this publication may be reproduced, stored in a retrieval system, or transmitted, in any form or by any means without the prior written permission of the publisher, nor be otherwise circulated in any form of binding or cover other than that in which it is published and without a similar condition being imposed on the subsequent purchaser.

 A catalogue record for this book is available from the National Library of Australia

National Library of Australia Cataloguing Publication entry

Creator: Pearson, Melissa author.
Title: Night Keeping/Melissa Pearson.
ISBN: 978-0-6480802-0-6 (paperback)
Subjects: Lighthouse keepers—Tasmania.
           Lighthouses—Tasmania.
           Families—Tasmania.
           Betrayal.
           Deception.
           Murder.
           Survival.

Cover artistry by L1Graphics
Cover layout and design by L1Graphics
Typesetting by Nelly Murariu, PixBeeDesign.com
Printed by IngramSpark

Disclaimer
All care has been taken in the preparation of the information herein, but no responsibility can be accepted by the publisher or author for any damages, resulting from the misinterpretation of this work. All contact details given in this book were current at the time of publication, but are subject to change.

The advice given in this book is based on the experience of the individuals. Professionals should be consulted for individual problems. The author and publisher shall not be responsible for any person with regard to any loss or damage caused directly or indirectly by the information in this book.

I would like to acknowledge the traditional owners of the lands of the Tasman Peninsula the Pydairrerme people and Seaford the Boonerwrung and Bunurong People And pay respect to their elders past, present and emerging.

I would like to acknowledge the traditional owners of the lands of the Tasman Peninsula – the Pydairrerme People; and Seaford – the Boonerwrung and Bunurong People. And pay respect to their Elders past, present and emerging.

I dedicate this to the women who
are my auntie's – you are everywhere.
To children born from women like my
mum – we are everywhere.
To men who are unheard – may your voices sing.
I ultimately dedicate this to the truth and raising it.
For us to rise too.

In consideration of the lives these events affected – those living and those deceased – Night Keeping has been written with respect and in honor to the truth.

The accounts and details have been presented with knowledge and research available at the time of writing. The events are based on the truth, but to protect the reputation, privacy, and well-being of those involved, names and identities have been altered.

It should also be noted:

The way one person feels may differ to those of another. That is certainly the case in this story. It is the position of the author not to dismiss or discredit anyone's account of their experience of the events portrayed in Night Keeping. I have listened without judgment and accepted as truth what has been described to me from the individual's memory. The following pages are filled with a composition of factual accreditation material and independent sourcing.

Where authentication cannot be carried out, it is accepted that readers will interpret their own findings. There is enough material to provide sufficient calculations and understanding. We have all experienced misinterpretation or denial when it comes to our word or our version of life. This story allows you to make your own decisions, just as the world does. Accept or ignore as you see fit.

But the story is told with faith, and it is suggested you read it as such.

To forget one's ancestors is to be a brook without
a source, a tree without a root.
~ Chinese proverb ~

You can't forget something you never knew. And now, I know.

PREFACE

I recall the day Melissa and I first met. It was over twenty years ago, and fate wove our paths together in a way for which I'm truly grateful. We were drawn together by a mutual passion for human endeavor and had both signed up to complete a master's degree in Sport Psychology.

On the surface, we seemed quite different, but as we got to know each other, we realized our foundational life philosophies are very similar. We can always count on each other for an alternative perspective, and I am so grateful for Melissa's friendship and belief in me.

This book is the culmination of many years of research and a lifetime of pain that Melissa has endured due to inheriting the family patterns of her predecessors.

The process of writing this book has been cathartic for Melissa. Drawing on an enormous amount of inner courage, she has shed many tears of frustration and pain as she penned these stories and imagined what it would have been like for the characters. Her imagination didn't have to stretch too far, however. Melissa has personally experienced too many similar events in her own life: abuse, denial, and cover-ups. During the creation of some particularly challenging chapters, there were days when she was unable to function as she processed the heaviness of the pain the characters inflicted on each other. Her own family members. Coming to terms with betrayal and witnessing the darkest side of human behavior was a huge burden.

But as she wrote and expressed, she healed. Without question, the value Melissa holds in the highest regard is truth. If Melissa were to have a personal motto it would be: 'The truth will set you free.'

Melissa was determined to convey her family's truth, which has been denied and swept under the carpet for too long. In doing so, she has set herself free. Consequently, she has paved a new path for her children, and for their children...

Another significant part of Melissa's motivation to tell her family's story was to share and bring to light universal human experiences that we all bear: vulnerability, shame, guilt and, in the end, forgiveness. These emotions are rarely discussed. If we are to move toward our ultimate goal of living from a place of love, we need to acknowledge the part these emotions play in determining our behavior and our life's path. May this book be a catalyst for you to heal your past hurts and live a life full of joy and love.

I genuinely wish that every reader of this book will be able to draw parallels from this story to their own ancestral history. The details may be similar, or they may be very different. I invite you to uncover any patterns that are playing out in your life that you've inherited via your DNA from generations before you—and that are not actually yours. It is with this awareness that you can start breaking those cycles and consciously choose a new path for you, your children, and your extended family. I encourage you to seek assistance from a therapist or practitioner to guide you through your healing process.

This planet is in dire need of many more people like Melissa. May she inspire you to find the courage to break free from the mold and walk your own path to make the world a better place, as she has. I sincerely hope this book becomes a significant part of your journey to doing just that: living your life on your own terms.

Stephanie Kakris

INTRODUCTION

One of the most commonly asked questions about *Night Keeping* will probably be: How much of it is true?

I can answer that for you: there is as much truth in here as I found. All the characters and significant events are true. They occurred. There are vast amounts of information available in the public historical record. I had conversations with people affected by these situations; they were many and were forthcoming with their recollections. I immediately and thoroughly took notes upon having these conversations to capture details and reference points for clarity. There are minor additions that express how someone may have been feeling to afford substance of insight. Psychoanalytical explanation takes its part, as does common sense articulation. This has all been done to provide context to the reader. I have also exercised my right to speculate on the stated outcome by suggesting that 'there are matters that are based on the truth.' This has been a measure of protection as this story is one of contention, and not all agree with its findings. The unfolding story is powered by the truth, not by what I manufactured. It's here you'll feel it.

Names have been changed as have some locations, but what has not been changed is that this story's destiny is predominantly set in Tasman Island, Tasmania, Australia. This identity is unchangeable, as to do so would subvert the story's essence of truth. And that I cannot and will not do. No longer will I withhold revelations, and I reject anyone's appeal for me to do so, no matter the reason. The island has secrets; secrets humans have kept. You will find them here.

This story took fifty years to surface, for the voices have been too scared. The carnage collected people and their courage in a collaboration of silence through the generations, unspoken until two turned to each other and said yes, we'll do it for fairness. For once and for all, we'll put peace and being to rest.

On the basis of genuinely caring, this is a life's account.

When the Night Keepers were watching out for others, who was watching out for them? No one, even though they, too, needed watching.

There was no protection from their infection, and that is only going to lead to a historical tale that's in need of a thorough correction.

Here it is, sorry for the wait; it took a while to release its courage from the chained gate.

CONTENTS

Take That, Her Fear	1
Central Role of All Things	11
Time to Find	23
He Was Hers	53
Bad Penny Brothers	77
Country Victoria Unearths a Hidden Gem	101
Then Along Came Another Man Called Phillip	111
Finding the Link and Following Him	123
Lighthouse Keeping—Who Said Isolation Is Only for the Incarcerated?	137
Man Left Behind	147
Plan Keeper Plan: Tick tock	155
Run Children Run: Time's Up	171
Arrival from a Departure	193
Does a Broken Man Mend?	215
First Try—Stranger Denied	221
Universe Plays a Hand	233
Two Shots Fired	253
Life after Death	275
Go On: It Does	297
New Year Carrying Cold Deaths and Old Habits	303
Dirty Man Stalking	319
Escape That, Her Life	329
To Summon on the Strongest Note	335
A Parting Share	365
Acknowlegments	366
About the Author	367

TAKE THAT, HER FEAR

As she sat there, rigid, she didn't know Kristen was cementing a memory in me. Pouring her undoing into me. I was around ten years old when it happened, and it doesn't move, the memory, just like she wouldn't move that night.

Nothing could have gained access to her state; it was too late. She was stone cold, frozen to fear. Recollections are crystal to the clear; it was Mother Dear whose true self appeared. Overtaken by internal cries she was rotten; to what inside her could not be forgotten.

By generational definition we became her victims from a lifetime of her victimization. It was apparent our mother was losing it. She was my first sight of disturbed. Tonight, in her performance of 'help me not,' was of course my initiation of 'one day I will.' Why did she behave in such a way? The short answer: her past had never left her. But to a ten-year-old's eye, there was no comprehension of how her mother was filled with such torrential lies.

Kristen's pierced in pieces this night, and fright isn't the explanation. Terror and irrational reaction is her truth, and to escape this maze, she uses me and him to serve as cover.

'Him' is my brother of a younger, and to this day – over thirty-plus years since – we've never sat and talked about this with our mother. She'd deny it anyway. Like that night, there's nothing she'd allow us to say.

This wasn't just a one-off. This was one in a series of behaving questionably, but this one... this was most definitely the most impactful.

Her behavior had perplexed me, and I never did receive an explanation. Not one. Well, not one that was plausible or offered of account. It was either 'it didn't happen', or denial's friend, 'that's not what happened'. And to be perfectly transparent, nothing of clarity was presented. There wasn't a choice or a chance to be or seek something different, it was 'put up with this' because that was what I was born into. What choice was there?

Difference came when I grew up and chose to face the 'why.'

To begin, an explanation.

I had to discover what I was searching for—she wasn't about to tell me. She still hasn't. What I've found came via investigation, research, and listening to people who would talk to me. For if I attempted to converse with her she would tell me: "I'm the one who lived through it, so stay out of it."

To that, I reply, "So did I."

I didn't see it as the personal massacre she did, but we each had our own version of the truth, yet she was the conductor.

I'll take you through the orchestra; see if you hear what we feel.

Through my middle childhood to early adolescence, it was all about packing the SUV and attached ski boat with camping equipment, then traveling to the river along the state border to water ski and simply exist. This occurred for every possible holiday that could be taken. When not integrated into all things tent, it was school, cross-country running, homework, chores, friends, Little Athletics, push bikes, and ice cream. There was Nana and Pa, skateboards, Fleetwood Mac, HR Puff'n'Stuff, The Banana Splits, motorbikes, Atari, playing footy and Blue Light discos. But for Easter, Christmas, and long weekends, it was camp by the river for weeks on end.

The group my parents belonged to consisted of regular school and social sporting-club friends and acquaintances. We had been going to this particular spot on the river as a group for the past five years or so. With most of the adults having had children, they all continued to holiday together. It was quite a tight group, and the families had loads of fun.

This night was no different. Skiing done for the day, boats and equipment packed up, dinners cooked and eaten, the congregation around the bonfire at the center of the site was in full swing. Each night the campers would come together and discuss all sorts of topics. Debates were heated and filled with laughter. There was always an alcoholic drink in someone's hand, and the kids would watch them get drunk. Some adults would fall asleep in their chairs. Some sang in assistance to guitar fumbling, while others were just comfortable to sit and relax and stare into the fire.

We children loved this time of night, because initially we would sit and listen and be a part of it and when it reached a boring point, we would race around the area playing 'What's The Time Mr. Wolf' or 'Murder in the Dark' or 'Hide and Seek.' No telephones, televisions or computers—just humans interacting.

It was the camp next to ours that changed everything and gave me an experience I have never been able to forget. This is quite possibly a blessing, as it was also the catalyst that presented me with an insight that, at the time, I did not fully understand.

An elderly man and his young Asian bride, who were city neighbors of camp regulars JJ and his wife Cheryl, had joined us at the river this particular year. The couple had come to a fierce and violent disagreement. The young bride had fled into the night, running into the surrounding bushland to protect herself from harm.

We, of course, were totally unaware of her desperate bid to escape. To our group, the evening was moving along as per normal. It wasn't until the two adolescent sons of the elderly man ran over to our camp, puffing, and standing in obvious fear. They stood at the fire circle and asked if any of us had seen their step-mum run through here. They wanted to find her before their dad did.

No one had seen the woman. We had heard the yelling and screaming but nothing that raised concerns — men and women yelling had been heard before. It was then that the older man appeared. Brandishing a rifle, he walked right through our camp, yelling the woman's name and telling her he was going to find her and kill her.

He disappeared over the small embankment and headed toward the bush where, we assumed, she would have fled. He fired off a few shots into the air. No one had a chance to react. We, the observers of actions foreign to our lands, just sat there unaltered.

Everyone just watched him in amazement, with no real concern.

As the shots echoed into the night sky, I was yanked from of my chair. Before I knew it, my brother and I were in our tent. We had been dragged forcefully away from the circle of fire without any comprehension as to why. Three empty seats sat as witness to our departure, while in our tent we were being served our own set of orders.

"Get to bed and go to sleep," was the command issued by our mother. No explanation, no change into pajamas, just shut in the sleeping compartment of the tent and the zip zipped closed. That was seriously it. Frog marched, shoved in, exit access denied, verbal communication silenced.

My brother and I—in shock from her actions, not the old man's—sat in the dark, baffled. We didn't understand the threat; we were just innocent kids. We sat in the dark, listening to voices yelling in the distance, and the fire of gunshots. We were aware of what was going on, but we were not scared. I thought it was just a stupid old drunk man who wasn't really going to do any harm. In my world, there was no way a man was going to shoot someone else. My mother's world, though, was completely different. But we had no idea what her world was like or what she had seen. We were sitting in our world and it had suddenly become quite weird.

The night was barely old, and it was not time to sleep. There were more stories to listen to as the adults entertained us that evening around the fire.

It was my idea to leave the tent and rejoin the circle. We were the only ones who had been removed, and I wanted to be back out there with everybody else. Others were still out there having fun. I don't know where our dad was during all this. What was he doing while our mother was being a problem? At this point, I should say that our mother and father do not drink alcohol. Mum, out of personal distaste, and Dad because mum gave him the ultimatum: stop your drinking or goodbye. So, no alcohol or drugs affected this evening's behavior.

In the tent in the darkness, I began to open the zip when suddenly we heard her voice snap, "Get to bed."

We were shocked she was still there. We had thought her long gone. My brother and I quickly put ourselves in our beds. Now we were terrified. What was she doing still here? Where was she exactly? We were being barked at, and while our mother had snapped at us before, this was quite something else.

We then waited for what seemed like long enough for a second escape attempt. There were no more yells from the bush, nor gunshots ringing off. The situation was well sorted and rested. The laughter and relaxation from the fire circle was well in jest.

This time, I was able to unzip the door, and we walked through the kitchen area toward the front flap of the tent—

"Get back to bed and stay there."

We both jumped, startled. She scared us so completely that we froze. The dictator had barked orders and we, the feeble servants, were caught on the spot. We readied ourselves for a final blow even though we didn't know from where it would come.

The entire scenario was absurd. We were just two gorgeous, well-mannered kids trying to free ourselves from something we didn't understand because it wasn't understandable. Standing there, I began peering through the shadows looking for her. I found her squashed between the round, yellow plastic bin and the quarter-sized camping fridge. Knees pulled up to her chin, she had her arms wrapped around her legs as if to make herself smaller.

Frightened by the vision of my mother resembling something not quite right, I returned to the sleeping area with my brother, and we soon fell asleep. Not a word has been spoken of this event.

Ever.

But I can still see her.

The following day it was all sunshine and skiing. The old man, his wife, and his sons went home. Friendly waves bidding them farewell. Like last night hadn't happened. Think nothing of it.

My mother was gone from behind the bin and the cover of the fridge, but she never explained a thing. According to her, it never happened. Not then. Not now.

It's baffling that something so stark in your memory, something you experienced goes acknowledged, not spoken of, not dealt with. You're left exacerbated. But it happened. Why did you do that to us?

I can only imagine how my mother, Kristen, was feeling that night because she wouldn't care to admit it. Not to you or me, or any Jiminy up a tree. In fact, she would go to lengths to discredit this account and erase it with one swoop of: "No it didn't."

It didn't happen.

To support her claim, she would recruit her son and husband, and then blame me with talk of nonsense and making things up again. Nothing's changed; she's singing her same tune. I've heard the playlist; it's full of tricks. It's her truth, because that's what she knew and how she herself grew.

What she doesn't see is that every time she speaks, she is explaining what she herself did for her own protection. She is explaining her own behavior.

For my own part, I am not good at inventing fictional characters. I could not make up such tales; at that I would certainly fail. I am only able to write truths. It is what I can do. I ask questions and summarize in an attempt to understand. I also make requests that memory offers me as little falsehoods as possible. For as clear as it can seem to be, memory can alter itself. Thus, I take into consideration that I may not know exactly what happened. I must do it this way because it is the safest most honest option. It is evidenced in the behavior of where I come from, and I am quite clear to all, that I rely on it.

There was no dialogue during my development about certain occurrences, and we were not advised of goings-on at all. My role model lacked the capacity to speak freely. I have lived with a massive hole of not understanding for most of my life. This isn't the only unexplained or unacknowledged action of my parents—there is an age of them. As an adult, free of control or harm by the people who raised me, I set about to mend the hole for myself, and the only way to do that was to hunt for answers, to investigate.

So that's what I did.

Today, I comprehend the terror she would have been reliving from that night. The flashbacks and the pain jolting through her would have been immense. She panicked—understandably so—and in her reactionary mind, did the right thing by protecting her young.

But she was also protecting herself. From her fears mainly, and you can now see the hold they had on her. She was being strangled by her past, no doubt. She was the only one who acted like she was out of breath. There were only three chairs vacant in the fire circle. My mother's decision dictated that. So, this was about her.

She had not sought professional assistance regarding her past, and she was suffering from irrational anxiety. The old man had no interest in her or my brother and me. He walked straight past us. She could see that, but her subconscious struck down any grasp of sense and whacked her out. No man, no gun, no bullet. Her own system psychologically fired at her. She was a weapon unto herself.

When I say we went through it too, I'm talking about this style of living. We weren't aware of her past at all. She didn't even tell us about her todays. She didn't tell us what was happening for her on any given day, let alone explain why she had us live this way—like this, like we did. We are the fallout from the explosion. She probably still can't see that because in her mind 'they' (my mother and her sisters) went through it. No one else.

I have heard this larking display and watched the full-body mannerisms that align with the declaration. There is a certain aspect of ownership they guard like a trophy. It seems warped to me, but it's not hard to see. If you talk to my mother or her sisters you will hear: "It happened to us, not you." That's ownership. It is truth, but its bold ownership first.

That stems from a sense of irrational title. Yes, it was a big deal in their lives. It was an occurrence that mattered, but at the time they did not receive the nurturing required, nor did they go through the healing process. Over their lifetimes, this has grown inside them— they have ignored themselves as others did. It was what they were taught. No healing had been done.

It is hard for them to quell a need to own and be owned by this distinct occurrence in their life. Hence, time that has passed has brought sternness toward the matter. Because that is the way with which it was dealt. Tragedies bring forth notoriety and attention, and there is an ownership worth acknowledging in that too.

Their feelings, their pain, their denied existence, their teaching or the reason for their eradication of empathy…will anyone hear them? The cries are their own.

From my point of view, this is, in truth, a sad story about a woman who lives through fear. It is even sadder that she experienced it first-hand. We weren't supposed to know it, and I wouldn't had I not endeavored to find out. The fact was at that time of her life, when she was hovering behind a fridge and bin, she was already a broken woman. She had experienced forms of physical and psychological abuse long before I was even delivered.

My question is: did we have a chance? My brother and I, did we stand a chance?

She didn't when she was born, and I can tell you why.

This is what happened to her and her tribe.

They didn't have a chance either.

CENTRAL ROLE OF ALL THINGS

PEARL JOYCE

Born: May 23, 1924. Beaconsfield, Tasmania.
Died: December 13, 1985. Frankston, Victoria.

Married:
David Smith, 1944. Beaconsfield, Tasmania.
Harrison Bennet, 1950. De-facto relationship. Tasmania.
Phillip Harper, 1959. Launceston, moved to Melbourne.
Hadley McDonald, 1965. Melbourne, moved to Tasmania.

Children:
First born male: Unknown (adopted).
Kendall Anne: December 25, 1950.
Kristen Nelly: July 26, 1952.
Kate Louise: December 16, 1953.
Kylie Tasma: May 4, 1955.

Occupation: Home keeping

She was someone else's before I knew her. She always was. I met her that way; she was forty-six years old when she first held my hand. Came and met me at birth. On that occasion, I became her worth and she in time was to be mine, but I couldn't tell you the age I was when I understood her to be my Nana.

That's what she was, how the sequence of life fitted us. I was her "Sparkling Kid" and she, it turns out, a caring ghost who carried far more than I could hope to understand in the moments I hung out with her. For she had many ghosts in her closet of shut-and-shunt-away life. With all the things I have discovered, it's a pity I cannot talk to her now.

From my discoveries, it seems Pearl was always someone's, and what a shame that has been. As you gather the history of a life and contextually place it—write it down—you can't possibly fathom its velocity, but it's there between the letters, the gaps that hold the words. It's all there; you just have to read beneath; read in, out, and under the time line. And there lies the truthful account. She is what happened; the story revolves around her. She doesn't exactly dance in the middle of it, more like spins with her head barely moving to see beyond the horizon. She didn't live open-armed and freely. She gripped firmly, just to be able to breathe.

As the child of light in her life, I wasn't expected to comprehend the enormous gaps Pearl had in her life, but what I could do was interpret moods and environments. I knew nothing of what was going on with my nana. I would suggest I still don't know all that happened to her, but as I grew up around her, I certainly felt her lay-low days and the 'leave-her-alone' ways.

I have vivid memories of her, and I declare they are fond ones. She didn't hurt me because she had no cause; I gave her no reason. I was one of the ones who unconditionally loved her back.

She didn't say much, and she wasn't heavy-handed, but you knew not to be naughty around her. I wasn't that way inclined, so we perhaps developed as a match. She was quiet and preferred to be alone rather than with others. She was the true definition of a loner, albeit always with a man by her side. And for as much as I remember her sadness, I can still see her smile. She was thinly built and drawn in her character. I knew her as this, and you don't wander in search for why or even grasp conclusions as to how that would be. You just play near her and say thank you when she hands you your favorite cola-flavored lollipop.

She would often tell me that she didn't really like people, but she liked children. That just made me feel even safer in her company. I was never in danger of harm when with her. And she and I spent enough time together for harm to get me if she wasn't guarding my innocence. But she was, and that part she got right. I am more than grateful for this because she didn't get to protect everyone.

Over the course of growing up, I often overheard it mentioned by adult voices that she was a grump. That was true. There be no lies here for you. She was a little cross—or to be blatant, a lot—and that was because she wasn't just sad inside, she was gutted.

Although this wasn't always the case. When around me she was often lovely, soft, delicate, and sincere. Maybe because I was her favorite grandchild, and probably because I spent the most time with her. To her I was polite, helpful, quietly-spoken, and possibly only one of the two or three humans she could trust in her life. Why and how she saw me as worthy of trust is because I trusted her. And this woman had a well-refined deceit detector... Or did she? She allowed two men to enter her life and desecrate it. In fact, she often didn't trust you before she met you.

She found it hard to trust herself and others; a riddled body of loss and torment had captured that capacity long before I breathed. To come close to her and then have her love you was a reflection of who *you* were, who I am. I passed her approval test over and over, and in telling her story here I have promised her I will do so again. But I have warned her spirit that as I locate misgiving behavior I will call her on it—adult to adult.

What I'll raise up front: she had good reason to not really like people. Her life was like an explosion of pain after an eruption of ache. That is unfortunate in and of itself. The way she dealt with how people treated her created a ripple effect that would touch us all, even today. To be true, she was as extraordinary as she was wrong. She was taken to places not many would be able to see, let alone look at. She answered herself at night and it's a given she didn't hear herself too well, but what she did is what she knew—she can never be taken down for that. She wasn't vindictive, nor did she seek vengeance. Aside from all the hurt in her heart, there was only love.

There was a game I used to like to play at her home—the home she settled into at the caravan park after years of running and hiding. She had a substantial collection of fifty-cent coins. It was worth something to her, and this something she let me play with. Only because she knew that the same weight would be returned to the jar after it was tipped out all over her floor.

I wouldn't steal any of them and I never did. She knew that.

I just used to play stack on stack or count them and I did so with these coins because she cherished them. And I guess as a kid I thought if I was allowed to be with them, I was cherished by my nana. And if I was cherished by her, then just maybe I would be cherished by my mum. Because my mum adored her mum, always had. That's one of the reasons I spent so much time with them. It was a three-generation interaction and I remember it very well. I would sit in the caravan on the floor, planning out my lines of coins while they sat in the annex, chatting over cups of tea.

I didn't retain all their chats. I can't imagine they opened up about the times she had loved four men. Or detailed what the love triangle was about. There was one man my mum possibly didn't know existed—David Smith, her mum's first husband. But she did know the other three: Harrison Bennet, her own dad; Phillip Harper, Pearls second husband but third love; and Hadley McDonald, the fourth love. Those men were no longer around to say hello to me or to pick me up and swirl me around in the air as I would have liked should we have lived together as grandfather and granddaughter. I didn't get the chance for that. However, the fourth was well alive; he was the man I grew to know as 'Pop,' but I don't ever recall him swirling me around in the air with laughter, as I can picture my biological and first step-grandfather caring to do. In discovering what I know now of him, I am glad Pop didn't. He was probably warned never to go near me, and he didn't. He never hurt me, but others he certainly abused.

This entire complex situation has many a moment of confusion. In both understanding and telling.

I would spend time in the late-1970s with Nana and Pop in Tasmania, and that was where Nana and I developed our strong bond. From around six years of age, I can see myself in her home. I recall bundling over Bass Strait during the school holidays to arrive in at the miniscule, isolated town of Derby. My time in Tasmania with Nana was as near solitary as her lighthouse-keeping days. The home was modest, and the games I played were from my own making. On the steps at the front of the home lived blue bottled bull ants. They were big, horribly ugly things with a bite that would have me screaming in pain—possibly where I learnt the expression of tantrums, because the sting on the foot would have me stomping around the stair path in rigorous expression.

My enemy—the ants—were distinct in that they had very shiny blue behinds, and these critters and I were at war. I would spend much time herding them about the pavement and smashing them with the various sticks I travelled the lands with. There were no children to play with, no animals of domestic or paddock stock to flock with, so it was ants or nothing. When I wasn't killing ants—such an endearing trait—I was pretending to be Huckleberry Finn along the Brycee River that ran through town. I actually did think I was him. I would make rafts out of large-logged limbs and wade through the shallows making up adventures as best my innocence could craft.

When that had run its course, I would go to the tin mine opening and play in the creeks stones and pockets of foliage. I am not sure how I wasn't bitten by a snake or cut my feet deep, as I was bare-hoofed all the time. I collected shiny blue stones for hours; I filled old glass peanut butter jars with them, cleaned the pebbles up, put clear water in the full jar and watched, transfixed, as I slowly span the jar in my hand.

I wasn't a bother to my nana at all.

She had one friend. I remember because we would go and see them at the bottom of the hill, but I do not recall anything of them.

There were two channels available on the television: the commercial station—channel nine—which was of no use to me as I did not bond with the character Humphrey B. Bear, who was speechless and annoying to my young and adventurous concentration span. Other shows were completely void of my interest, which left the remaining station—channel two, the government programmed one. Nothing there for me at that age, so it was outside or with Nana.

One time, I was possibly learning about chores and we were in an outside area doing linen washing. I got my arm caught in the rolling pins of the washing machine. I do remember crying and my nana saving me. I still grease off those ancient machines when I see them in antique stores, even though the whole incident was possibly my entire fault.

NIGHT KEEPING

She had, at some point, bought me two miniature rabbits that were plastic toys that I could play with in the bath. I also remember playing with them in my bedroom. I still have them.

That was generally how I spent all my time in Tasmania.

It is timely to mention here that nothing sinister happened to me in Tasmania. Of this I am grateful and fortunate, as after discussions with my family, Tasmania held a most sinister threat, whose identity and behavior I had completely no idea about. Not a clue.

It is explained in pages to come when it fits the story line—it's bloody horrific and it boils like fury in my veins.

There is a part of me today that would like to know if my mum made a pact with my nana to ensure I was protected. Unequivocally, there was a grotesque monster that was way too close to me when I was all alone.

Eventually Nana and Pop relocated permanently to Victoria to be close to my mum and us. The strongest early memory I have of that period is burning my bottom on the heater at the family home in Karingal, and Nana putting butter on my bum to soothe it. This is a distinct memory of mine; she was rather nurturing to me. By today's standards, butter and burns are a no-no, but back in the 1980s, it was still accepted practice.

There were many other times of togetherness. My memory is clear that I loved her, and she loved me. There have been days since her passing—over thirty plus years ago—that I wish she was around.

Then I could ask her questions only she could answer.

I clearly remember the night before Nana let go and left us. I asked that my mother, Kristen, take me to see her in the Frankston hospital. She had been battling bowel cancer for some time and I was never comfortable with death or serious illness; thus, I could not bear to show much interest. I didn't have the capacity to deal with it. When I deliberately asked to be taken to see her, it was a rarity.

We were at the hospital and I was shown to her room. I sat with her and told her I loved her, and she heard me. I truly believe I knew she was going to die the next day, or that something was guiding me. I assuredly know this. I went when I didn't want to go, and when I did she left with death.

Upon my asking, my mother was so overjoyed that I wanted to see my Nana that she took me shopping at Myer that same evening and bought me clothes. This pair of rarities collided, and people acted kindly to one another. I received white summer shorts and a top, which was an odd form of mothering I was granted from her. Nana passed away around eight the next morning. I remember Kristen receiving the phone call. Tears flooded her face and splashed on the floor, soaking small portions of the carpet.

What pain I witnessed.

A small gathering came to a church to usher a person off with words of their worth. I wonder how she valued herself. Not much, I'd say, for she wasn't a co-habitant of self and worth.

She was a private person, and at her funeral she was the first dead body I had ever seen. I wish I never had, as it's a memory not yet faded. You don't get rid of that, you can't, it's not there to go. Her open casket was in a room, and I was encouraged to go and view it. I stood with her pale, drawn face and body clothed in a cotton dress, her hands on her chest holding a carnation.

This was the second time I said goodbye to her in under a week.

The rest is a blur. I think her daughters had breakdowns after that day, and carnage flowed to us all.

But it absolutely has to be said, memory has holds.

As you grow old, not only do they come, but so too does adult ability. And in that rational, adult spirit, I would care for another visit with Pearl and I'd ask her: "Were you comfortable being open for display on the day of your funeral given that you were such a concealed person?"

It is not my most poignant question, but it was an ironic end to her last day of visibility. When all her life she hid as best should could, at death she was found.

I can see her in the last months of her life, the hospital surroundings and her resignation. It is inarguably true she had battled since breath itself. She was long past tired and at the gates of ready. She wanted reprieve from her shit life.

I sit here now knowing where she came from, and I absolutely wish I knew then what I know now. I just can't help but think about what went with her when she left. So much unsaid. All answers fled with her last exhale.

One thing is for certain: her pain and suffering came to an end. But so did her voice, her story. Yet knowing she didn't speak then of the decisions she made, leads me to assume she wouldn't have spoken to me anyway, even though it would have been her Sparkling Kid asking for answers.

Nana came from a place of 'to not speak,' and she adopted this to perfection. Of course, it had deliberate repercussions. Not healthy ones.

Although I wasn't directly told where she came from, as children we overheard. I don't remember the specifics or circumstances; I wouldn't have understood anyway. But I stashed those words in my memory. They would sit inside me unchanged for decades, waiting.

It came to a point that when I was researching the details of events, I was able to say: "No, that didn't happen" or "It happened this way." I knew I was right, because I'd heard the details when I was little. Like the dinghy, the rocks, and the fisherman, I knew before I was told.

In short, my memory served time until it was ready for release.

It was the context I exhumed which, unfortunately, is disappointing for the next generation growing up with adults who do not speak of the past. Sometimes we do not get to share the true self of the person we look up to. We are born into an environment and we are stuck, much as our parents who were born into theirs.

This consistent pattern creates suffering. And it repeats. I can only suggest that Nana suffered in her silence, as have her daughters, and the daughters of her daughters. Memories and emotions, though, don't go anywhere. Even when they are locked in silence, they survive inside forever.

On that universal fact of experience alone, I would like to sit with Nana to hear her story in her voice.

It is important to know that one of the first things I discovered about this person called Pearl was that she not only used silence to rule her life, she commanded the same from her own. It was suggested to me there was a reason her daughters—Kendall, Kristen, Kate, and Kylie—known as the Four Ks, didn't speak openly or freely about their history and the events they overcame. Their mother had made a pact with them for silence.

The pact was made early in their lives and it was instilled in them without exception. Though some of the Four Ks live in each other's daily lives, they have only ever spoken briefly about their experiences. Silence still lives in them, for they were bred that way.

Such a pact would only serve Pearl. It was a means to conceal her untruths. I wonder how much that silence has hurt her daughters. From the very beginning, I learnt that Pearl had a history of lying, and with that came a deceptive style of living. Therefore, the fewer people in her life, the less likely she was to be found out or held accountable… and the more she got away with.

It is a similar trait I grew up with in Kristen's life. Her main response to anything she remotely didn't want discovered was: "That never happened." And when that didn't stop the questions, she shifted to: "That's all in the past. That's over and done with, that's gone. Life moves on. Move on."

Both methods are a control tactic because they don't want to be answerable for their behavior at all. Nor face what is inside them as a result. This was the suffocating and restricting environment Pearl and her daughters lived in. Unnecessarily toxic, it stamps out the individual expression of experience. Little to no recognition exists in that atmosphere.

Today, some of Pearl's daughters won't ever hear a harsh word said of her in their company, but the facts are facts, with or without smoke screens. Pearl has some answering to do in this story.

From start to finish, she is the central character of this entire tale. She is the problem, the source. As I write now, I feel the drudgery of it. It's a drain on my energy, as I have worked for years to remove myself from any of her direct or indirect problems. I am struggling during this chapter because of the pull of the energy associated with it. And I *loved* my nana, but I cannot deny a truth. It is a best-delivered script.

It is Nana who meets the men and takes to being intimate with them and then births her daughters. This creates a tie from mother to daughter and daughter to mother that will be everlasting and powerful beyond any life experience or personal needs of the children.

She is the matriarch, the one who calls the shots.

She is the key to everything.

Even me.

TIME TO FIND

FIRST TASMANIA TRIP

Trip One
Depart Victoria, Monday August 17, 2009.
Return Victoria, Tuesday August 25, 2009.

I went for answers as I realized I knew nothing.

So, I yelled to her in a heaven you'd hope she'd be in. "Nana, I don't know anything about you! Where do I begin?"

I went straight for her death. Where else would I go? It was all that was available to me. I obtained her death certificate and worked backwards, identifying her parents—their names and where they came from. I then hired a genealogical researcher to track and record the family tree, and from that I was able to identify family members.

Once I had names and dates, I went to the archives of death notices in the library. Through the public notices of sympathy and mourning, I was able to locate those who cared about them, approaching them to meet.

From there, I went to every public department I believed would offer me any information and scrolled through volumes of archived material, followed all avenues. Some days I walked away with nothing, but others were a bounty. Electoral rolls helped locate living family members, and to them I sent cards advising who I was and why I wanted to chat. I sat and I foraged and I didn't give up.

While tracing and learning of Pearl's family members, it became apparent she had a strong association with the Tasmanian lighthouses. She lived as a lighthouse keeper's wife for years. So, I researched everything to do with lighthouses in Tasmania. I gathered whatever I thought was relevant—articles, books, people's names and titles, pictures—all on the living and deceased. It would teach me of a life that had its impact on mine.

The same method I used to find Pearl's family, I applied to lighthouse discovery. Again, I ploughed through government departments and public records, and was able to locate several living locals involved with lighthouse preservation. I knew discussions had to be had with these people.

Sitting staring at the piled documents, it was clear: I had to go to Tasmania.

So I did.

First, I made written contact with all these strangers and simply told them the truth. I was earnestly investigating, tracing Pearl Joyce and the path she trod that was her life. Once I said I was the first grandchild of Pearl and her second love, Harrison, I was assisted greatly. I soon learnt many people knew of the situation that caused so much havoc, and all of them were happy to help me. And they talked as soon as I arrived.

It was an incredible set of events.

Once it had been established that my interest was genuine and of good intent, I had many people come forward and offer their assistance.

I received an incredibly generous gesture from a woman who welcomed me into her home, and who would be a most valuable source of information. Not only did I like her company, but she had spent time living on Maatsuyker Island with my family. She remembered Pearl well. Here, I was staying with a woman named Emerald who was a living testament of a time I was searching for. It was magic.

This first trip had me in Tasmania for ten days. I caught the boat over, landing in Davenport before driving down to Hobart to stay with Emerald. I couldn't believe she had a hot lunch ready and waiting at the table for me. We warmed to each other, sharing stories of what I knew thus far as she regaled her recollections. It was an amazing beginning of many discoveries.

Emerald also had a gift for me—three black-and-white photos of Pearl and the Four Ks amongst the rocks of Maatsuyker Island.

I never knew what Pearl and the Four Ks looked like during this time, and here they were. To be honest, Pearl looked a mess—lackluster and downtrodden, riddled in suffering.

The photos provided insights into the life of the woman I wanted to know, but I was not beside myself with joy to see her distressed in this way. It hurt. Her daughters are all happy and generous with their smiles and their bather-clad, tanned and healthy bodies. But here in my hand was part of a map I was creating, and just like with art or history, to create purity it requires all facets. Here, this piece showed hell before the shots were fired....

Hell.

The next day I ventured to more unknown lands to meet a man I had been conversing with over email and phone before my voyage across Bass Strait. Jason Brook was one of the longest-serving and most recognized lighthouse keepers in Australia, and he had an abundance of information about everything relating to lighthouses and those who watched them and watched from them.

He was a character as prominent as a light tower himself, and he and I got along like best mates. When I arrived, we greeted each other with open arms. His lovely wife Lorraine had made us pumpkin soup for our first day of banter. We sat in the lounge and shared information. We agreed, we disagreed, he opened floodgates to emotion he had not shown anyone before, and I listened to his story and was brought to tears myself.

Jason had much to teach me, and I had much to teach him from my findings. Between us, we made a good start into understanding what had happened on the islands. He had immense insight into the running of lighthouse posts as per government rules and regulations. Jason also taught me about what it was like to live on an island amongst the Keeping community.

He shared a secret with me.

When he does talks or trips to the Tasman Island tower, he regales people with the story of my grandfather. He couldn't believe that man's first granddaughter was now debating with him in his lounge room. I, for one, was glad to be. Not only did Jason and I serve each other's intellectual minds, we also sorted through information and found the answers we needed.

Three days I sat with him, and not once did we feel uncomfortable or strained. It was mutually respectful to be in each other's company.

Every night I returned to stay with Emerald, and we would discuss the day's findings and she would offer her memories when they surfaced.

On one of my last days, I spent the entire day sitting in the public records office in Hobart trawling through the official lighthouse islands' logbooks. They are large, old, leather-covered logbooks that held the embarking and disembarking dates of my family to the islands on which they were stationed. For the first time, I came as close as

I had ever been to my grandfather. As I turned page after page, I learnt of his movements and his daily chores. Then I was reading his handwriting in the Tasman Island logbook.

I touched the old ink and said, "You were here, Harrison. You touched this page and inscribed the day's events as they happened, years ago."

Here I was, coming from a place of unknowing, and now I was sitting as close as I could ever get to a man I never knew existed.

I said my goodbyes to Emerald and hugged her with much care; I truly feel she was an angel. For the second part of my trip, I needed to head back to the top of the state.

In any country, there is an aspect of driving in the countryside that offers purity of gathered collection and reflection. This trip was my first, and I didn't know what discovery I would make next. I had no clues. Maybe that was another bonus in a journey where the expression 'you don't know what's around the corner' was my true experience. There's no curveball here; this is an outright strike-rate of oncoming 'what's' from me.

Most of the remains of Pearl's origins were now resting in the Beaconsfield cemetery. That's where I was going. I must say I am not a regular frequenter of burial areas; this was simply a mark of respect and an introduction—to headstones as it may be. When I arrived at the cemetery, I was starkly alone. In the middle of nowhere, in a small isolated country town. It was purely silent as I stood looking across the contained mass of old and new graves. It was confronting.

I had no idea what I was looking for other than the surname 'Joyce,' so I began to walk the rows, peering at headstones, faded and worn. The presence of energy was quite unmistakable; I was incorrect to consider myself alone, even with the dead. I could feel something next to me, walking with me. It was ever-present.

After acknowledging aloud that I could feel a presence, I located Pearl's mother and father, Joseph and Carol. There they were. Two people who had existed quite well in their lifetimes but who were never mentioned in mine.

It was only that their names were on Pearl's death certificate did I know them. These people were significant in the life of a woman who was significant in mine, and yet I had never heard of them.

I cleaned up their graves and spoke to them. Then I found Pearl's sisters. On their headstones were the names of their children.

"There were more," I exclaimed, meaning more family members. I found Pearl's brother; he too had a child. More again. I wanted to meet these relations, so I took photos of all the headstones.

As I exited the graveyard, I turned and bowed, thanking the unseeable for having me for the afternoon. The dead don't speak, but they leave a trail to follow—if you're looking, that is.

This trail led me to a new town where I arranged a meeting with a woman who was keen on the Joyce family history. She was willing to help wherever she could. I set myself up in George Town, but I didn't much warm to the atmosphere or some of the locals, especially after an incident on my first night.

I walked from my hotel to the main strip, looking for some hot soup. None could be found. The only offering was pizza or an abundance of grease, which I couldn't stomach this night. Pizza was not the only choice on the menu. Apparently, I was too. Once my dinner was ready, I walked with it in hand back toward my hotel. I had just been to an automatic teller machine and was placing my wallet in my jeans' pocket when two adolescent boys, who had been in the takeaway, shop with me minutes earlier, walked past. They strategically placed themselves to the side of the street, so I had to pass them. They followed me.

I knew exactly what was going on; I was being rounded up. It was near six in the evening, and dark. No one else was around; it was me and them. I knew I was vulnerable unless I showed them otherwise; and yes, I was scared.

They began whistling at me and walking faster as I stepped up the pace. Menacing behavior can be intimidating and stressful, but I kept walking and did not answer any of their lewd comments. Sensing I was about to be pounced on, I spun on my heel, startling him.

He stood an arm's length away. I was still holding my pizza. His friend was five steps away.

I looked at this creep and snapped, "I am not a woman you want to fuck with."

He just stood there, fear in his eyes.

His friend said, "What did she say?"

"She told me not to fuck with her."

Neither spoke.

I was staring straight at him. "Don't think I wouldn't turn around to face you if I couldn't wreck you. Now fuck off."

He turned immediately and quickly walked away. He didn't say a word to his friend, who soon followed. Once I felt I could, I turned, and when I reached the street corner to my hotel I ran until I was behind my hotel door with chain and lock latched.

Then I cried.

I hate violence, both the threat of it and the times when I must call on my ability to use it. Even when I need it to protect myself from others. It's not who I am, but I do have the ability to defend myself. We all have a survival skill within, that saves us like mine saved me that night. And yes, I would have smashed his head in without hesitation. I am glad he walked away.

The next day I met with Eve, the woman who had information on the Joyces. We spent the afternoon exchanging information, and she was an absolute gem.

She told me of attending school with the Harper clan, and she remembered Pearl, Harrison, Phillip, and the Four Ks. She was another living source of information. We went to look at the Eddystone Lighthouse tower together, and the quarters where my family started their Keeping life. She then told me about other family members who lived in George Town. She rang them and explained who I was, and if they wouldn't mind meeting with me.

They agreed, and before I knew it I was in Pearl's niece's living room. With warmth, I met Rose Lowe and her husband Bryce. Rose was the daughter of Pearl's sister, Laura Jean.

"Whoa," I said. "You knew my nana. Hang on a minute, you also knew my grandfather."

Oh my god, I was about to burst. They stared at me, perplexed, then quickly realized I came for information with the openness of good intent. Rose and Bryce told me more than I ever expected to find, including the names of living relations and their contact details.

Rose openly gave her memories. She remembered fondly visiting her nana and pop's home. She loved them dearly, as they were good people and she was always given a treat when she stopped in at Joseph and Carol's. She smiled with her memory and said that after devouring her treat at Nana and Pop's house, she would duck next door and get a treat from her Aunty Pearl and Uncle Harry (Harrison).

She said they were lovely to her, and the home was always neat and tidy. She loved going there, and vaguely remembered a bassinet in the room. Rose sat back, and as I watched her, she smiled again with her head slightly tilted back, her eyes staring toward the roof. She giggled as she recounted how lovely it was to go into both homes, and how those who lived there were lovely to be with.

Then she was quick to tell me, "It wasn't a nice turn to be at her Aunty Et's home."

Another sister of Pearl and Laura Jean.

Rose told me it wasn't like the others, that there was something about it that never felt right. She never got any treats, and her uncle Glen was a strict man who would prefer children were seen and not heard.

But as for Pearl and Harrison, she couldn't get enough of them.

That night Eve took me out for dinner at my hotel's restaurant, and we had a lovely, safe night. The day had been wonderful, and she reflected her approval with her smile. Eve walked me to my room and we ended our time together, as the next morning I would head to Launceston to see if I could meet Rose's sister, Eleanor.

I had only found out she existed the day before, but it was with excitement that I knocked on the door. She wasn't home, but that didn't matter so much to me. I knew she existed, and I would be back to see her and the others I had discovered.

After leaving a note on Eleanor's doorstep, I went to meet my cousin Chrissy in a town just south of Launceston. I had arranged to spend the day with her and her children. When I arrived, I was met by my cousin and her little daughters with love. It was beautiful. We sat down for fresh chicken sandwiches and happy banter. Then her mum—my aunty—arrived, and the warmth left. She was the youngest K—Kylie—and although she didn't remember much because she was only two years old at the time, she had a lot to say. She was also a staunch supporter of the second K, my mother Kristen. Kristen and I had a strained connection possibly since the day I was born (or not far from).

In Kylie's company, the day was abhorrent, so when I was able to leave, I took off fast. All I wanted was to get as far from her as I could, and that meant getting the hell out of Tasmania.

So, I high tailed it to the ship's wharf and sought to change my return ticket to a day earlier. It was permitted, and home-bound I sailed.

I landed back in Victoria and the relief surged through me, so did all the information I had gathered—I had a bounty.

Pearl was born in Beaconsfield, and her school years were spent at St. Xavier Catholic Convent School, but I am unaware if she furthered her education past primary levels. I do know she grew up in this area, and thus was amongst the blue-collar workers' way of life in her young and adolescent years.

Beaconsfield was populated with males either working as miners or 'wharfies' (those who manned the wharf), which was located at Beauty Point, just down the road from where she lived. The women were mainly home-keepers, and nuns schooled the youth.

It was a very small town and still is. It would be made famous by the 2006 tragedy of a mining shaft collapse, with the survival of two men and the loss of one. Beaconsfield wasn't well-known when Pearl walked the streets, but she was, and so was her family. She was close to her three sisters, Laura Jean, Et, and Nelly. They were accompanied by their brothers, John and Lindsay. She was far from alone, although I cannot gather the nature of the relationships—whether they were virulent or supportive. Perhaps they were both.

The environment she lived in was reserved and simple. Not a lot gained her attention, and there was not a lot of much anything else but the comings and goings of regular country life. Men worked, women stayed home with babies, and the pub was the local relief center. However, as with most things, it's what lies beneath the surface. Somewhere in Pearl's life, she was either tainted by another's actions, or she simply had a predisposition for the lifestyle behavior that was to come.

Her father's name was Joseph Harold Joyce. He was born in Tasmania in 1884, and was one of eleven children to George and Kate. It is said that his family was known by the surname Plummer before going by Joyce. He would remain in Tasmania until his death at the age of eighty-one in 1965. He was tall and solid but not obese. Much like a gentle giant. Joseph worked the gold mines in the Lefroy and Beaconsfield regions and then became a waterside worker on the wharf at Beauty Point. Here, he was a well-regarded foreman who had a valuable amount of respect from fellow water staff. This respect and the value of his position extended to the Beaconsfield community.

He was welcomed as 'Big Joe' who had a soft and giving heart with a work ethic that didn't stop. Because he worked hard, he was able to establish substantial land ownership along Christian Street, the main strip of Beaconsfield. Near his death, he gave it to the community and it became a public space for all. This was by all accounts an example of how he was in his life: a generous, giving fellow. That is certainly what I have heard from relatives who spent time with him.

Carol May (Nel) was Pearl's mother. She was born in 1881 and lived a grand eighty-nine years before passing on December 3, 1970. All her six children were listed on her death certificate: John was in Melbourne, Laura Jean in Beaconsfield, Et in Launceston, Lindsay across the river in West Tamar, Nelly in Launceston, and Pearl in Melbourne.

Carol was described as albino in pigmentation and of tiny frame. She was cared for by her daughter Laura Jean toward the end of her life. It was said she used to sit a lot of the time. Sit and stare. Wasn't ever violent in disposition. A quiet woman who didn't ask for much.

Looking after her mother took its toll on Laura Jean. Laura Jean herself had a harsh life and was raised by her father's mother. There is a huge irony, as it was Laura Jean—the eldest daughter—who cared for a mother who did not raise her.

Laura Jean had her arm amputated for medical reasons. She was a navy nurse, who unfortunately suffered from chronic seasickness; thus, went on to be a psychiatric nurse. It was requested of another sister, Nelly, to care for Carol to give Laura Jean a break. By all reports, this 'sent Carol around the twist' and, horribly, Nelly also fell to psychological instability and required housing care in a facility herself. The details here are terribly nebulous, and I don't know everything. What I can glean is there was burden and fallout. Pearl and her brothers are of no mention.

Together Pearl's parents were considered "lovely people." This has been said numerous times, and I believe it; I've heard nothing but. This is an important consideration because to understand Pearl is to know and understand where and who she came from. I have not heard anything about violence or alcoholism in either of Pearl's parents.

I have heard, however, that they were heartbroken by Pearl's life; it caused them much pain. This is a genuine theme, as there are seven independent adults who have said the same thing. It was Joe who tried to help Pearl. He sent her money and allowed her and Harrison to live with them. They watched Pearl's pain and it travelled into their hearts.

One of Joseph and Carol's grandchildren told me of the time she was cared for by 'Nana Nel,' that she would go over to Beaconsfield from George Town and be cared for by Carol regularly. She clearly recalled being given empty tins to play with, and her Nana Nel would have an afternoon sleep every time. She remembered being in the house when Nelly and Pearl would come home from school. She quipped that she was so scared of those nuns from Nelly and Pearl's school.

If for any reason Carol had to make her way to the top of the hill to speak to the head of governance at the Catholic school, this young granddaughter would hide because the nuns frightened her so terribly. She still shakes her head at the memory, "Oh, they were terrible," she says with a shudder.

She tells me that her nana and pop were the loveliest people. They always put a hot meal on the table for anyone, and one of them was always there for whoever needed them.

There, I had it. A family tree for Pearl. I had seen the family home where she and her four daughters had resided near Eddystone Lighthouse; I had surveyed the town where Pearl, Harrison, and Phillip had presumably met, but all certainly lived. Established that the Harper family and my family were in close proximity to each other and possibly interacted. I had been to Eddystone Lighthouse and seen the quarters my family lived in at the beginning of their lighthouse tenure. I sat across from people related to Pearl and who absolutely loved Harrison—wouldn't have a mark against his name. I had photos of my family to forward on to an aunty I respected very much—the only one who talked to me—and I had confirmation Pearl was raised in a loving home.

This was a lot, but not the lot. A meeting of all living Joyce family members was being arranged and I was to return to Tasmania for this.

It was to not only to meet the family members, but also because I had made a promise to Jason Brook. We had spoken of General McArthur and how he declared, "I shall return." We had forged a special bond over being true to your word. I declared I would return. Jason would be waiting for me, and I wasn't going to disappoint him or the Joyces.

SECOND TRIP TO TASMANIA
Trip Two:
Depart Victoria, Monday, October 5, 2009.
Return Victoria, Thursday, October 8, 2009.

The Joyce family meeting happened when my Melbourne researcher came through with a vast amount of information on my family tree. My heritage map was forming thoroughly. The researcher was good; she was really good.

Pearl had many family members, and it was to them I wrote asking if they would care to meet and talk with me, explaining I was researching my family and I'd really enjoy hearing from them. They agreed, all of them. I contacted Rose's sister Eleanor; she had received the note I left on her doorstep, and I would stay with her during this trip to Launceston.

I was going to fly over the sea this time, as the previous boat trip back to Victoria had been hideous. I was thankful for having a cabin to myself, as I was so unhinged by my seasickness that the toilet and I were quite familiar with one another by the time I reached my destination. Washed out had a new meaning and breakfast was a threat.

Neither Eleanor or I knew what the other looked like. That was fine, as when I walked through the terminal gates I saw two smiling women holding a note with 'Melissa' written on it. I smiled, and we said hello and hugged. She had with her another relative I had not met.

The woman's name was Taylor and she was the daughter of Nelly, one of Pearl's sisters.

I was abuzz with anticipation, and the welcoming attitude of my family lifted my spirit. This was truly amazing. They existed—and I was with them. We went to Eleanor's home, where I was made to feel welcome. She was a lovely woman. Cups of tea were served, and discussions commenced straight away.

For the next four days, Eleanor and I were inseparable. She was her own treasure chest, with photo albums of family I had never even known about. Amongst them were photos of Pearl as a younger woman. I would never have seen them had I not walked out my front door and into hers.

As I flicked through the pages, Eleanor explained whom was whom. For the first time in my life, I began to see Pearl as the person she never spoke about. She had never shown us this woman. Ever.

Eleanor agreed to let me have the photos printed. I was thrilled by this, for both research and personal reasons. For the first time in my family's life, I was going to be in possession of photos no one else had. It was a gift I was going to give to Pearl's daughter, Kendall, the eldest of the Four Ks. She was the only K who supported my quest and thus was the one I returned to after every trip to share what I had found. On this return I had jewels she never dreamt of seeing.

The next day, Eleanor and I drove out to Beaconsfield and returned to the cemetery. I announced at the gate, "Hello, I am back", and we entered and cleaned up the Joyce gravesites.

Eleanor then drove me around the township of Beaconsfield, telling me where Pearl went to school. Then she had me standing in front of the house Pearl grew up in as a child, which was next to the house Harrison had built for them to live in after their first-born, Kendall, arrived. Eleanor was amazing; she knew so much. She was taking me places I couldn't have dreamt of seeing. She even took me to the wharf where Pearl's father, Joseph, had worked.

Next, we pulled into someone's driveway and made our way to the door. Before I knew it, I was sitting in the home once occupied by Pearl's brother, Lindsay. I was in Pearl's brother's home, and I hadn't even known she'd had a brother. We were discussing all matters regarding Lindsay's life, and I found out he had a son named Ray who lived in Hobart. I think I started spinning a little; there was so much to learn. Eleanor and I had lunch at the bakery then sailed back toward her home, where I sat in front of the heater, staring at the carpet. Warm and full.

The next day was bigger than the first. I would be treated to a moment I would never forget. All the Joyce relatives and their respective partners had gathered at Maureen and Daniel's home. Maureen was the daughter of Et, another of Pearl's sisters. I was amazed, as here I was in one room with so much of the history I was searching for. I went from not even knowing where to start, to meeting the family and listening to them speak of their memories. It was phenomenal.

I was working my way through everything to establish what happened to my family—who did what and when. In this room, I was told as much as could be; no one held back. That was just the way I needed it and asked for it to be.

The lunch-spread Et had put on was a banquet of old-style cuisine with salads, cold meats, and the most scrumptious caramel banana tart I'd ever consumed. The view we had through floor-to-ceiling windows showed the ocean and the white-tipped waves, which were quite amazing given we were talking in part about what had happened in the oceanic environs. It was almost like it participated in the discussion.

My family asked as much of me as I asked of them. They knew a lot about Pearl and her family, but I filled in gaps they had not been able. It was a day of discovery. I sat with people I would never have sat with had I not offered them my hand to take. We all had each other's hands that day. We agreed the story was tragic. Only one man in the room didn't like my grandfather; everyone else loved him, and they didn't have a bad word to say of the man whose memory they stored.

That night more relatives travelled to Eleanor's home to meet and talk with me. It was wonderful, just wonderful. One relative, a second cousin named Lucinda who didn't speak to her sister Taylor, came over and we sat facing each other, talking, connected, even with her sister Taylor in the background.

Another relative, Kerry, who is Taylor's daughter and who also doesn't speak to her mother, made the two-hour drive to be with us. She and I went on to become friends, and we laughed, my goodness did we laugh together! A lot of discovery on both sides was happening; it was a most liberating and dynamic atmosphere.

My time with Pearl's side of the family was coming to an end. Before I left, I told them all how extraordinary it was for me to have been with them. It was because of their open, welcoming nature that I drove away knowing more about my nana. It was cemented that she came from an upbringing of silence, where her own mum, Carol Joyce, wouldn't tell her left hand what her right hand was doing. Pearl was a prodigy of silence. She was a vault of secrecy, and I think part of that was due to hiding her lies and protecting herself from embarrassment. She was ashamed, but she needn't have been. Just like the man I was about to meet.

I had a date in Hobart I had to get to. Eleanor dropped me off at the car hire and I drove to meet Ray, the recluse who didn't talk to anyone. He had agreed to meet me. I was lucky, very lucky, but I was also persistent and polite in seeking to meet with him. I came in peace and of good will; he saw this and said, "Meet me at 1400 hours at the hotel I go to daily."

I could do this; I could find the hotel and walk through the doors. When I did, he noticed me instantly, and for reasons other than the fact it was obvious I was an out-of-towner.

As we hugged, he said, "I knew straight away", and "You are a young Pearl."

I smiled, but I didn't agree. We sat together, and he was superb. Reclusive, shy, reserved, and hard as hell to speak with at length, but when he did open up, he was gold. I can replay our conversation with laughter at any time. We spoke for nearly three hours, and in that time, he told me that he was raised by Pearl's parents (to Ray they were Nana and Pop Joyce), and when Harrison built the house next to Nana and Pop Joyce, Ray lived alongside Pearl and Harrison for a considerable amount of years. He was a living part of my nana's past.

As he spoke, I watched his facial expressions and listened to the tone of his voice and the flow of his words to help gauge whether he was telling the truth. Nothing in Ray's manner gave me reason to doubt. He was shy and considered and had no cause to harm others—alive or dead—so when he spoke, I believed him.

He looked at me and quietly said, "Pearl was paid to have sex with men in Melbourne." Those words issued calmly.

"Oh my god," I said just as calmly. "You just told me my nana was a prostitute."

He nodded. "Yep."

"Are you serious? My nana had sex with men for money?"

"Yes. That was general knowledge."

"Wow." I said that a few times.

He could see I wasn't upset by the information, but I was completely comfortable hearing his memories. He then told me Pearl's own father would send her money to be sure she was looked after whilst she was in Melbourne.

"But if Nana was earning money in the sex-with-men scene, why did she need money sent to her?"

"She wasn't earning enough."

From this we assumed that Nana wasn't turning enough tricks, so to speak.

"I am not shocked, but I am shocked," I said. "Wow... wow."

I wasn't shocked. I had heard references to her sexual patterns previously, but no one had come out and told me so directly. She was paid to have sex with men. I asked Ray if he had knowledge of her being raped in her early years or sexually abused. He did not. I was looking for any association or connection between previous life incidents and current self-worth, or if what Pearl was doing was survival.

Before sitting with Ray, I was of the impression Pearl had numerous partners, but I never made the connection that she had previously tried to make a living from it.

I was surprised by several aspects of this information. The fact that her father knew what his daughter was up to shocks me, but I don't judge either Joseph or Pearl. I am not them and I was not around at the time. All I can do is interpret what I've been told, and piece together meaning and reason.

How and why Pearl came to feel comfortable offering herself to men is for her alone to know. She may have just been that way inclined. She may have found the attention she received fulfilling, and realized she was useful in an area of her life, and either enjoyed it or used it as a means of fortitude.

There is much degradation of prostitution in our society, yet it is one of the oldest professions of our existence. I am not sure how much Nana involved herself in this profession, but there was a pattern where she had many male partners and a reputation for it.

Her daughter Kendall has told me Pearl was a woman who couldn't live without a man in her life and repeated the 'loose morals' stance. I have had a male family member tell me he didn't go into Pearl's George Town house for the "special hot dinners, if you know what I mean."

I had never heard the expression, and assumed Nana wasn't a good cook. I was clueless, and playing a guessing game as to what it meant. It wasn't until a conversation with another family member who overheard the comment that I was able to process the meaning. Because she explained it and stared at me until I reached a point where it clicked. But even then, I didn't put 'paid' and 'have sex' together; I just put 'had sex' with 'many but no one ate together'.

This was in reference to where Pearl and Harrison had lived in George Town from 1951 to 1955. She had a reputation then, but she had begun this style of behavior long before.

I was right about one thing: she could not cook.

Numerous relatives have told me the names of several men Pearl was involved with, including a man called Algi Deli—the town's butcher, who lived across from her in Beaconsfield. She was particularly fond of him.

She left Beaconsfield in 1941 and married David Smith in 1944, who would be her first husband, but not her first lover. I do not know much about David Smith, other than that Pearl was twenty years old when they married, and they had a son who was adopted out to care.

Her husband worked on the ships that crossed Bass Straight from Tasmania to Melbourne—the *Turana* and the *Nirana*. From her marriage in 1944 until she met Harrison in 1950, we assume that Pearl went back to Melbourne, as she was not heard of or seen by her family in Tasmania until she returned to Beaconsfield in 1951 with

Harrison and baby Kendall. I am not sure what became of David Smith or her first son.

At her father's deathbed in 1965, she was heard twice in separate instances by her nephew, Ray, and her niece, Eleanor, saying that she wished that he would just die so she could go back to Melbourne. Joseph was in the Beaconsfield hospital, and her attitude at this time was less than appropriate.

Ray described her as 'cold.' He told me she said she "just wanted him to hurry up and die." Ray looked at her and thought, *now I can see your true colors; I know you now.*

He had his opinion verified on this occasion. He had not warmed to Pearl at all through his lifetime as a member of the Joyce family. When Joseph died Pearl was forty-one and living in Eden Road, Seaford. She had well and truly gone through hell by now and was enduring the psychological stains of life.

Life events had clearly hurt her, and death too often she had met. She was also well involved with Hadley McDonald—her fourth long-term partner. I am considering that she returned to Beaconsfield, Tasmania, without the Four Ks, as by now Kendall was herself well-cemented as the mother of the house.

In 1965, Kendall was 15, Kristen was 13, Kate was 12, and Kylie was 10. Their mother was away, behaving with hostility toward a man that provided for her. Or did she have reason to not have empathy for him? I wonder why Pearl didn't care for her dad at his deathbed. I have no explanation or answer.

Ray described Pearl to me as an unattractive woman who was indifferent and not normal. He told me she was unsophisticated with a very cheap way about her. She would wear very thin, un-styled cotton dresses that would just loosely hang over her and were less than appealing. She didn't care for herself much.

There is a junction here I am unable to bridge. I understand how these comments arise and the reason for their formation, as I knew of my nana as a plain-styled character myself. It is accurate she didn't appeal to the high-end of fashion or labels, and dresses did simply hang off her as they had her own mother. That heritage worked its way down the generation. But as a prostitute, would she have not cared for her appeal? I would have thought so.

Ray's account, however, does tell you a lot. There wasn't a lot of care and nurturing back in her childhood and adolescent days. Her self-care system wasn't flamboyant or robust. Ray remembered she was always very skinny, and yes, this is accurate too.

In my memory I can see her brushing her hair. Her dress sense was as nondescript as her lifestyle. She cared not for material things, and was incredibly quiet and withdrawn. She most certainly kept to herself.

Ray was right; I saw it myself.

I asked him if he thought Pearl and Harrison loved each other, and Ray sat in thought for a moment. "Yeah, I think they did in their own way."

"What do you mean?"

"Well, they were both weird and indifferent people." He went on to tell me that they spent a lot of time drinking together and each was as bad as the other. Ray described Harrison as coarse in nature.

When I pressed him to elaborate, he said, "Oh, I don't know. He was just coarse."

After speaking with him further, Ray found Harrison unapproachable, strange, and emotionally unstable. These words were from a man who was quiet and reserved, sophisticated and observant. Ray was very quiet as a child and still is as a man. That way, he told me, you can see people for who they are. He would know; he was the child no one wanted to see. He became the master of seeing by not being seen. I relate to this man more than he understands.

Out of genuine interest I found out about him. His father, Lindsay Joyce, Pearl's brother, and his mother Olive Bourke became parents when Ray arrived on February 8, 1938. With Lindsay being a young nineteen year old, and Olive even younger at sixteen, they were thrown into parenting. Unable to care for their son, and Lindsay going to fight for his country in World War II, Ray was taken in and raised by his grandparents, Pop and Nana Joyce.

He became their son and lived with them from birth to approximately nineteen years of age. When Harrison and Pearl arrived in 1951, as an astute thirteen-year-old Ray recalled a lot. The Christian Street house they all lived in was a small, weatherboard home that would be considered suitable for an outdoor shed by today's standards. They occupied this together for some time until it was established there wasn't suitable room for Pearl, Harrison, and baby Kendall.

Harrison then built a small two-bedroom home next to Nana and Pop Joyce's house and they lived alongside each other. This was where Harrison began to become part of the Joyce family, and he was well-received by all (bar Ray and Daniel Olgilvie, Pearl's brothers-in-law).

Ray watched Harrison build the family home in Beaconsfield with recycled materials. He did so all by himself, which Ray was very impressed with. Ray recalled that Harrison was very good with laboring and was a hard worker. Before they knew it, a home was next to his home, and from there he watched how dysfunctional his aunty and uncle were. He still has a low opinion of them both.

Ray is comfortable telling stories of his life; I see he was a considerate, kind boy and man. He was different in that he loved music and played the piano and acoustic guitar. He loved classical music and the quiet, gentle life. He was his nana's favorite, and he remembers helping her keep the house running. He polished the floors with her and cut the firewood and generally helped out. He said that it was Nana Joyce who did everything, and it was she who kept the house and family going.

Ray was raised by two women, and when he wasn't with Nana Joyce, he was with his other nana, Amy Bourke—Olive's mother. Nana Floyd was a quaint English lady who showed Ray how to play the piano and live a life with etiquette and style. He never knew he had a father until Lindsay came home from the war. Nana Joyce asked him if he wanted to meet his father, and he was shocked by this.

"Father? What father?"

The situation was explained to him, and therefore Ray met Lindsay. Lindsay adored Ray and they quickly bonded, but Lindsay soon met his second wife, Claire, and lost interest in Ray. Lindsay and Claire married on the May 9, 1952, and this entire experience hurt Ray deeply. He therefore felt an intense sense of rejection that has quite possibly lived with him since his birth in 1938.

He lived out his adolescence with Nana and Pop Joyce. He described his pop as a very big man and obese. "He was a plodder who didn't have a need to do things in a hurry or concern himself with hard work about the house." In Ray's eyes, his pop did nothing but work as a foreman at the wharf at Beauty Point, which gave Joseph a lot of responsibility and respect around Beaconsfield.

Joseph was so giving to Pearl that Ray remembered him sending her money, and Rose and Bryce remembered him sending Harrison and Pearl boxes of vegetables and fruit when they lived in George Town after leaving Beaconsfield. I have learnt they would have come from their son Lindsay, as he was an avid produce grower, and established a large market garden that had many fruit-bearing trees, and harvested vegetables year-round.

This information all came from a man who lived it and I don't have a need to press its authenticity. Ray was an absolute light in a story filled with too many shadows. How lucky I was to hear his voice before he left Earth.

Before I knew it, I had to leave. I thanked him for agreeing to sit with me. He was a lovely man. Unfortunately, his spirit was rocked by a sequence of life events as a child and young adult in relation to his father. Ray wasn't entirely embraced or supported for who he was; he had no choice—he was born that way. The last thing I told this gentle man was that I would accept him and his way any day. We hugged, and then I had to bid him farewell.

For there was another man waiting. I knew he would be staring at the clock, sitting at his front window waiting for my imminent presence.

Jason Brook and his wife Lorraine were expecting me for dinner. As I arrived at Jason's home, I was buzzing from what I had just heard from Pearl's nephew and from seeing Jason and Lorraine again. We hugged each other and said our hellos and stood in the kitchen as I shared with them what I had just been told.

Jason's immediate reaction was, "Yes, I have heard that."

"Go on," I said with exuberance. "Do tell."

He said he had been told the story by one of his head keepers within the lighthouse community. Cyril Mater was the man he was referring to; a much-admired man who taught Jason a lot about keeping a well-run island, including how to be a good lighthouse worker and leader in a confined environment. Cyril was placed at Tasman Island to clean up the island and stop the fighting amongst the workers who called it home. He was a straightforward, by-the-book sort of man.

Cyril Mater knew Pearl had a reputation and told Jason that she was "on the game" and "very much a lass." All these descriptions point to a repetitive pattern of behavior her daughter Kendall was unfortunate enough to notice at the young age of ten. Yes, even she was aware of her mother's behavior; from twigging in childhood to acknowledging it in her adulthood. It was true, my nana pleased men frequently.

These patterns have been mentioned over and over. I get it. "She had loose morals." This has been said numerous times and I think I've heard all I need.

Jason recalled that Cyril met Pearl in George Town in the 1970s. He insisted Jason steer well clear of this woman; he was adamant. Jason admits he was curious, but he took his commander's words seriously and obeyed them. He never met Pearl, but he remembered her and her reputation for the rest of his life. She was undeniably well-known.

After this conversation, I still had way too much energy for my body to contain. If anything, Jason's descriptions supported what Ray had told me. I didn't think Pearl should be shamed. I declared that I needed to free this energy and only a run was going to do it.

Barely containing my excitement, I put my running shoes on and headed straight for the highest of the hills overlooking the bay. When I reached the top, I stretched my arms out and put my head back, giving myself to the elements. I breathed in deep with a power flowing through me. I felt like I was on top of the world.

I ran back to Jason's where we all sat down to a hearty meal. We talked more until I hit a wall of tiredness.

That night I went to sleep thinking: *Well, my grandfather was a murderer and my Nana was a prostitute.* There was nothing I could do about that but smile. Their lives had no reflection on me today. Best of all, I did not judge either of them. It is what it is. With that I slept soundlessly.

The next morning, I had much to ponder. Jason and I sat for a day of discussion and theorizing. With the wind whistling outside, we bunkered in for banter. I stayed a few nights and we tied up as many loose ends about the paths of Pearl and her men as we could. There were several queries that could only be answered with 'who knows' or 'I'm only guessing,' but together we did our best, and we uncovered what we could.

On the morning I left, Jason cried and told me to go quickly as he doesn't like goodbyes. He has a very good reason for that. One of his parents gassed themselves in an oven. It's one of the reasons I know what an honor it's been to have met such people, who welcomed me into their own homes and shared their life views with me.

This was all capped off by something I have always wanted to experience. I boarded the plane to Melbourne near dusk and as we flew through the clouds, I peered to my left to see if I was could catch the Western green tinge. I did, and I cried because it was one of the most emerald green spheres I have ever seen. It was supported by yellows, oranges, pinks, and purples. It really was a kind of magic. The perfect end to this journey. A gift, even.

Back on Melbourne soil it was time to piece together all my findings.

I had established Pearl was born and raised in Beaconsfield by two loving parents who have a kind legacy. She would have encountered tough measures throughout her schooling as the nuns were strict and fierce. This did not benefit the church's calling as she was not religious or worshipful at all. That system failed, and I was never to say grace or cross my heart at her insistent gesture, for she didn't believe.

She resided in Tasmania from birth until adolescence. I can place her in Beaconsfield in 1941 at the age of 17, as Eleanor remembers speaking with her. Pearl promised Eleanor that "she would come back get Eleanor and bring her to Melbourne after the war." But Pearl never did. Eleanor has always despised Pearl for breaking that promise.

This is most certainly the time when Pearl left Tasmania for Melbourne. Why would Pearl have to promise something on her return if she wasn't leaving? It is from there that she engaged in sexual relations with men that founded her reputation as being "on the game."

I have not uncovered any reason why Pearl was so cold toward Joseph at his deathbed. Out of all the siblings, it was only Pearl who left Tasmania for the mainland, and she did so as soon as she could.

Where she stayed and exactly what she did whilst she was in Melbourne is not traceable; all I have is that she was paid to have sex with men, and when she was short of funds her father sent her money. At some point from 1946 to early 1950, she met Harrison and gave birth to Kendall in Melbourne in December 1950. Then she returned to Tasmania, and I am not clear on why she did this other than it was to be with her family.

Presumably Pearl lived next to her mum and dad for a period of two years, and then in 1952 she, Harrison, and Kendall moved to George Town, a small fishing town not far from Beaconsfield. They rented two houses during their time in George Town—one at 200 Low Head Road, which is approximately just shy of a mile (1.5 kilometers) from the Low Head lighthouse and keeper's quarters. It was also close to the station that housed the pilots who boarded the aircraft carriers during World War II. The other home they lived in was close to the town center on Goulburn Street.

Kristen was then born and their third daughter, Kate, followed in December 1953. Pearl had a short break from childbirth, but now had three children under the age of three. They were joined by their fourth sister in May 1955, and the family was complete.

After the succession of childbirths, Pearl and Harrison left George Town and stepped into their first appointment as a lighthouse family on April 17, 1956—a month before Kylie's first birthday.

In April 1956:

Harrison was thirty-eight years of age

Pearl, thirty-two years of age

Kendall, five-and-a-half years of age

Kristen, nearly four

Kate, two-and-a-half

Kylie, just one year

Pearl and her family had close to four years in the George Town community. She is remembered by Maureen, who was another niece of Pearl's.

Maureen said, "Wherever Pearl went, there was trouble. She was always fighting about the girls, meaning her daughters."

This is similar to what April Hagen (Harrison's sister) wrote in her letter to Margaret Barnes (Harrison's first wife). She says it was Pearl who caused the problems on the lighthouses, and that is why they had so much trouble. Maureen went on to say that Pearl attracted the wrong sort of people and couldn't be on her own. Kendall says the same.

It is a fair picture I am procuring of a woman who was cold-hearted at the death of her supportive father but prior to this moved interstate to live next to him for years, and who did so by choice. She married a man called David Smith and had a son who she adopted out and provided no trace of either's identity when they parted company. She fled her hometown to the mainland where she provided sexual services for financial gain, met a man called Harrison in this working scenario, and the two of them grew fond of each other to the point where they had a daughter and moved back to Tasmania together. They lived near her family and were proud of their four daughters. They embarked on an isolated endeavor of a life of lighthouse keeping.

With character references saying she was a troublemaker and had loose morals, what could possibly go wrong?

HE WAS HERS

HARRISON JAKE BENNET

Born: May 11, 1918, Collingwood Victoria
Died: December 2, 1960, Seaford Melbourne
Married: Margaret Barnes June 8, 1945, Benalla Victoria
Children: Joshua Bennet, May 5, 1945-January 13, 2009
Defacto: Pearl Joyce 1950-1959 Tasmania Island region

Children:
Kendall Anne, December 25, 1950
Kristen Nelly, July 26, 1952
Kate Louise, December 16, 1953
Kylie Tasma, May 4, 1954

War Service: World War II
Enlisted: October 21, 1939
Discharged: October 4, 1945
Region: Middle East, Greece, Papua New Guinea
Regiment: 2/5 INF BN
Occupation: Lighthouse Keeper

I didn't know my grandfather. There was a zero-tolerance embargo enforced on his existence.

Not once did Pearl say, "Hey Sparkling Kid, let me tell you about your grandfather, your mum's dad."

There were no photos, no direct discussions, definitely no stories, just overhearing a surname and mention of Tasmanian islands.

His four daughters didn't know much about him either.

That may be largely in part to the fact that he himself wasn't exactly raised with pride or self-esteem. Violence and rejection were daily tasks to overcome for him; these he mostly ingested in silence. This man wasn't given a chance whatsoever. He was destined for pain, and that became his reality.

The other reason the Four Ks not knowing anything about Harrison is that from the time they left him behind at Tasman Island, they disowned him in name and biological right. Therefore, this information may be met with much the same attitude—they couldn't care less...or maybe, they might.

For a long time, he was the monster who beat their mother. The one who left them with a legacy that would follow them day and night. While the Four Ks want to disown it, there is truth in it that affords answers now. Even today, Kendall states: "Don't judge me for what my father did."

I look at her and say, "I never have."

My knowledge was of a bad man named Bennet, and a good man named Harper. But I had no idea who was who and how those men fit into the family. The concept of my mother having a father did not present itself.

From my childhood memories, I knew my mum and her sisters escaped from an island in a rowboat with the help of the supplies man. But was that memory accurate? It told me my nana formed a friendship with the supplies man, that she told him she needed to get off the island and he agreed to help. One night, he rowed over to where my family was and spirited them away. That was all the knowledge I had, all a child could manage to retain.

There is not a lot of accuracy in terms of the complete picture, but it is close to the truth. Not once did that story include the concept of a grandfather. He really didn't exist.

I had heard of Bennet, but never made the blood-relative connection. And you did not say that name aloud or ever dare ask how it related to you.

I didn't know about Harrison until I had his death certificate in my hand. The only reason I discovered him was newspaper articles named him. Neither my mother nor immediate family told me.

It may or may not please his daughters to know that not all those who met Harrison thought ill of him. Contrary to his engraved, one-way reputation, I met with people who could not understand the thoughts of those who spoke negatively of him. There were several individuals who would swear by his loving and caring nature. One Joyce relative even challenged me to never let another tell me my grandfather was a loathsome sort.

In fairness, I decided to go and meet my grandfather.

From newspaper articles, I discovered there were court documents and inquisition files on this man and the situations surrounding him.

I sat in the Public Records Office and stared at the small, folded bundle before me. There were a few thoughts circling in my mind: *This is all it comes down to,* and that this small, folded bundle was only one amongst millions that sat on a shelf, archived. Such a small, uneventful bundle contained the information that altered so many lives.

I had been waiting for close to three decades to know what my grandfathers looked like. Although the images in these documents were not the best way to be introduced to Harrison or Phillip, I hadn't another option. There were no photos of Harrison, but an aunty had been concealing the only available photos of Phillip. Access to the public files was my only chance.

So, at the age of thirty-eight, via two black-and-white crime scene photos, I met my biological grandfather and my step-grandfather.

I opened the envelope and placed the contents before me.

It was Harrison I saw first, and while the image was confronting, I said, "Hello." I tried to look past the blood and the bullet hole, but they were quite a prominent feature of the headshot. It was taken on a morgue slab in the basement of the Frankston hospital. There he was—my mother's father; bullet hole in skull and all.

One striking feature stood out: Harrison's nose. My mum has that nose, my Aunty Kate and Kylie definitely have that nose. It is unmistakable—long and pointy. I even have a version of that nose. But Kendall doesn't. Then again, you can have different features and still be related.

It is true, throughout the years there had been some conjecture as to whether Kendall had the same father as the other sisters. Even Kendall suspects she is not Harrison's daughter, and as I stared at the photo I, too, saw how Kendall's father was a mystery, because I didn't think I was staring at him. The suspicion was that Phillip, my step-grandfather, was Kendall's biological father. I was open to the possibility, but how on Earth did Phillip and Pearl know each other before Harrison and Pearl did? I haven't found anything to tell me they had. It might just be family conjecture. No more to it than that.

I kept staring at these photos and noticed that my dead grandfather was dressed in his best clothes. "You dressed to die," I said out loud. Yes, he had.

His bow tie, clasped around his crisp white shirt, matched his suit jacket. He was clean-shaven, and his hair was neat. He was older than I imagined. He also appeared to have a swollen and bruised left eye, which was older than the fresh wound to his forehead. Had someone hit him before he shot himself? Had he been warned not to come near my nana? Or, had he fallen recently? An observation that would never receive an answer.

So that is how I met my grandfather. In a public office after a silent stint of staring at a package that contained reports and photos. Waiting for courage and readiness to reveal an identity.

It was now time to meet Phillip; he was in the envelope, too. I put Harrison's photo aside and drew Phillip before me. This image was as confronting as Harrison's, and again the blood and bullet wound were prominent.

He was too young to die.

He was a handsome man. Still in his sleepwear, his hair was longer and straighter on top and slightly messy—probably because he hadn't prepared himself to die that morning. He was still in bed when a man came to his house intending to kill him.

His clothes were white, but there was blood soaked around his neckline. And the entry point of the bullet had left quite an indentation in his forehead.

"I wish you hadn't died," I said to him.

It was disturbing to see these pictures, but I was satisfied that I now knew what my grandfathers looked like. I knew their faces; could picture who I was reading about in the court documents. Knowing was much better than not knowing.

But it comes at a cost; its damage done, and I had to declare this murder-suicide was far from over.

To be truthful all of it hurts, but it only hits after a while. Then comes the deferred pain. I didn't know what was happening until I began to speak aloud.

"I think I'm holding it together all right," I said, "given that today is the first day I have seen my grandfather."

With or without a bullet in his head it was a long-awaited introduction. Before I could rationalize it, the sadness came freely. I thought of who my grandfather was, what he did and what he didn't. I wished he hadn't shot another man and then himself. I wished he hadn't died too.

Why did I ache so much for never meeting 'the bad one?' And why did I wish he had lived? For if Harrison had lived, I would have had a true grandfather. I would have had two grandpas on my nana's side, because Phillip Harper's heart would have continued to beat, too.

And my mum would not have hurt so much. Her ability to genuinely love died when he died. She didn't just lose two dads in December 1960; she had been shot as well.

And then she had us—my brother and I—and she wasn't anywhere near repaired. The bullets are in all our heads still.

She couldn't give herself to us completely because she had lost something so treasured as an innocent child. She is an adult, but on many occasions, I have seen the frightened little girl whose stepdad was shot in the family home, and then her biological dad had shot himself not twenty meters away. She never had time to heal.

This is where it all started. It's the little girl hidden between the yellow bin and the fridge on that camping trip.

It's why we are here.

As time passed following the occasion where my mum had been huddled up behind a bin at the camping site, I learnt the concept that every side has another. To discover the truth of a situation, one must have all the various sides, angles, and versions before you pass judgment. Thus, I went searching for the other side—Harrison's side. It was time to access his death certificate and go from there.

I found those who knew of Harrison. Again, I also had the exceptional work of the genealogical researcher. Lists of family members were given to me—I had blood relatives in hand. One side of my tribe was broadening. Harrison had brothers and sisters and a mother and father, and all of them I would come to learn about.

Knowing what we know of Pearl fairs less in comparison to what I unfold in Harrison's life. There's decades of it. Horrid account after horrid account. A clear representation that for every action there is a source.

More often than not it's another's behavior that is precipitated by another's actions. The ripple effect. It is the undeniable influence of where we are from. Who it is we have come from that teaches us how to behave. The standards that are acceptable and those that are not. Our parents, of course, and other influential role models directly and indirectly show us what is acceptable through their behavior. And what is it they are showing us? Did my mum show me how to hide behind a bin? Or was she showing me how to be crippled by emotional weight?

Consider this: they are often teaching through behavior via the lessons they learnt in their youth. With this universal acceptance of learned behavior, it is reasonable to infer that Harrison never had a chance.

He was born in Collingwood. His father was Jake William Bennet. Jake was born in South Australia on the February 9, 1882 and died in 1935. Harrison's mother was Frances Mary (nee Davis-Lee). She died in 1930.

Together, Jake and Frances Mary had six children:

> Harrison Jake Bennet born May 11, 1918;
> died December 2, 1960
>
> Charles Harold Bennet born October 19, 1919;
> died 1982.
>
> Jason (Jack) William Bennet born July 24, 1911;
> died November 16, 1944
>
> Mary Gwendoline Jones born 1916;
> died August 17, 1957
>
> April born August 26, 1909; died January 21, 1981

They resided at 60 Abbott Street, Abbottsford.

Harrison's father had a menacing nature, equipped with rage and aggression that manifested in thorough beatings of his children. I have listened to the stories of how it was to live in this man's home. How had the Bennet children existed beyond their young years? How had they not had their last breath beaten from them?

Their survival may be attributed to their cunningness—an adapted survival resource that would have taken numerous forms, such as hiding before their father got home and curling into a little ball to protect themselves when caught by his need to thrash something. What a terrible existence to endure.

He worked at the local brewery and drank beer to an alcoholic's excess.

What I have come across in my research is that their father was the source of torrential abuse. One living relative described him as a "violent bastard." And in the early 1920s, what are you going to learn from one violent bastard? How to be a violent bastard. There was no dial-up helpline, no psychological assistance for the survivors of violence, and there was no talking of the matter.

If you were waiting for your mother to save you, she more than likely could not as she, too, was under the control of the "violent bastard." What she could probably do for you, as she loved you, was keep your shoes clean, make sure your socks were darned, tuck your shirt into your shorts, brush your hair, and occasionally hold you as you cried in pain and fear.

Harrison and his brothers lived this. When I received the images of the family I saw it straight away. Even when the dead can no longer speak, the photos do.

Harrison learnt violence from watching and being subjected to violence. He "grappled a woman's throat," as stated by Pearl, because he would have witnessed this action by his father. He thrashed in anger and had a volatile streak because he was his father's son.

Let us then assume—and in part, securely accept—that Harrison was a violent man. Not having been beaten by him myself, I am not directly affected by his brutal hands and I do not fear him or his memory. But I know this from the silence and the glimpses of his memory I have seen in my mother and aunties. He was bad, and he hurt people he loved. He hurt his children on occasion, he hurt the woman he was romantically involved with, and he hurt the families he left behind. That being said, there is one point to be made for the picture to be in focus: Harrison was also hurt.

He may have been woken from sleep with a beating. He may have avoided it some mornings by either hiding under the bed or racing out the door to school before being seen. Who knows how many times a day he had threats and fear strangle his throat? I am absolutely not making excuses; I deplore his behavior, but for the truth, he has the right to have his side told.

One time he and his brother Cameron were being beaten so severely in the lounge room that Harrison was curled up in a ball, watching his mother from under his arms wrapped over his head. She didn't move to save him; he doesn't flee the whacks across his back. He remains there till his father exhausts himself. Then Cameron and he are left to lie in pain. The emotional damage would have been soul destroying.

He grew up in the streets of Collingwood and Richmond, presumably attending primary and secondary schools in that area. I have not uncovered any further details of his life during his childhood and adolescent years. However, I do know at the age of twenty-one he enlisted for service in World War II. An examination of Harrison's service records confirms he qualified for the following awards:

> 1939-45 Africa Star, Pacific Star, Defense Medal, and War Medal
>
> 1939-45, Australia Service Medal

He served with the 2/5 INF BN in Greece from April 9, 1941 to May 1941. Thus, he would also be eligible for the Greek Commemorative Medal.

On the October 21, 1939 he was registered in the army then discharged October 4, 1945.

The battalion Harrison served in was quite significant, as it was one of two to be in combat against all the King's enemies during World War II. He fought the campaigns in Libya against the Italians, in Greece against the Germans, in Syria against the Vichy French, and in New Guinea against the Japanese.

The 2/5th Battalion formed on October 18,1939, and Harrison was part of it by October 21. He trained at the Puckapunyal barracks before departing April 14, 1940 where he sailed across seas to arrive in the Middle East on May 18, 1940.

It was a harsh environment; arid, hot and blowing of whipping-like sands. His company undertook further training in Palestine and Egypt before its first campaign in the advancement against the Italians in Eastern Libya. They were there for the months of January through February of 1941, having successfully participated in the attacks at Bardia and Tobruk.

By early April his division was deployed to Greece to resist the oncoming German invasion. It was a fierce confrontation that saw the Australians withdrawing from its initial defensive positions at Kalabaka to the port of Kalamata, from which it was evacuated on the 27th April. It must have been horrific seeing approximately fifty transport drivers being left behind to become prisoners of war.

The battalion rested in May, but by June that same year they took part in the campaign in Syria, including the explosive battle of Damour that delivered the defeat of the Vichy French forces. In Syria and in Lebanon, Harrison and his battalion remained as part of the garrison force until January 1941.

From the war of sand, the battalion left for the jungle and fought against Japan. They were then deployed to Milne Bay in Papua in early October 1942 but did not cross fire

NIGHT KEEPING

with the Japanese until the end of January 1943, when they joined the force of defending Wau, in New Guinea. This was a bloody and viscous battle that saw the Japanese around Wau defeated in February. From here, the embattled men charged towards the drive at Salamaua and were ruptured and relentless in the gun exchanges at Goodview and Mount Tambu in July and August.

Just stop for a second and imagine how much gunfire the men have heard in three years. What they've seen, smelled and felt.

It's both gut-wrenching and character wrecking. One doesn't go through those battles and come out the other side the same. No one does.

Harrison remained in Papua New Guinea until July 8, 1944 before his return to Home Base Camp Pell. Located in Parkville Melbourne it was an army camp named after Major Floyd J. Pell, a US airman killed in 1942 defending Darwin against a Japanese air attack.

A member of his unit summed up the service of the 2/5th Battalion when he stated, "We won no Victoria Crosses, we were not famous, but we proved ourselves at Bardia and for sheer dependability and duty well done, we have no better." A conclusion; well worth its mention.

From the August 20, 1944 to September 19, 1944, Harrison was classified AWL. Which meant he was 'absent from where one should be but without intent to desert.' It was his first AWL charge, and it was correct as he was in Rosedale setting up his brother Jason's business. He did this and then continued to a town across the other side of Victoria—Benalla—where he met a woman by the name of Margaret Barnes at the local pub, the Tarax Bar.

He entered into a sexual relationship with Margaret and their son was conceived. He also met Jill Mead. She would return to him and help in his life right when he needed her years from this moment. For now, he had to face the music so to speak.

FIRST COURT MARTIAL

His first court martial gave an insight into his life. I was told of his court martial in a way that implied he was a "no good loser;" that the court martial was proof that he wasn't any good as a man. As I began investigating Harrison's service record, the court martial raised questions about his character. But I soon learnt to not believe everything you're told.

The first AWL was about his brother Jason, and so is the second. Harrison put his brother before himself.

The court martial transcripts give dutiful insight into what happened.

Corporal H. J. Bennet, L.T.D. Camp Pell of Unit 12 AUST Small Ships Coy, stood before the court of the Department of the Army Melbourne to be answerable to the Attorney General's Department Canberra October 3, 1944. He faced the charge of A.A. 15 (1) A.W.L. from August 20, 1944, to September 19, 1944. He pleaded guilty and was thus found guilty and received 60 days of detention from October 3, 1944. It is believed the court was properly convened and constituted with qualified and eligible officers and the charge sheet was drawn correctly, and it discloses an offence against the Army Act by a person amenable to military law. The charge found that Harrison absented himself from Camp Pell on August 20, 1944, without leave until he surrendered himself back at Camp Pell at 0800 hours on September 19, 1944, to Sergeant A. Hazewinkel.

Not only was Harrison sentenced to 60 days of detention, he was also sentenced to forfeit 13 days of his pay while awaiting trial. His record of offences registered on his court-martial sheet tells us he was charged previously with the following:

>AWL: six times
>Disobeyed a lawful command: three times
>Conduct to the prejudice: twice
>Failed to appear at a place of parade: once

He attended court at 0930 hours on October 3, 1944, and gave the following evidence:

The summary of evidence is read, marked Exhibit 'K,' signed by the President, and attached to the proceedings. The Defending Officer advises Harrison whereupon he admits that he is the person named in the AAF Mob 3 and Certificate of Surrender, attached to the Summary of Evidence. Rule Procedure 40 (A) is then complied with.

Question to the accused: Do you wish to give any evidence or to make any statement with reference to the charge or in mitigation of punishment, or as to character?

Answer: Yes, I wish to give sworn evidence in mitigation of punishment.

Harrison then gives sworn evidence and the court hears Harrison's reasoning for leaving his post as per against Army regulations. Harrison declines to call any character witnesses but continues with: "on the 20th of August I was on leave and I got a letter from my brother saying he was in distressing circumstances regarding financial matters and he asked me if I could help him out. I decided to do so, and I bought him some machinery. He is a woodcutter and carter at Rosedale.

"I bought him a truck and put 80 pounds' deposit on it. I bought him a drag saw at 50 pounds, four horsepower stationary engine at 27 pounds. A 13/4 h.p. stationary engine at 17 pounds and a saw bench and belt at 20 pounds. That is approximately 190 pounds altogether. At that time, I had approximately 300 pounds in the bank.

"My brother is a married man with one child and another on the way. He was very worried over his position. I had so much at stake I wished to see him firmly established and then I surrendered myself to Sergeant Hazewinkel at Camp Pell. I have been in close arrest at Royal Park since the 19th of September."

After hearing this, the prosecuting officer declined to cross-examine Harrison and he was examined by the court with the following questions:

> Question: Could this not have been done whilst you were on leave before the 20th of August?
> Answer: I never got the letter before, Sir, and I never knew the position.
>
> Question: Haven't you been in touch with him before this period?
> Answer: I had been in touch with him, but he never mentioned his position to me.
>
> Question: Did you make any application to LTD for some extension of leave?
> Answer: I had an extension of leave of 14 days, that brought my leave to, I think it was, the 19th or 20th of August.
>
> Question: Couldn't you have done everything that was necessary in that 14 days?
> Answer: No, Sir, I never had the time to do it.
>
> Question: Why couldn't you have done all this? Why couldn't you have placed the money at his disposal and let him buy this machinery?
> Answer: It was my money, Sir, and I wanted to see it spent properly.

Question: He was in a better position to know what was required, wasn't he?
Answer: I had a fair idea what was required myself, and I had done that sort of work before the war.

This was the completion of the information gathered at the hearing, and Harrison tells the court he does not want to have his evidence read over to him. The various certificates and registered documents were tendered and verified by all parties, and the defending officer representing Harrison addressed the court on the question of punishment by stating that: "He had nearly six years' service inclusive of a period in Middle East and New Guinea and asks for a fine." Harrison was asked if he would like to address the court and he declined. The court then closed for consideration of his sentence.

Harrison was sentenced to undergo detention for a period of 60 days.

From Harrison's testimony, we can see that he answered the questions put to him in a straightforward manner. He was telling the truth and was prepared to face his punishment. He not only surrendered himself, he surrendered himself in uniform and returned once his personal matters were sorted. He set off from his responsibility to help a brother, and he would have known the consequences for doing so. Yet his duty at that time was to use his own money and put himself at risk of reprimand to help another. He acted with consideration and knowledge. He did not trust his brother, and with the information I have uncovered on Jason's past behavior, he had good reason to take responsibility for his investment. It was an investment on Harrison's behalf, as we learn from his court testimony in his next court martial.

Because he does it again. He flees Camp Pell a second time and is registered AWL from the April 22 to June 12, 1945. He found himself in Benalla, getting married to Margaret Barnes, and being at the birth of his son Joshua, born May 5, 1945. His marriage to Margaret Barnes proceeded on June 8, 1945, and he surrendered to the Richmond police station on June 12, 1945.

SECOND COURT MARTIAL

After serving his 60 days of incarceration from his first court martial punishment, Harrison returned to his service duties before he was called to be answerable to a second court martial. Private H. J. Bennet, L.T.D. Camp Pell of Unit 12 AUST Water Transport Coy, stood before the court of the Department of the Army Melbourne to be answerable to the Attorney General's Department Canberra on June 19, 1945.

Harrison faced the charge of AWL from April 22, 1945 to June 12, 1945 at the Hawthorn court. He pleaded and was found guilty of his charges.

The proceedings were the same as the first court martial, and documents and presenting officials were sworn in and qualified to be present

The court sentenced Harrison to 60 days detention, which was a valid sentence. He forfeited one day's pay while awaiting trial. The court recommended immediate suspension of the sentence.

His record of offences, registered on his court martial sheet tells us that he was charged previously with the following:

AWL: six times
Disobeyed a lawful command: three times
Conduct to the prejudice: twice
Failed to appear at a place of parade: once
DCM held at Hawthorn AWL: 60 days.

The court proceeded through its formalities and representatives stood and were sworn in. Harrison was asked if he objected to be tried by the President or any other officers whose names that he has heard. He answers "No," and the Major President of the court begins proceedings at 0925 hours. As the charge sheet was read, it was heard that Harrison left without leave at 2359 hours on April 22, 1945 and did not return until he surrendered in military uniform at the Richmond police station at 2100 hours on June 12, 1945.

Harrison was asked if he wanted to give any evidence or to make any statement with reference to the charge or mitigation of punishment, or as to character. He answered, "Yes, I desire to give sworn evidence in mitigation of punishment." Again, he declined the opportunity to call upon any witnesses as to character. He gave the following evidence before the court.

"I am 27. I am married and have one child. In August last year, my brother decided to start a business after being discharged from the Army. He asked me to help him finance it, so I helped him, on the understanding that when I got out of Army I should be in partnership with him. It was a woodcutting and carrying business in Rosedale, Victoria. Two months after we started this business he was killed in an accident.

"I applied for leave, which was granted. 14 days of compassionate leave, without pay. He was killed when the truck skidded in loose gravel and crashed through the bridge into the river. He was drowned. That truck formed part of the partnership assets.

"I was granted this leave to try and sell the business as a going concern, or to carry on myself if I could get a discharge. If I could have carried on myself, I could be sure of his wife getting a living. He left a wife and two children. His wife had no relatives in Australia.

"I did not get a discharge and reported back to camp, leaving her to look after the selling of the business. Which she could not do, as she did not know anything about what it was. I came down myself to do it.

"The truck at the time was still awaiting repair. I eventually sold the business and am waiting now for them to pay out the money on the business. I had about 200 pounds in it. I did not apply for leave the second time to sell the business; I knew that I would not get it. I was not too sweet with the CO of the unit.

"Another reason why I stayed away was I had a girl in trouble and was informed by the police that she was naming me as the father, so I married her on the 8th of June 1945. I returned to camp immediately when we came back to Melbourne. I surrendered."

Harrison's brother, Jason Bennet, was discharged in March 1944. He served alongside Harrison and their other brother Cameron during war time. He returned to Australia and died in tragic circumstances on March 16, 1944. And on that: what of Jason? How much happened to Jason? I found him to be unfathomable. He, Jason Bennet, is significant to his brother, and therefore we need to find out about him. I detail the reasons why after completing the picture of Harrison.

Back at the court case where Harrison was cordial and responsive.

The prosecutor stood and began cross-examining Harrison.

> Question: You say on this occasion you did not apply for leave because you knew you would not get it?
> Answer: Yes, Sir.

> Question: Didn't you consider it worthwhile having a go?
> Answer: It was not much good having a go; I was not too sweet with the CO of the unit.

Question: Why were you not too sweet with the CO of the unit?
Answer: I was an NCO at one time and I was reverted to the ranks, and he took a very poor view of it.

Question: You have been in the army a long time.
Answer: 5 years and 8 months, sir.

Question: You should know by now that there is a correct way to do things, shouldn't you?
Answer: I know that, but it was no use me putting in for it because I knew I would not get it if I did put in for it.

The prosecutor retires from questioning and the defending officer declines to re-examine. The court then asks Harrison to be answerable to the following questions.

Question: Your reason for surrendering was that you intend to carry on?
Answer: Yes, sir.

Question: You feel you are fixed up at home now, you can go on fighting?
Answer: Yes, sir.

Question: Do you know where your unit is?
Answer: Brisbane, sir.

This was the end of the information gathered at the hearing, and Harrison told the court he did not want to have his evidence read over to him.

Various certificates and registered documents were tendered and verified by all parties and the defending officer representing Harrison addressed the court on the question of punishment by stating that, "The accused has seen active service in Middle East and New Guinea. Total service nearly six years. In light of past record and of his sworn evidence that he will soldier on, he deserves leniency."

Harrison was asked if he would like to address the court and he declined. The court then closed for consideration of his sentence.

Harrison was taken from the Richmond police station June 12, 1945, and placed under the command of Major Commander of the Metropolitan Troops Corp D. Naylor. He was placed under close arrest upon charges against him being investigated by his CO on June 13 to Camp Pell where he was placed under open arrest at the depot. A certificate tendered to the Hawthorn Court by the camp staff officer states that: 'he has performed normal duties and his conduct has been good.'

From this disciplined action, Harrison returned to service. From July 16, 1945 to September 17, 1945, he was in Tasmania with his regiment on water transport duties.

By October 4, 1945, he had been discharged from the army. He then went to New South Wales, where he remained for a short period. In the summer of 1946, he was at Musslebrook and Denham, New South Wales. On February 12, 1946, I can place him at 'Ridgelands' in Musslebrook, working where he had his RAS badge stolen from his coat at a dance in Denham. He may have stayed there longer or returned to Melbourne. I cannot place him again until 1950, when he introduced Pearl to Thomas and April Hagen, his brother-in-law and sister who resided in Jameson Street, Richmond. He met Pearl somewhere in that time line. By April 1950, they had conceived Kendall as she was born in December.

On May 4, 1951, a statutory declaration regarding his stolen RAS badge listed 1 Gore St., Fitzroy, as Harrison's residence. It was mentioned to me that this area was a red-light district. It seems suitable that Harrison and Pearl met in this area, given Pearl's livelihood. They may have been in a relationship for years or known of each other for years prior to conceiving Kendall.

By mid-1951, Harrison had moved to Tasmania with Pearl and baby Kendall, to live with Pearl's parents in Christian St., Beaconsfield. He built their own home next to his in-laws' dwelling and obtained employment at the local wharf with the help of his father-in-law.

After a successful time with his in-laws, he took his family in late-1951 or early 1952 to live in George Town until April 16, 1956. Kristen and Kate were born in Launceston, while Kylie was born in George Town. On April 17, 1956, Harrison and his young family commenced their first station as lighthouse occupants at Eddystone, Tasmania. This is day one for the new lighthouse keeper.

I came to learn Harrison had a Jekyll and Hyde nature. Charming and confident, yet desperate and broken.

His behavior was not unique. His two other brothers, Jason (Jack) and Cameron, were equally troubled and ultimately self-destructive. According to a living relative, Harrison, Jason, and Cameron were peas in a pod. When they returned from the war, they were "piss heads" and saw a lot of each other. That included before, during, and after the war. It makes sense for Harrison and his brothers to be close, as they were rejected by their incapable father from a young age, only to be raised by their sister, April. There was a desperate need to belong in each of them. Drinking would have been a friend, just as it had been their father's companion.

I am of the opinion that Harrison did what he wanted when he wanted. His testimonies at his military hearings do show he had valor. His movements upon his return from fighting for his country are varied; he moved about frequently and in many directions. He married a woman he didn't care for and paid to rescue his brother's business, which he intended to invest in himself once discharged from the services. It all changed when he met Pearl. He stopped for her. He went where she did; he didn't run off. He stayed. Why? Because he loved her.

When Harrison moved interstate with Pearl, it was more than likely he just wanted to belong, and Pearl genuinely had his heart. He didn't love Margaret Barnes, although he had married her and had a child with her. He didn't stay with her, but perhaps left with ease and relief. He remained with Pearl, not for just one child but four, and this time he didn't leave his children behind because he wanted to be with them.

He was more than likely emotionally unstable; he was back from the war, which would have affected him severely. However, it cannot be discounted that he was unstable before he left for the war due to his turbulent childhood and adolescence. He had lost his brother Jason, and was an alcoholic. And above all else, he had taken to Pearl, who herself was not of the most nurturing and wholesome nature. They made a good pair. It's no wonder they gravitated toward each other.

The truth is they did make a good home in Christian Street, Beaconsfield, I have heard their home was a welcoming place. There are stories of drinking to excess and catching taxis home roaring drunk, but there is no hint of violence. Not yet.

Eleanor, remembered a lot about Harrison, and they are fond memories. When I asked her if she recalled any violent behavior by Harrison, she said with exuberance, "No, not at all. I've never heard anything like that Melissa." This was truth based on her experience, and she was more than happy to tell me stories about Harrison.

During Eleanor's pregnancy with her son James (and following his birth), her then-husband, Bruce, was messing around with other women. Eleanor was the first to say that he was a good man, yet also a ladies' man, but Eleanor finally left him as he was unable to stay faithful.

On this occasion, as she was giving birth to her son Bruce, Harrison found out that Bruce was with other women and took much offence. Harrison made a point of letting Eleanor know that he was going to give Bruce a hiding. This tells me Harrison believed in fidelity and in giving a man a smack to the head when he stepped out of line.

Eleanor also said Harrison "was a good boxer."

Intrigued, I asked her to explain.

"Well, he used to box in those side show tents. It was the Harry Paulson boxing tents and whenever he needed money he would box and win. He knew how to fight, and he did all right, too."

This was interesting as Harrison would have learnt how to box throughout his childhood and possibly in the army.

Eleanor also remembered that he worked hard and that he loved his girls.

He is also remembered for attending to his responsibilities and working at the wharf, and by doing this he acquired the funds to move the family to George Town, along the main road near the Low Head Lighthouse. Harrison began working at the Australian Aluminum Production Commission (AAPC) as a painter. According to Daniel Ogilvie, who was Harrison's brother-in-law, all Harrison did was sit on one of the towers and throw nuts and bolts at the seagulls. He wasn't committed to his job. Daniel said there would have been a truckload of nuts and bolts in the bushes below the towers. Harrison worked there until he joined the lighthouse community and became a keeper.

Although there are varied accounts of his character, he was employed constantly and served his family in that regard. I saw commitment to a woman, but I am fierce in defending the rights of women, and I want to know if he had hit her yet. When did he start hitting her? And what would his disrespectful excuse be? I also wanted to know why he chose to take his family to isolation. There is conjecture that he moved in this direction because he wanted to remove Pearl from inklings of her previous behaviors. If she was on a remote island, she couldn't serve 'hot dinners' to frequenting men. This is just speculation, and I have nothing to support it. It is a question worth putting on the thinking table, though.

We are nearly on the islands, keeping watch of night, but before the pages take us there and before we meet Phillip—the third man involved in the triangle of love and deceit—it is important to learn about Jason. The two men are entwined, born together and buried together.

Harrison has outright stated he did not trust Jason, yet he helped him wherever he could. This shows how Harrison interacted with people and isn't farfetched as a model for how he gets along with Phillip.

BAD PENNY BROTHERS

JASON BENNET (HARRISON'S BROTHER)

Born: July 24, 1911, Collingwood Victoria
Died: November 16, 1944, Rosedale, Victoria

Married: Felicity Lakes

Children:
Josephine, 2 years at death
Ordett, 3 weeks at death

War Service: World War II
Enlisted: 1940, Darwin
Discharged: March 1944
Region: Middle East
Regiment: 2/6 Field Regiment Artillery, Gunner
Occupation: Woodcutter

Jason was the eldest of the surviving Bennet boys. Born close to two years after his sister April; he was in trouble before he knew it. Delivered with the spirit to stand up for himself, he was a challenge to his abusive father, Jake. It wasn't long before he was promptly considered too much to handle and was permanently not welcome in the family home. Jake and his mother, Florence, made Jason a ward of the state. Whether he was criminally minded as documented when just fourteen years old, is up for debate. But quite frankly, it seems to me this man was a niggly, conniving, nasty sort. I am all for compassion, but Jason was something else.

When I looked upon his photo, I saw it—the spirit energy of menace. Yet he had a wife, children, and a brother prepared to put himself out—even to the detriment of his legally obligated duties—to help him.

I met Jason via court documents.

On August 17, 1925, a letter written by Senior Detective J. Owens for Superintendent Campbell of the Victorian Criminal Investigation Branch stated that:

1. I have to report for your information that Jason William Bennet is under committal for trial to the Criminal Court at the present sittings.

2. His parents reside at Abbott Street, Abbotsford; his father is employed at the Victoria Brewery, East Melbourne.

3. Bennet has a bad record; he was committed to the Reformatory School by the Children's court, Collingwood, on the 25th of March, 1925, on a charge of unlawful possession. He has since been charged with larceny but as he was a ward of the state, these latter matters were not proceeded with.

4. He was caught thieving by his parents and they state that he is out of control. He has been given up as hopeless by everyone that has had charge of him, and he has also threatened to poison his parents before this offence had been committed.

5. The authorities at the Reformatory Schools for Boys state that they consider that he requires much stricter supervision than is enforced at the Schools.
6. Would Mr. Campbell please forward this report to the Crown Law Authorities for their information?

He was fourteen, and what he had done in that time was astounding. Come August 16, 1926, at the Melbourne Supreme Court, Jason William Bennet—at the age of 15—was charged with administering poison so as to endanger life.

Who did he poison? Was it his parents—he's threatened to poison them— or someone else?

Whatever he did, on August 10, 1926, Jason was committed to trial by the Justices of Stratford to face the charge of causing to be taken poison with the intent to murder. This was a capital charge under section 8 of the Crimes Act 1915. During the committal hearings, Jason pleaded not guilty to the charges, but while he was in the Sale Gaol, he ended up changing his plea.

He wrote from Sale that he intended to plead guilty at the trial, and this was witnessed by the governor of the gaol, Mr. Rowe. While awaiting trial, he was taken from Sale Gaol to Pentridge Gaol in Coburg. Jason was assigned counsel under the provisions of the Poor Prisoners' Act 1916. During the trial, there was no requirement for witnesses to attend as he was to plead guilty. He was committed at the Children's Court, being under the age of 17, and it is indicated in the brief that the plea of guilt is a good one.

He faced a number of charges, to all which he pleads guilty.

1. Administration of poison so as to endanger life.
2. Maliciously administer poison to be taken by Harold Richards.

3. Inflict grievous bodily harm for the said Harold Richards.
4. Endanger the life of Harold Richards.

Jason was sentenced to three years' hard labor and was to receive five strokes of the birch. The evidence during the committal hearing reveals much about Jason and how he came to be in Gippsland. The prosecution called six witnesses to testify against him:
Charlotte Richards
Harold Richards
John Ford
Charles Garrett
Bruce Owens
Jake Makay

The court was offered the following exhibits:
A: Tin of cocoa
B: Bottle of strychnine
C: Post office receipt
D: Tube of strychnine
E: Bottle of water and strychnine
F: Cardboard box and bottle of strychnine
G: Statement of accused

That was my introduction to the life of Jason Bennet. Now to try and make sense of it. To do that I had to read Jason's handwriting and somehow believe what he scribed.

He told the court how he came to be in Gippsland. He commenced his testimony by declaring that he was a ward of the state and that on June 29, 1926, he came to Stratford with a lad named Fred Gunn. They had escaped from the reformatory school, Royal Park, the previous week. While they were at school, Fred Gunn had said to Jason that while he was working at Stockdale, he found out how to get some traps. He told Jason he had a gun and one cartridge at his parent's home and asked him if he wanted to escape the reformatory, get the gun, and go to Stockdale and go trapping together.

Jason said, "All right."

On the night of June 23, 1926, the two young boys climbed over the fence and went to Gunn's home in Richmond. They retrieved a pea rifle then headed to South Yarra where Jason stole a bike before moving on to Malvern. They slept in a timber yard for the night. The next morning, they travelled to Armadale, and Fred Gunn stole a bike there. The two of them then cycled to Gippsland, obtaining food along the way. It took the two boys six days to travel to Stockdale. On June 29, Fred Gunn took Jason to the Richards farm, having told him of his previous work there.

During this time, they met with a Mr. McDonald, a neighbor of the Richards. He told them that one of the boys would be able to get a job there; they would just have to go enquire. Fred told Jason that he should be the one to get the job and that he would go on with the trapping as planned. He then assured Jason that he would remain about the area for a couple of days and then go trapping.

Jason agreed and went on to the Richards' farm, where he met Mrs. Charlotte Richards. Upon meeting her, he asked if she would employ him. "Any chance of a job?"

Mrs. Richards then asked Jason if he was a friend of Fred Gunn and continued by telling Jason that she was scared of Fred. Jason told his first lie to Mrs. Richards, stating that he did not know Fred Gunn. With that, the Richards gave Jason Bennet a job.

Fred remained in the bush and was seen the next day by Mrs. Richards while she was outside with Jason. On the instructions of Mrs. Richards, the two chased Fred. As Jason was running, he deliberately did not catch his mate and Fred escaped into the bush. Fred came out of the bushes that night and met Jason in the Richards' yard, where he asked Jason to fetch a can opener to open some fish. Jason gave his friend the opener and Fred was not seen again until the son, Harold Richards, caught him in the loft and handed him over to the police.

Jason continued to work at the Richards' undetected. He was not given up by his friend, Fred. Jason remembered being at the Richards' for two weeks, working hard and doing his chores, when Mrs. Richards started growling at him.

On Tuesday night, he was asked to put the bread tub outside along with several other requests at the same time. Jason commenced to do what was asked of him. He had not yet put the bread tub outside when Mrs. Richards started pushing Jason around. Jason told her to leave him alone and said that he would leave. Mrs. Richards then advised Jason that he was not permitted to leave and that she would not let him leave until he got his clothes that had been ordered that afternoon. A traveling draper called Mr. Boucher had arrived in the area that day and came to the farm, whereupon Mrs. Richards ordered Jason a suit.

They sorted this situation out and the two of them got along well for the next couple of days. Then Mrs. Richards started picking on Jason again, this time about "his people." Jason tried to defend his family and told Mrs. Richards that his people were all right and that his sister went out with a boy.

Mrs. Richards then said to Jason that "his people should look after his people's sister as she wanted minding." This, like the other situation, was settled and things were fine again for a few days.

Mrs. Richards told Jason to clean out the shed. He was to remove the feathers from the shed and burn them. He did this then returned to the shed and continued to clean up.

Mrs. Richards came to the yard and saw the feathers scattered all over the yard, approached Jason and told him off, saying that he had not set the feathers alight and they were scattered everywhere.

She then hit Jason with the rake and told him to clean up the mess and stayed to assist him. During the clean-up, she pulled a bottle off the shelf and said, "This pink strychnine does not kill the foxes like the white does." She then proceeded to pick on Jason about the feathers. After the shed was clean, she entered Jason's room and pulled two blankets off his bed and told him that he didn't deserve so many blankets as he was "used to sleeping under trees and that."

It was Jason's responsibility to have the potatoes peeled prior to 1700 hours (5p.m.). When he failed to accomplish this, Mrs. Richards saw fit to continue her tirade whilst he stood at the basin doing his tasks. As befitting his nature, he tried to stand up for himself. He told Mrs. Richards that it wasn't his fault and that he was trying his hardest. He had been working all day long.

Mrs. Richards told Jason not to speak to her that way then hit him. Jason had had enough of her cruelty and told her he wasn't going to stand for it much longer. Mrs. Richards again told Jason he wasn't going anywhere until he had paid off the suit.

The next day was a Sunday, and Harold Richards and Jason decided to go and rob a beehive. Mrs. Richards made it clear to Jason that she did not want him to leave, but he did. He paid for it with a tirade on Monday. Mrs. Richards took the day to tell Jason how worthless he was and generally picked on him to the point that Jason told her again that he was not going to stand for it anymore. As he was being belittled, his thoughts turned to escape and retribution.

He decided to put the strychnine in the cocoa. Simple as that.

That night, the family ate dinner together and Jason went to the shed at 1900 hours (7p.m.). He got the bottle of strychnine and scraped some out with a stick and then returned to the kitchen, which was now empty. He put a quarter of a teaspoon into the cocoa tin and placed the cocoa tin back onto the dresser. At some point, he sat down and began sewing a pouch, and then Harold returned from the post office.

Jason promptly asked the family if they would like a cup of cocoa. Mrs. Richards didn't, but made herself and Mr. Richards a cup of tea then left the kitchen. Jason now insisted that he would make Harold a drink of cocoa, but Harold said he'd make his own after finishing his chores. Once finished, Harold made himself the hot cocoa, and upon taking the first sip, remarked at its bitterness. Harold then asked Jason if he knew anything about it.

"No," Jason lied then went to bed.

Jason listened to the movements of the house, then heard Harold go to his mother's room and ask if there was anything on the cup that he drank from, to which she said no.

Harold told her the cocoa made him feel sick. His mother told him to take a good drink of castor oil and she got up and went to the kitchen with her son. She asked him what was wrong, and he told her that he thought he had been poisoned. Maybe out of guilt or deviate pleasure Jason got out of bed and went to Harold in the kitchen and asked him what was with him. Harold again stated that he thought he had been poisoned, and with this Jason ran to the McDonald residence to ring the doctor and ask him to come see Harold.

They fetched the horse and when they heard someone calling out. Jason met Harold on the road and took him to the McDonald's home.

Jason then told the hearing that he put the poison in the cocoa because of the way Mrs. Richards had treated him. The reason he let Harold drink the cocoa was because he thought if one had it, then the lot might as well. He also didn't want to alert Harold to the poison as it would have foiled his plot to poison them all. He finished his statement by saying that he did not know his actions would result in such seriousness and that he was sorry for his behavior.

That concludes Jason's point of view.

Now to hear Mrs. Richard's.

Charlotte Richards presented her version of meeting Jason Bennet and welcoming him into their family home. She stated that she met and came to know a lad by the name of Frederick Gunn about two months earlier. He had come "from the schools." He stayed with the Richards for two weeks before they had him returned.

The Richards were familiar with the reform school network and may explain why Mrs. Richards belittled Jason so. The Richards may have used the reform schools as a means of free labor—work in return for a bed at night.

She told the hearing that Jason Bennet had been with them approximately five weeks, only taking him on when he'd lied and said he didn't know a young lad named Gunn. She then drew attention to the events that unfolded on the 26th of July, a Monday afternoon at 1600 hours (4p.m.). She and her sons, Alf and Harold, and Mr. Richards and Jason had a drink of cocoa together. No one had any ill effects from the afternoon beverage. That evening at about a quarter to nine she was in the kitchen with Harold and Jason. Jason stated that he was about to make Harold a cup of cocoa, and she asked him if he would have a cocoa, too, and Jason replied, "I don't take cocoa at night." She made herself a cup of tea and took this to bed. The next thing she recalled was Harold at her door, asking if she was awake. She got out of bed and assisted her son. When Jason got out of bed, she asked him to go to the McDonald residence to get the horse and buggy, as they were the closest neighbors at two miles away. Jason did this. She remained with Harold until Doctor Ford arrived.

The following morning, she asked Jason if he knew anything, and Jason replied, "No." Mrs. Richards produced the strychnine bottle from the shed and the cocoa tin. She had given the two items to Constable Bruce.

Harold (Harry) Richards now had his turn to recount his experience.

He was a farmer at the Stockdale farm and the son of Mrs. Richards. Harold came into the house at 1115 hours for dinner. Although this is lunch time to us today, this was dinner time in the 1920s. She then told him that if he waited for Jason to get it for him, he would wait all day.

"This is because Jason is slow," Harold said.

Jason was peeling the potatoes at the time, when Mrs. Richards said, "Look at him peeling these potatoes; he has been there ever so long."

With that Harold heard a splash and the rattle of a dish. Mother said, "Look, he has kicked the dishwater and potatoes under the bench."

Mrs. Richards then prepared Harold's dinner, which he ate before returning to his work duties.

Harold returned at a quarter to five, drank cocoa with everyone, then after tea (which is dinner), took the mail to the post office, returning at a quarter to ten.

Mrs. Richards told Harold she was having trouble getting Jason to bed, to which Jason replied he was waiting to make Harold a cocoa. The cup Harold made his cocoa in is one of the cups his mother and father used for their own tea not ten minutes earlier. Harold refused Jason's offer to make the cocoa and made it himself.

NIGHT KEEPING

Harold consumed half of the cup and said, "By Jove, Jason, this is terribly bitter. I have never tasted anything so bitter before."

Jason replied, "It was bitter like that at dinner time."

Harold corrected him. "It was not bitter like that at lunch time." He threw the rest of the drink out and sat in front of the fire. Jason went to bed.

As Harold was resting by the fire, he felt a twitch across his back then his limbs began to feel numb. He realized something was not right, so he took a drink of cod liver oil and washed it down with fresh milk. He then went to his mother's room and asked her about it.

He deteriorated quickly and told his mother he needed help. His mother and Jason helped him walk along the road toward the McDonald's home. Jason ran ahead to fetch the horse and buggy while Mrs. Richards and Harold continued on. Harold had four fits as he was walking. He estimated that they were close to an hour and a half on the journey when his mother called for help not 200 yards from the McDonald's house.

This places the time at around 1130–1145 hours. That gave Jason an hour and a half to run or walk two miles to fetch a horse, and presumably upon fetching the horse and buggy he would have returned in a faster time.

It appeared that Jason did either not go to fetch the horse and buggy as stated, or he did but with the intention of taking as much time as he could to not assist the dying Harold. Much like when Jason faked his attempt to catch Fred Gunn.

The doctor was not called until Harold and Mrs. Richards arrived at the McDonald residence. There are a lot of inconsistencies. Would the doctor not have been alerted when Jason initially arrived at the McDonald's property?

Jason didn't have the horse and buggy with him, when Harold and Mrs. Richards came across Jason along the road. Mr. McDonald wasn't with him. Jason answered Mrs. Richards' call.

Harold said, "Come here Jason, I want you."

"I can't find you. I don't know where you are," Jason replied.

This is surprising. Jason was familiar with the area, and there was one road.

Harold told Jason, "Follow straight up the road; you must come to me."

Jason appeared and once they arrived at the McDonald's house, Harold immediately had a fifth fit. It was then the doctor was called, and Harold was treated.

Harold was shown the bottle of strychnine and said that the bottle had been in his room for the last 12 months up until July 16, 1926. Then some of the strychnine was removed and the cork sat on the bottle differently.

The discrepancy between Jason's behavior and Harold's account illustrates a calculated intent to murder. He's hiding, he's sneaking around, he's lying, he's making out he's assisting when he isn't. I don't give credit for Mrs. Richard's belittling of him, but this is pure orchestration of criminal infliction. This is the threat he made to his parents being carried out when an opportunity arose.

Following is Doctor John Ford's account:

The doctor was not called until a few minutes before midnight, and upon hearing the news, made his way to the McDonald residence at Stockdale. Ford immediately identified signs of strychnine poisoning, and evidence that an emetic had had a good effect. The muscles of his lower extremities and his back were in a state of absolute rigidity. Harold's jaw had been firmly closed until the emetic acted. Harold was unable to walk, and when the doctor helped Harold to his feet, Harold fell back. His pulse was very slow, and his body was perspiring freely.

NIGHT KEEPING

Ford stayed with Harold for close to two hours, waiting until the effects of the poison had passed, and administered more treatment to eliminate the last of it. At this time, Dr. Ford received the tin of cocoa from Jason Bennet and the boy named McDonald Junior. This tin was forwarded on to the public analyst department by registered post.

The time it took Jason and McDonald Junior to fetch the tin of cocoa implies that Jason did not attempt to get the horse and buggy to assist Harold. The two boys achieved this journey twice in less time. We can assume that McDonald Junior was asked to accompany Jason because Jason was untrustworthy.

Jason's intent was for Harold to die.

With premeditation, processing, and behavior, it is clear Jason was the first of the Bennet boys to wish certain death upon another. He was, by all accounts, lucky to not be the first murderer of the Bennet clan.

Charles Garret was next to deliver his findings.

Mr. Garret was the government medical legal analyst. He received the registered parcel sent to him by Doctor Ford on July 28, 1926. The parcel was labeled registered No. 534 Stratford and contained a tin of cocoa with the Windmill Cocoa label on it. He weighed the contents at 1¾ of an ounce and began analyzing its contents. He noted there were a number of colored crystals he submitted to chemical analysis. They were pure strychnine. He then removed 60 grains (or about 1/12 of the portion), made a quantitative examination and found that it contained about 1½ grains of strychnine. The cocoa contained equal to 19 grains of strychnine.

On the evening of August 9, 1926, Detective Owens handed Mr. Garret a corked white glass bottle labeled 'bottle found in creek at Stockdale 9/8/1926 J. N. Bruce.' Mr. Garret commenced examination immediately, finding a muddy-colored fluid that had a bitter taste. It contained a crystalline substance: strychnine. He was handed another parcel that contained a blue glass bottle labeled 'poison, pure strychnine.' This was the bottle from Harold Richard's bedroom. Mr. Garret found the contents of this bottle consisted of strychnine in a crystalline form which was similar to the strychnine present in the tin containing the cocoa. The bottle contained about 100 grains of strychnine. A fatal dose is from ¼ to ½ a grain of strychnine.

How did Harold live?

Senior Detective Owens now took the stand.

Owens traveled from Melbourne to Gippsland to interview Jason Bennet, presumably from the Stratford lockup. Upon introducing himself to Jason he asked if he knew of anything to do with the poisoning out at the Richard's.

Jason told Detective Owens he knew "nothing of it," to which he was told that he "might as well tell the truth."

Jason's cunningness kicked in, and he told the detective that it would "have to be proved that I know something about it."

Detective Owens looked Jason in the eye, letting him know who was in control, and said, "Don't worry, we will prove that. But I want you to tell the truth. You are in a very serious position and it is a very serious charge. If you have done this terrible thing we only want to understand you state of mind, so that you can be trained and put on the proper course so as not to do such things as this." Detective Owens offered Jason care and hope, and that was enough for Jason to then speak.

He told the officers that he put the strychnine in the cocoa. When they asked him why he did this, Jason told Owens it was because Mrs. Richards was always picking on him. He then told the detective that he got the strychnine from the bottle in the shed.

Detective Owens then went to Stockdale where he spoke with Mrs. Richards and Harold. He returned with the bottle and showed it to Jason, who confirmed this was the bottle out of which he took the strychnine. It should be noted that this did not coincide with Mr. Garret's findings.

Detective Owens had to return to Gippsland, this time to the Sale Gaol where Jason was detained after his confession.

On Sunday, August 8, 1926, Detective Owens once again sat in front of Jason. "You did not tell me the truth about the strychnine."

Jason, ever the unfettered liar, said, "Yes, I did."

So, the detective had to inform Jason that science had truth on its side and the strychnine in the bottle was not the same as the strychnine in the tin of cocoa.

Jason continued to lie. "Yes, it is."

Detective Owen demanded Jason tell him the truth. Jason realized he couldn't bluff his way out, so told the detective about the second bottle of strychnine in the shed he used for the cocoa, and that he had then thrown the bottle in the orchard.

"Which part of the orchard?"

Jason said, "Near the bottom."

"Where about?"

"Near the creek."

"Can you get any more definite about that?"

"It might have gone into the creek."

"Tell me where it is; we must find it."

"It is in the creek near where I buried some cats that I drowned."

The detective left Jason in his prison cell and drove to Stockdale on August 9, 1926, and with the assistance of Barry Clements, he recovered the bottle. He then drove to Melbourne and gave it straight to Mr. Garret when he arrived that evening.

Mounted Constable Jake Makay and Senior Detective Owens conducted their initial interview of Jason Bennet on July 31, 1926. But the detectives were already mounting a case against Jason with the tin of cocoa and the first bottle of strychnine. It was not until science revealed Jason's lie that the detective returned to Jason, at which time he was charged and transported to the Sale Gaol to await trial. The remaining witnesses delivered their statements on August 10, 1926. The trial was heard at the Melbourne Supreme Court on August 16, 1926.

This event demonstrates Jason Bennet's calculating nature, even at age fifteen. This young man was beaten as a child, plausibly neglected and rejected by his parents, and grew into an untrustworthy and unstable person. He was seriously tainted by his introduction into this world. It was said that Harrison was the 'bad penny' of the Bennet men, but I think he shared this label with Jason.

'A lot' doesn't begin to cover how much lying Jason did during his life, and he didn't go far from one gaol to another.

Did you pick up his statement about drowning cats? I know some would say that is the way of the land, but a certain predisposition would be required to do that.

Where did he go from here? He was incarcerated from 1926 to 1933. The Metropolitan Prison received Jason on August 14, 1926 where he was taken to Pentridge Prison in Melbourne, Victoria on September 4, 1926 to serve at the governor's pleasure.

At this time, photos were taken of the young Jason, who was described as 4'10" in height with a medium weight range, blue eyes, brown hair, and a fresh complexion. He was young and slightly innocent in these photos, especially his profile portrait. It was stated that Jason could read and write and was born to follow the Church of England. He was classified as a laborer and was sentenced to three years' hard labor and the infliction of five lashes with the birch. He was ordered to serve his sentence at the Bayswater Reformatory School.

On November 29, 1926, Jason was taken to the Bayswater Reformatory and stayed there for a short period before he again jumped a fence and escaped. On the run from his conviction, Jason found himself in country Victoria in the town of Castlemaine, where he was caught breaking and entering. He was charged and tried at the St. Kilda Children's Court on November 17, 1927, where he was convicted and ordered to serve his new charges that carried a three-month incarceration term. He returned to prison to serve the unexpired portion of his sentence of three years as per the order of November 29, 1926.

On November 17, 1927, the Castlemaine prison received Jason, and as he was a security risk, he was taken to Pentridge Prison on May 18, 1928, and remained incarcerated at his Majesty's pleasure from 1928 to 1932. He received a lengthy list of offences and additional sentencing during his time in Pentridge.

Pentridge: penalty for offences was two days in solitary confinement.

> January 21, 1929: Failed to obey an order
> June 24, 1929: Misbehaving during divine service
> August 15, 1929: Disorderly conduct
> February 24, 1930: Failed to obey an order
> August 11, 1930: Using indecent language
> August 27, 1930: Making unnecessary noise
> January 5, 1931: Talking during exercise
> January 31, 1931: Failed to obey an order
> February 1, 1931: No remission, no warrants to discharge
> November 23, 1931: Disorderly conduct

On September 7, 1932, Jason was taken to Beechworth Prison in country Victoria. His photo was again taken in

June 1932 and his demeanor was far more hardened than the photos taken in 1926. He had profile and frontal images and a photo of himself standing with arms by his sides, staring at the camera. His profile image was of a man who bared a striking similarity to his brother Harrison.

He received two recorded offences during his time at Beechworth. On September 7, 1932, and January 23, 1933—for removing vegetables. Jason remained in Beechworth Prison until he was released on parole December 15, 1933.

It is estimated that Jason spent up to or more than 28 days in solitary confinement.

Any way you view the charges and the reasons for why Jason was convicted and sentenced during this period, he spent a good deal of the first 33 years of his life incarcerated. He was told what to do and how to do it, put down, controlled, and ordered around for 33 years. He may have been raped; he was certainly beaten. He was an unsavory character, and I would not choose to become acquainted with him, but equally I do not think he was ever given a fair chance from the beginning.

From 1934 to 1940, Jason stayed out of trouble. He was six years out of prison, but I have not been able to confirm what he did in that period.

Then, as was the national call, he joined the army and spent a free life fighting for Australia.

In 1940, Jason enlisted to serve Australia in World War II. He was deployed to the Middle East in the 2/6 Field Regiment Artillery as a gunner. During this time, he met his wife-to-be and married her at the age of 30 in 1941, while serving time as a soldier in Lebanon. He and Felicity (Flick) welcomed their first daughter, Josephine, in 1942. Jason continued his service and Felicity remained in Lebanon with baby Josephine until she boarded a ship bound for Australia. She and the young child arrived in Australia April 9, 1943, on the ship *Port Lee* into the care of April and Thomas, where they waited for Jason's return.

NIGHT KEEPING

Jason arrived home on March 23, 1944, on compassionate grounds. These grounds may be based on the welfare of his wife and child or to do with his own psychological state. The reasons are unclear, and I have no documentation to offer any insight.

He returned to Gippsland for work, and Felicity and young Josephine remained in Melbourne, making a home at Heidleberg Road, Clifton Hill. Jason must have commuted from the city to the country, which left Felicity with a young baby and an absent husband. Is that happiness? Or, was it just the way it was? They had their second child, Ordett, within three weeks of Jason's death. Felicity remained in Melbourne and raised her two daughters; she remarried and had a third child and moved with her family to Marrickville, NSW.

As we saw in Harrison's chapter, Jason established a wood-cutting business in Gippsland. He was still the drinker, and on this occasion, he sat in the pub having a few, not knowing how close his end was—November 16, 1944.

He'd lived a hard life till now, but it's quite clear he was happy. At the start of the month, he had travelled to Melbourne and visited April and Thomas. He was in good spirits and good health as stated by Thomas on November 17, 1944.

Possibly the last man to see Jason alive—along with Jason's friend, Michael— was the Railway Hotel assistant manager, Jake Cunningham. He told the inquisition that at 1415 hours, Jason and Michael called in at the hotel and asked about an order for firewood. They then had two drinks each. Left the hotel and returned at 1600 hours that same day and sat talking in the parlor. They had three or four more drinks each.

Jason left at this point to attend to business in town then returned at 1700 hours to pick Michael up where the two spoke of returning to Rosedale. As they were discussing plans to leave, two other men named Birmingham and Linden entered the hotel and the four men sat and had a round of drinks together. At this time, Jake went off to the shed to milk his cows. It was 1730 hours. As he was bringing the cows from the paddock across the road, he saw Jason and Michael in the truck. He stated that they were sober and not displaying any effects of drinking too much. Jason had asked for a bottle of beer to take to Jack Gove. Jake filled a bottle of draught beer for him and the two men drove off.

The first witness to see the truck was Nigel Bertram, a line foreman with the postal department. He stated that around 1730 to 1800 hours, he was in his dining room and saw a red truck travelling toward Rosedale at about 40 miles an hour or faster. He stated that it was travelling faster than trucks usually travel along that road, and he and the house were almost enveloped in dust.

They continued to head south and passed Phillip Jennings' house. He was 14 years old at the time and had just left school to help at home. He noticed a truck at 1750 hours travelling at a fast rate. He was in his mother's driveway leading up to the house driving a wagon. He was only a quarter of a mile from Rainbow Bridge, where the truck was heading. He thought the truck was travelling faster than vehicles usually travel along that road. He looked back toward the bridge and saw the truck swerve and go over the side. He watched the front of the truck drop down toward the water.

He then called out to his uncle, "There's a truck gone over the edge of the Rainbow Bridge!" Then, with his uncle and another man, went to the bridge and saw the truck upside down in the water.

The uncle, Thomas Jennings, ran straight into the water and pulled open the driver's side door. He noticed there was no movement inside the truck and estimated that he would have only taken three to five minutes to get to the truck from the time his nephew called out to him. He also noticed there was no movement in the body when he first grabbed it. He assumed the man was dead, but he still felt around in the water inside the cabin. He caught hold of a man's leg and tried to pull him out, but the man was caught.

The second man with them was Harold Whatmough who, with Thomas, was trying to pull Jason Bennet out of the cabin. They could not see Michael in the passenger's side as that side of the truck was lower in the water. Failing to free the body in the driver's side, Thomas got on his push bike and began riding toward the O'Brien's house to call the police. With the phone out of order, Thomas rode back to Rainbow Bridge and Mrs. O'Brien continued to try and ring the police.

Back at the lagoon, a third man, Frederick Fitzpatrick, arrived and the two men made another attempt to free the body from the driver's side of the truck. Frederick was able to remove the driver's wristwatch—the time on the watch was 1800 hours when it stopped working. He then saw Constable Draper heading toward the bridge. It was now at least half an hour since the truck first went off the bridge.

First Constable Jake Draper of Heyfield arrived at the Rainbow Bridge after 1830 hours. He noted that a red, three-ton motor truck was lying wheels up in the water on the right-hand side of the bridge. The truck was submerged except for the front wheels and front mud guards. It was resting on the top of the cabin with the tray part balancing in deeper water.

Draper entered the water and felt around the cabin, trying to free Jason. He found that Jason was caught by his left leg, which was over the gear lever with his toe caught under the button of the self-starter. He was able to release

Jason and brought him to the bank and commenced artificial respiration then asked another man take over resuscitation before reentering the water to search the cabin.

He found Michael, removed him from the truck, took him to the bank, and laid him next to Jason. Michael was huddled in the opposite end of the cabin to Jason. Draper stated that both men were completely under water and probably dead upon his arrival. The rescuers tried to resuscitate both men until Dr. Brent arrived and pronounced both men dead. Jason was wearing a gray pullover with gray trousers and tan shoes. Michael was wearing a blue coat, gray pullover, and trousers with military boots. The constable then examined the dead men's bodies and found that Jason had a bruise on his left shin where it had been against the gear lever, and he had a small abrasion on his forehead. Michael also had an abrasion on his forehead above his right eye.

The constable then investigated the crash impact site. He noted the bridge was approximately 170 feet in length and 14 feet wide. There were two sharp curves within 100 yards of the bridge on the Heyfield side. He could see the truck's tire marks and noted the truck's left wheels were being driven on the loose gravel at the side of the road. It appeared the wheels were skidding as they turned to the right and on to the bridge, and these marks continued across the bridge in a half circle and through the railing on the right side.

There were marks on the bridge that indicated to the Constable that the truck stood on its end near the edge of the water about 16 feet below the bridge, and then somersaulted into the water. Its impact broke the two panels on the bridge, the roof of the cabin was dented, and the front damaged. The Constable did not sense there was any cause for suspicion of the motor accident and subsequent deaths of Jason and Michael.

Jason died from accidental drowning whilst confined in the cabin of a motor truck that had fallen from a bridge into deep water. Sitting next to him was Michael Joseph Jarrett, and he too drowned in the incident.

At 1830 hours, the legally qualified registered medical practitioner Oscar Brent attended the scene at Rainbow Bridge. Upon his arrival, he saw two bodies on the bank of the lagoon receiving artificial respiration from helpers. He noticed the partly-submerged motor truck near the bank of the lagoon and saw that the side railing of the bridge was broken.

The next day—November 17, 1944—Dr. Brent did a post-mortem examination of both bodies and concluded the men's cause of death was drowning. He found that Jason's skull was fractured and that his lungs were waterlogged. He had a bruised left thigh and a small abrasion on his forehead. The skull fracture indicates Jason was almost dead before hitting the water. He was laid to rest at Charlton cemetery.

Upon all this Harrison had a lot to tend to. He left his barracks to tie up his brother's woodcutting business. I wonder how this death impacted him. We know Harrison didn't trust Jason but gave him money and intended to go into business with him once he was discharged from the army. There was a bond there; I wondered how strong it was.

There is credit to the account that Harrison hadn't displayed the ability to forge or maintain strong bonds with anybody, including the woman we are about to meet. If there was going to be anyone who provided evidence of Harrison's ability to strongly bond, it would have been her. Wouldn't marriage and a child do it? No, that doesn't count, and just as confronting and hard as that is, this woman had much the same wary disposition as Harrison.

She, too, was to have a mighty distant guard. When I knocked on her door, my god was it up.

COUNTRY VICTORIA UNEARTHS A HIDDEN GEM

This search was more a hunt. I had pointers indicating different directions, and like a bloodhound I searched until I found. This trip was one such occasion. I had nothing more than a need to know, and for some that's enough. Even though I had such a dogged nature about me as I travelled up the Hume Highway, doubt did visit my thoughts. I didn't want this trip to country Victoria to be a waste of my time or my finances. I didn't have all the details I needed; the car and I were venturing off together somewhat blind.

What I did have was names and addresses, and the determination to knock on strangers' doors and introduce myself.

No one knew I was coming, as I had been unable to locate the key individual I needed to speak with. I simply assumed she was in the same town her family had grown up in—the town where she had married my grandfather. That was it; that was all I had. That, and the hope she had remained in a small country town.

I stayed in a modest hotel and organized the street names and family members I needed to see the following morning. Unfamiliar with the town, I drove a couple of the streets I had earmarked on the map; quite honestly, I had no idea where I was going. Maybe I was being guided by the unseen. Either way, I stopped the car to find out which home was closest.

I was one turn away from Drew Street, and before I knew it, I was looking at the front yard of number eight. I didn't know if anyone was home, nor what to expect, but I had to move forward.

An adolescent girl opened to door to my knock. "Yes?" she said.

My introductory spiel began. "Hi, my name is Melissa, and I'm researching my grandfather's family. His surname is Bennet."

With that, an older woman poked her head around from the kitchen whereby I continued to explain that I was looking for my uncle's family—that he was my grandfather Harrison's first son.

The older woman ventured closer. "That's my husband's dad," she said. "Come in, have a seat."

I had found Joshua Bennet's only son, Mitchell Bennet, and I was sitting with Mitchell's wife Joanne and one of their daughters, Lisa.

I was welcomed, and we sat and chatted for nearly an hour. The irony was, they had been searching for Harrison but could not find anything, and here I was with all the information I could give.

I told her that I knew Joshua was born May 5, 1945 and was Harrison's first child. Harrison married Joshua's mother—Margaret—on June 8, 1945, but Harrison disappeared after the required marriage and left no trace or explanation for leaving his wife and son behind. It also assumed it left a gap of understanding in Joshua's life and the lives of his offspring.

I discovered that my uncle died a sad, lonely man and had been beleaguered by self-loathing. I can't help but think that may have had something to do with never having been loved by his biological dad.

Joanne told me she cared for Joshua in the later stages of his life. He passed away in January 2009 at the age of 63. The doctors said he had drunk his body to ruin. Even in hospital, Joshua had to have a drink and it was Joanne who provided just what he needed. There were many times when her caring efforts were unappreciated, but she was still there for Joshua and Mitchell as they needed.

I learned that Joshua married Maylene Bamford, and during their union she was subjected to abusive and controlling behavior. When she left Joshua, she made it clear that she was genuinely scared to be near him.

He did have a dedication to his son's sporting ability and watched Mitchell play cricket and football on a consistent basis. Photos of Mitchell and Joshua show two men sitting happily together, both smiling with eyes aglow. Joshua had a soft spot for the granddaughter I was sitting with. She was his favorite, and he didn't show her any of his rudeness or arrogance. So, he had a caring heart and a love for other people, and I am sure he had many other positive characteristics. He loved fishing and worked for the CRB. Joshua was a laborer; employed to build and repair roads and bridges and concrete in the Benalla district, where he was also laid to rest. May peace be with you, Joshua.

I told Joanne I hadn't yet located Joshua's mother, Margaret Barnes, and she was someone I really wanted to meet, as she could tell me about my grandfather—and when I found her I hoped she would.

It was Joanne who gave me the golden key, the missing piece's home address, and, "she would be at home", I was told.

On my way to Margaret's I picked up a walnut and sultana cake from the local baker then drove straight to her home. Before getting out of the car, I said, "Okay Harrison. Help me out here." I was about to meet his first wife; the least he could do was ease the situation.

The door was open, but the security screen locked. I knocked firmly.

"Yes?" the lady said through the protective screen.

"Is that Mrs. Margaret Barnes?" I asked politely.

"Yes."

As I began my introductory spiel, she told me she was in the middle of her lunch, that it was a bad time, and she had a doctor's appointment.

I was getting nowhere. I think I bordered on pleading with her and asked her if she wanted me to come back after she had finished her soup. I told her I wanted nothing from her and wasn't selling anything; that if it was her wish, I would place the cake on the doorstep and leave. But all I really wanted was to know about my grandfather.

"Come on then, you might as well come in," she said with a sigh, and opened the door.

That was touch and go.

I explained I was Harrison's first granddaughter and was looking to meet his son Joshua; unfortunately, I was a few months too late.

Then I produced her marriage certificate, and we began to have the most revealing conversation. Only a handful of people knew this information. So, after making tea and cutting the cake, we settled in the lounge room, agreeing the cake was good. It feels honorable having a stranger feel safe in your company. I pride myself on that and understand you must be genuine in your intent. Here I was, arms out saying, 'X-ray me, and see it all, I come in total peace and respect.'

I recounted my research and retraced my steps to Margaret, explaining my endeavor to find out about Harrison. I told her I had recently visited Harrison's nephew Gary (April's son), and he was a very lovely man. This was comforting to her.

"April wrote to me," she said.

"Have you still got the letter?"

"No, I don't think I have, I don't think I kept that."

At some point during our conversation, she began to trust me then went in search of April's letter. She was shuffling the contents of a box when she said, "You are in luck dear. Here it is; I kept it." She returned to her seat, unfolded the eight-page letter, and began to read to me.

The letter was dated and addressed as:

14th April 1961 April Hagen to Margaret Barnes

It was written in honesty and meant for care. What is shared in the following is from what I heard.

April apologized for not writing sooner, but she had been unwell and was only recently starting to feel better although she was still dealing with her ailment. She told Margaret about how after the shootings and inquisitions, the Bennet family's hands were tied. They kept their truth silent to protect Margaret and a woman named Jill Mead, and didn't want to get dragged into the mess of the situation because what was reported in the papers was inaccurate.

April spoke of how she, Thomas, and Cam did all they could to help Harrison, but when he came home from the Islands he was not a well man. She said that upon his return to Melbourne, "he intended to marry a woman you know of, in Jill Mead." Jill and Margaret were friends from working together at the Tarax bar in Benalla. This was where Harrison had boarded, and how his and Margaret's paths crossed. He also met Jill Mead at this time.

April told her that Harrison had been diagnosed with cancer of the liver, and given two months to live. Jill was to marry Harrison and care for him in his final months. They planned to marry after Christmas 1960. Her letter explained that he was "so ill" there was nothing anyone could do to help him. He was in pain mentally and physically. She continued by saying, "Who are we to judge?", and supported the loving Harrison she knew, as did her husband Thomas and her brother Cam.

She said, "[she and] Cam did all they could to keep him happy." They gave him money and kept him with them as much as possible, but he was a saddened man and missed his daughters terribly. With the knowledge of his incurable cancer and not knowing where his daughters were, Harrison attempted suicide. He fed a pipe from his exhaust into the window of his car and was not far from death when a passerby noticed and notified the authorities. "That passerby returned him to us and thank God for Harrison's survival."

Had the passerby not seen the car, Harrison would have died. Harrison had his car taken from him and was put on strict restrictions, which was part of the two-year probation period he had to abide by. He had to be at the Richmond home at 6.00 pm each evening and report to an officer of the law each day. He did not advise the court of his cancer status and instead decided to find his children to say goodbye, then marry Jill and let cancer take him.

What April was writing and explaining to Margaret was absolutely accurate. As Margaret looked up from the letter she was reading, she told me of when Harrison came to see her not long before all this happened.

Harrison had arrived at Margaret's home unannounced and asked her if he could take his then fifteen-year-old son Joshua Bennet out for the day. Margaret said that she would ask, and Harrison took Joshua to Shepparton for the day. He returned his son to Margaret then came home to Richmond.

Margaret never heard from him again but learnt of his fate in the papers over the following days. "I only knew what was in the papers," she said, and then read the truth when April's letter arrived four months after the shootings.

What Harrison did was exactly what he intended. He said his goodbyes to his son, now he wanted to say goodbye to his daughters.

April informed Margaret that Harrison had made an impassioned plea at the court suicide hearings, and the Judge said that the case was a terribly sad matter, but he could do nothing of it as Harrison was not married to Pearl and therefore had no legal standing. This broke him. He was failing everywhere. He was the biological father to four daughters but had no rights. He couldn't marry Pearl because he was still married to Margaret.

The letter goes on to explain that April told Harrison's wife-to-be, Jill Mead, to assist with her father's moving of the family home from Frankston to a newly-acquired residence in Essendon. Harrison naturally helped the Mead's move—he put his hand up straight away. In a remarkable set of circumstances, Harrison told the van driver of his plight during the long journey from the old residence to the new. As Harrison was crying his story out to the patiently-listening driver, the man suddenly turned to Harrison and said, "I know where your girls are because I moved them." Imagine the bets on that occurring!

The removalist then gave Harrison their address.

The next day Harrison went to the Eden Road address he had been given and asked Pearl to see his children for the day. Pearl agreed, and Harrison spent the day with his daughters. He returned them home safely and asked Pearl if he could see them again. He left Seaford and was home in time to meet his probation. April describes this was the happiest she had seen him. He was bubbly, over the moon.

The following days were joyous, but then he was struck another blow. He received a solicitor's letter telling him to stay away from his daughters, and April described how deeply he was hurt and maddened by the letter. She had never seen him like this and said the man who had signed the solicitor's letter signed the death warrant of Phillip and Harrison.

April and Thomas observed that on the night of December 1, 1960, Harrison was depressed and went to bed around midnight. April heard Harrison get up and leave the house around one in the morning but thought that he could not get to sleep and had gone wandering. She went back to sleep.

Harrison, on the other hand, went to Eden Road and sat in his car outside until dawn broke.

The police found the solicitor's letter in the pocket of Harrison's suit jacket. He was dressed in his best clothes with a matching bow tie, and a crisp white shirt. He was clean-shaven, and his hair brushed and in place. It was Harrison's last stand. His heart had been torn apart and was physically and mentally wrecked. He had nothing to lose. He was a dead man walking.

The police located the solicitor and gave him a severe dressing down. In April's words, the police said the man's signature wasn't so tough now.

April then told Margaret that Harrison died a broken man, and that she, Thomas, and Cam paid for Harrison's burial. She was sorry Harrison had taken another's life and warned Margaret of Pearl. "She is a snake in the grass."

She said Pearl put Harrison through much angst while on the Islands. She kept fighting with others and causing trouble and that is why they had to keep moving from island to island. Pearl had told the Bennet family they could see the girls whenever they wanted, so wondered why Pearl didn't extend that to Harrison. Maybe none of this would have happened. April told Margaret that she and Joshua were welcome and would always be welcomed as part of the family.

That was the end of the letter.

It was handwritten and well-composed, with much respect for the truth and for Margaret. It is a testament to April's character—a beautifully-souled woman who was caring and honest. It is a true account that upholds Harrison's intentions, and is a cherished gift of Margaret's. She wouldn't let me have it.

In my time with her, I found Margaret to be an honorable woman with strength of character and a capacity to survive. She had a child out of wedlock in times where it was frowned upon; admitted she got herself into a bit of trouble, but she stood up for herself and made her life a credible one. She worked three jobs at times and found love with a man named Barry, and with whom she had two more children. She is now surrounded by loving grandchildren and great-grandchildren.

She recounted her time with Harrison as being "young and stupid", and their required marriage was not made in heaven. They had a son, but never lived together after the marriage. Harrison wasn't violent toward her and didn't drink alcohol. Yet he never stuck around to watch his son grow.

THEN ALONG CAME ANOTHER MAN CALLED PHILLIP

AND HIS SURNAME WAS HARPER

It's sad. I thought I was part of this clan; that's what I was raised to believe. No truth in it whatsoever.

I have no bloodline from my second grandfather, not even any ties or links; though in my eyes we were related. While I was unaware we had no blood ties, what I did know was this man was the good one.

Pearl and the Four Ks lied, not just to us but to themselves as well.

Again, I am starting with the dead, but this time I knew to search the cemetery. As a kid, when we drove past this cemetery, my mum's composure would change. By doing so, I came to understand that someone in there mattered to her. She may have been unaware she did this, but for years I observed her change in demeanor when we passed. Mum would either go silent or make a sad, negative comment. I cannot remember her exact words, though.

It became a land of significance; one that had answers, but it was years off in knowledge for me.

It's now thirty-plus years later, and with time, honesty, and determination on my side, I researched who was there.

I had two names from the inquisition documents, and the genealogical researcher once again came up with directions. So, I went searching amongst the numerous headstones, just so I could say hello.

May 9, 2009 was a cloudy and chilly morning when I decided to find my step-grandfather, Phillip Harper. All these years and I had never ventured into this cemetery. My first visit I brought my children and a friend; I was nothing like my mother when it came to parenting; I had an open and honest method that revolved around inclusion.

So, Jasmine (nine years old), Caleb (seven), and Suzan and I went. They sprinted up and down the rows as I systematically walked their lengths. The children were randomly calling out to each other. "Have you found it?" or in Caleb's case, "I found it!" When we rushed over to him, the headstone held a completely different surname, but he got 1960 right, which he was proud of. An hour had passed, and the children were beginning to feel defeated, but I kept telling them we had all the time we needed. There was no rush; we were not going to give up. After I had surveyed the second section, I was starting to feel slight frustration too and yet awareness that I had looked at approximately a thousand headstones of people whom others loved.

By now Jasmine and Caleb were playing a respectful game of hide and seek and were yelling out, "Ready or not!" followed by laughter and squeals when found by the other. I was looking at how many lives had passed, and how much sadness each would have left behind.

Suddenly, Suzan, who was searching the last section, yelled out "Melissa! Melissa!" She began jumping up and down and waving her arms around. "I've found it! I found it!"

Relief overcame me. We all ran toward Phillip's headstone. Here he was, and next to him were his mum and dad. So close to the road. I have driven past this man countless times without realizing.

I began cleaning up the few weeds and moss that were on his gravesite and then cleaned up Agnes and William's headstone. Suzan went and found Morris Harper's headstone—Phillip's brother—and I was left alone.

"Hello, Phillip," I said, then explained that I guess I would have called him Pa or Grandpa, or maybe Pop. I told him I would have liked to have known him, and was aware he died unnecessarily and way too early. I said I believed he was a good man, and that I would find out as much as I could about his life. I then thanked him for saving my nana's life.

We left all feeling happy to have found Phillip, and rapt with each other for not giving up. There was laughter and a sense of accomplishment. The experience was definitely a positive one.

Now it was time to find Phillip's family and listen to their stories of him.

His full name was Phillip Patrick Harper. His mother was Agnes Harper (McHugh), who died in 1961 at the age of 72. His father was William Harper, who died in 1968 at the age of 68.

William Harper was a hard worker, and served his country during World War I. He would be known in the later part of his life as an ANZAC. Upon finishing his service, he was offered a soldier's settlement as a lighthouse keeper for King Island. Upon taking up this duty, he married Agnes McHugh in Launceston. He was the lighthouse keeper on King Island for many years, and in their steadfast marriage had seven children: Phillip Patrick, Jarrod Desmond, Anthony William, Morris, Elma, Beatrice, and Lilly. Lilly was born on King Island.

From his tenure on King Island, William took his family to Swan Island, Low Island, Bruny Island and Maatsuyker

Island. They were lighthouse royalty—well-known and well-established.

It had a foundational impact on them. Due to the style of lighthouse living, the Harper family was close, and they followed each other in their trades and vocations. Beatrice followed in her father's footsteps and joined the army, as did her brother Jarrod and sister Elma. Beatrice and Midge—a friend of hers—served together in the army in Hobart, and Midge eventually became Beatrice's sister-in-law, having married Jarrod.

Phillip became a carpenter, completing his apprenticeship in Burnie. His brother Anthony (Tony) also becoming a carpenter. Lilly was a receptionist and manned the telephone exchange.

When asked, Jarrod would say that Phillip "was a great mate of mine", and it was obvious that he missed his brother. His good mate was irreplaceable. It was Jarrod who introduced Phillip to the lighthouse-life of Tasmania. From Jarrod's perspective, he was helping his brother and by doing so, could also share that with him. He enjoyed being side-by-side with Phillip, just as they had been raised. Jarrod was a strapping young man, and had learnt much from his father regarding the skills required by a keeper. He went on to have an admirable career as a lighthouse keeper before serving as a soldier in World War II.

Phillip was a great carpenter and had no shortage of ideas and business endeavors to make his mark as a self-provider. After completing his apprenticeship, he bought a truck and went into business as a timber carrier from the pine forests of Tasmania. He worked very hard in his chosen field and carted much pine in a short time. Unfortunately, he was not as diligent in keeping his paperwork in order and was soon under the microscope of the taxation office of Australia.

His brother recounts, "He got into trouble with the tax office." Phillip was a "complete doer but was shocking at bookkeeping." He continued to run his timber carting business but found it hard to get ahead with his financial situation and nearly ran his truck into the ground, as he did not have the income to pay for maintenance repairs and to pay his tax bills as well.

His brother Jarrod suggested that Phillip get into relief keeping in the lighthouse network "to get himself on top."

Phillip eventually moved to mainland Australia and started work as an ice block provider for the community. This was, in Jarrod and Lilly's opinion, a "disaster". The problem being that from the time Phillip dropped off the ice blocks, they would melt in the summer heat and his clients wouldn't pay. He left this venture and traded as a much-respected carpenter in the Frankston and Seaford areas.

Jarrod told of how Phillip was a very fast builder and would have houses put together in no time. "He used to do it all; he would put the framework together and put it up."

There is a juncture I haven't been able to pinpoint but I know it's there somewhere. When did Phillip cross paths with Pearl and Harrison? Or when did Harrison and Pearl cross paths with Phillip? They knew each other; they must have. If not by association then clearly by direct friendship, as I've been told. Some say they didn't know each other until they were on the islands as night keepers.

Was the aligning of those three lives when Phillip and his family were living in George Town? Did Phillip meet Pearl and the Joyces then? Was it when Harrison was in Tasmania on water transportation duties from July to October 1945? Or was it when Phillip was in George Town doing his carpentry schooling, anywhere from 1949 onwards?

Phillip was born in 1929, making him twenty years of age in 1949. Pearl and Harrison arrived in Beaconsfield, Tasmania, in mid-1951, but moved to George Town in late

1951 or early 1952 and remained there until April 1956. Before Phillip moved to the mainland to work in the Frankston/Seaford area, had he met Pearl and Harrison? I can account for them being in proximity in similar year spans. Was the population so grand that their paths were mere specks? Or, was the population small and did they know each other? Was the connection via family members? George Town was small and remote—then and now. Where did they meet? Someone knows.

I was about to meet some people who would perhaps have the answers I was seeking.

I met Lilly in early May 2009, not long after Mother's Day that year. Her brother, Tony, whom I found in the directory gave me her address and phone number. It was as simple as that.

I'd grown up believing I was a Harper, and while I was excited to meet Lilly, I still felt unsure as I knocked on her door. I stood towering over the very petite lady who was my stepfather's sister. Aware of the height difference and hoping not to intimidate her, I stepped back and offered her a smile and an explanation as to who I was and why I was there, and that I had nothing but love on my side.

She welcomed me inside, and I was stunned by her beautiful home. Lilly had surrounded herself with old wares and antique crockery, and the theme was authentic in heritage. Everywhere I looked, I was taken back to the early stages of settlement, but with class and style. Everything had a place, and the old-style oven was cooking a brilliant fire that smelt fantastic. She had me sit, and we had a pot of tea together. I remember telling her that I had just visited her brother's grave and had cleaned it up. I explained how I came to know there was a man of significance in the cemetery, but I wasn't sure who he was and how exactly he fitted into the family. I had heard stories and knew a little bit about him, but now I wanted to know more, and she was my first point of call. To me, the Harpers were family.

It was a weird contorted moment. I told her I had thought we were related, but knew we were not. I wasn't sure how that was; as my understanding was that I had no association with Harrison Bennet as the biological means to my existence. Lilly pulled a strange face and told me we were not related.

I sank slightly as that bubble of untruth popped, and I sat there not disheartened, more embarrassed. Embarrassed for the lies I had been fed. If anything, I felt exposed, but from the embarrassment I wanted the truth.

We sat and talked for some time, and Lilly was happy yet cautious. It was apparent she was not being exactly forthcoming. She'd known me all of two hours and was obviously protecting her family.

But my intentions were obvious—who was I? Where did I come from?

To me, Phillip was a very important part of my family, and sitting with Lilly was the closest I had ever been to the man in that cemetery. I remember one of the times we passed the cemetery, I had asked my mum why she didn't go and see the person inside. I do not recall a response.

I told Lilly that I had stood at Phillip's grave and said hello, and how I wished he had never been murdered, that I was sorry for it all. Of how I wished he had lived, as he would have been a great man to call my grandfather, and I had only heard good things of him.

I asked her to tell me what she remembered of him, to just speak freely so I could know my step-grandfather.

"Well, he was Mum's favorite," she said with a lot of conviction and perhaps a tinge of healthy sibling rivalry.

Agnes loved her son very much. He was number one in her life.

"His murder took its toll on Mum," Lilly said, "she suffered immeasurably."

Agnes died not long after she buried her son. It could be said that she, too, died when Phillip did.

It was hard for Lilly to tell me this, and I did not push the matter further, as I sensed that the pain was ever-present. I acknowledged how terrible it must have been, and how for the Harper family the loss was irreparable. It was a sad moment, and while I wanted to know more, I saw the glaze come over Lilly's eyes, and I respected that boundary.

I asked her about his life, and she said, "Well, he loved a good time. He was a handsome man, and everyone liked him." He was a popular fellow who had goodness in him that attracted the attention of female admirers and a large social network. "He would do anything for you. You know he was always helping out," Lilly said to help me understand the man my nana fell in love with. He was a hard-working, honest man who did not have an aggressive nature, and there is no argument from anyone that he was my nana's savior.

I was privileged to be in this woman's company, and we spoke for hours. When I left, I told her I would see her again.

The information was stacking up on all sides, pieces of the puzzle fitting together.

As previously mentioned, Phillip was in substantial financial trouble due to problems with the taxation department and his failed business ventures. I uncovered new information from Lilly on our second meeting.

Three months after our first meeting, I discovered Lilly was there in Seaford the day the two men died. She was the voice of the Harper family, and the effect the shootings had on them.

Prior to our second meeting, I sent Lilly several cards and watched her progress as she spent some time in hospital. I spoke to her and her brothers, Tony and Jarrod, on the phone. I researched full time for three months, and

I learnt much more, and hoped Lilly wouldn't be as wary and withhold information this time around.

Lilly was out front waiting for me, and I took a quick assessment of her mood. She was different. There was a smile on her face that reassured me I was welcome. We sat and talked for nearly five hours, and this was a much better sharing than the previous visit. It felt quite natural, given that I had just lobbed into her life unannounced and said, "So let's talk about something painful."

I sat at the table and sketched up the family tree forward from her mother and father—Agnes and William—and then we spoke about each individual. She told me various stories of her upbringing. With William being an ex-serviceman, he was readily accepted to work the lights of Tasmania. William Harper was twenty-five when he embarked to serve his country in World War I. He enlisted in the Australian Commonwealth Armed Forces on the June 11, 1915 and served in the 57th Battalion. He returned to Australia on March 28, 1919. This leaves very little time for William and Agnes to have met, gotten married, and moved to King Island in 1919 as stated on Agnes's death certificate. They began a family when their firstborn (Margaret Beatrice) arrived December 11, 1921. Beatrice was joined by her sister Elma in 1922. The two sisters were joined by Lilly Gladys in 1928, who was born on King Island.

Lilly recalled being on King Island, Maatsuyker Island, Swan Island, Cape Sorrell, Eddystone Point, and a long time at Low Head, where William Harper was the head keeper. As a young girl what Lilly remembered was the winds while being on the ship then boarding the small dinghy to disembark on Mattsuyker island—she thought it would have high sides to protect the people, but it didn't.

She was very frightened, and remembered clinging to her mother as she was being carried. This would have been between 1930 to 1935. In 1929, Phillip Patrick, the first son of the Harper men, was born in LaTrobe, followed by Jarrod Desmond in 1931. Then Anthony William in 1934. The last child born was Morris Douglas, in 1936 in Burnie.

From this we can see that the Harper family has well-established roots and connections with the North of Tasmania. They spent a lot of time on King Island. The younger Harper children—Lilly, Phillip, Jarrod, Tony, and Morris—attended the George Town primary and secondary schools from the years 1938 (December 14, 1938, as stated in logbooks) to approximately 1946.

From the record books of the Swan Island and Eddystone Point lights, it can be established that on June 1, 1936, William and his family arrived on Swan Island and disembarked later that year on November 29, 1936.

Staff as of June 1, 1936, A Trickman HK, William Harper LK and S Brown LK.

On November 29, 1936, lighthouse keeper Harper and family left the station.

On May 27, 1938, the Harpers return to Swan Island and keep their post until

December 14, 1938, where they head for the Low Head post.

On November 26, 1938, the Swan Island working party arrived. The lighthouse keeper, Harper, packed up.

December 5, 1938, Harper furniture to landing.

December 6, 1938, wireless duties Harper.

December 8, 1938, Harper belongings carted to the landing.

December 14, 1938, at 1600 hours, lighthouse keeper Harper and mechanic

Calestone left for Low Head.

From 1938, the Harpers spent six years at Low Head, and it wasn't until January 22, 1947, that the family arrived on Eddystone Point from Cape Sorrell.

Eddystone Point logbooks:

January 22. **1947**: William Harper arrived at Eddystone Point from Cape Sorrell on January 22, 1947.

July 13, 1947: Mrs. Harper went to the station for medical treatment.

July 17, 1947: Mrs. Harper returned to the station.

They would all eventually move to the mainland in Melbourne, Victoria, and orchestrated plane fares from Launceston. The majority of the Harpers took up residence in the beachside suburb of Seaford. Here they remained, and Phillip travelled to Tasmania to be a relief lighthouse keeper. That's when it all really started to end. And end it did, for just about everyone.

FINDING THE LINK AND FOLLOWING HIM

I am not convinced Phillip, Pearl, and Harrison didn't know each other prior to meeting on the lighthouse islands of Tasmania. But I do not have anything to tell me otherwise. So, I follow Phillip as much I can because he is the triangle's link. I have established he went to primary and secondary school in George Town, where Pearl and Harrison lived for years. Phillip also did his carpentry apprenticeship in George Town at a similar time Pearl and Harrison were there. Did they really not know each other?

How could this be when I have heard people tell me they were friends?

Phillip attended Lilly Harper's wedding in Melbourne on December 15, 1956. By this time, he'd had an accident in the truck his sister Beatrice had bought him, and coupled with his tax office issues, he needed money. As mentioned his brother Jarrod suggested he take up relief work as he was well-established in the lighthouse community and infrastructure. He did so, and went to the islands.

Assuming the three had not met prior to this, this is how they do.

From January 1957 to July 1959, Phillip Harper was a relief keeper. He spent from January to March 1957 as a relief keeper then, as stated in the logbooks, on March 16, 1957, Phillip took up residence at Tasman Island.

From Eddystone Point Log Books

R Harper has come from Melbourne and leaves Eddystone Point for Tasman Island.

Arrives:

January 4, 1957: to Gladstone for lighthouse keeper Harper.

March 13, 1957: lighthouse keeper Harper to Gladstone for stores.

The above are the documented movements of Phillip; he was stationed at Eddystone Point Lighthouse and went to the township of Gladstone to purchase supplies for the Eddystone Point workers. He did this twice before leaving his tenure on Eddystone. From there he arrived directly on Tasman Island.

Departs:

March 14, 1957: lighthouse keeper Harper to Tasman Island.

Cape York arrived 1400 hrs. and work completed at 1800 hrs, being ready to leave to take Phillip Harper to Tasman Island.

The *Cape York* was a ship that circumnavigated Tasmania, working to deliver the lighthouses with supplies and for the use of employee transportation.

Phillip was picked up March 14, 1957, and taken down the coast to his destination at the southern-most tip of Australia.

From Tasman Island logbooks

March 16, 1957 to July 12, 1959: RP Harper lighthouse keeper.

Arrives:

March 16, 1957

Attending Cape York.

Light keeper Mater left station.

Relief keeper Harper embarked.

Cape York embarked Hobart 1245 hours.

This 'Mater' is Cyril Mater, the man who largely taught Jason Brook his lighthouse skills, and the one who warned Jason to stay away from Pearl. He is leaving as Phillip is arriving. They cross paths, they know each other. They help each other with the unloading and loading of the Cape York. This is no easy feat on Tasman; it's arduous and lengthy.

There is nothing else of mention until he departs.

Leaves:

July 12, 1959: down the Zig Zag track.

I have not located any other documentation through the government logbooks that discloses where and what Phillip did on the Islands of Tasmania. All I have is that he arrived. That's it.

Reference documents and first-hand accounts helped me work out when he left the island. I cross referenced the above with Harrison and Pearl's documented lighthouse occupation. In doing so, I learnt a lot about Harrison and Pearl's life, and life on lighthouses.

All new light house employees begin at Eddystone Point; Harrison and Pearl were no different. As Eddystone is still partly connected to the mainland, it is not as confronting in displacement as areas such as Tasman—or any of the others that are dots of land in the middle of circling seas.

Logbooks state:

Eddystone Point

April 17, 1956: Bennet and family arrive at Eddystone Point.

Commence lighthouse occupation from 1430 hours.

April 20, 1956: Bennet' effects arrive at station and special mail off Gladstone.

June 5, 1956: Instructing lighthouse keepers Skipper and Bennet in compiling of monthly returns.

July 10, 1956: Checking equipment with lighthouse keepers Bennet and Skipper.

August 6, 1956: Carting lighthouse Skipper and Bennet effects to South landing 0900-1200.

Cape York anchored 1245.

1300-1700 working Cape York.

Light keepers Skipper and family and Bennet and family departed station 1700 hours.

Cape York departing bay at 2015 hours.

Maatsuyker Island

August 18, 1956: Cape York arrived 0730 hours commenced unloading to shores of effects.

Keepers Jeff Skipper and Harrison Bennet and families disembarked.

Lighthouse keepers Morrah and Hornsby families and effects embarked.

Mail dispatched.

Mechanic and Kirkwood and Flude serviced Jeep.

Work completed 1645 hours and Cape York departed 1670 hours.

Carting stores.

Whim to station.

Worked on phones.

September 26, 1956: Head Keeper Croswell embarked per mail boat at 0545 hours.

Commenced half-night watches between Harrison and Jeff.

Harrison has taken over from Croswell, the Head Keeper, and writes the entries from September 26 to October 14, 1956. In this time, Harrison and Jeff share the duties as light keepers and are the only two families on the island for approximately twenty days.

September 27, 1956: With the Head Keeper gone, Harrison and Jeff declare a public holiday.

Played a game of croquet.

September 28, 1956: Butchered sheep for meat supply

Throughout all the entries, Harrison is the only keeper to use 'butchered' when noting the death of stock for consumption. All other keepers use 'killing.'

October 15, 1956: Head Keeper disembarked 'flying scud' arrived at 1600 hours. (Meaning the Head Keeper, Croswell, returns to Maatsuyker.)

December 2, 1956: Head Keeper Croswell leaves Maatsuyker.

Head Keeper Jackson and family arrive.

This arrival is important as the Jackson family and Pearl make for good friends. Presumably they first meet here then go on to have strong bonds when together again on Tasman.

> **December 10, 1956**: Checking ledges and stores with light keepers Skipper and Bennet.
>
> **January 3, 1957**: Mail boat arrived.
>
> Mechanic Flude landed 0615 hours.
>
> Mrs. Bennet and two children embarked.

Pearl and two daughters, presumably the two youngest—Kylie and Kate—leave for a break. Where do they go? Family in Launceston? They are gone for seventeen days.

At this point, Phillip is on Eddystone Point and has been a part of the lighthouse community, and radio communication within and between islands.

> **February 20, 1957**: Mrs. Bennet and two children disembarked 0145 hours.
>
> Attending mail boat 0115 hours to 0250 hours.

Pearl and her two children return. Note the reference to Mrs. Bennet. They're not married, but to unsuspecting folk they are. Pearl returns willingly; does she really have to? Kendall and Kristen are still on the island with Harrison, and she may return for them but if she was in a situation that was perilous, why would she leave two daughters there in the first place? Was it battered women's syndrome? I am left to assume, which is never a definite. At this time there was no violence between Pearl and Harrison.

> **April 15, 1957**: Jackson, Skipper, and Bennet painted the outside of the tower.
>
> **November 3-6, 1957**: Jackson, Skipper, and Bennet paint the inside of the tower.
>
> **November 30, 1957**: *Cape York* arrives 0430 hours.

Head Keeper Jackson and family embarked, and relief keeper Barry Armstrong and wife Emerald, disembarked. Here is where Emerald meets the Bennet family. They share Christmas 1957 and see the New Year arrive together.

Emerald handed me four original photos of herself, Pearl, and some of the Bennet daughters, with Jeff and Billy Skipper holding a young Kate when I stayed with her. I later gave these to Kendall, and she had them sized up. She and her sister Kristen enjoy spending time looking at them today.

These photos were taken as the families shared time together at the island's shores from November 30, 1957 to June 24, 1958. That was the period the Armstrong's relieved on Maatsuyker. Emerald was nineteen years of age.

In the photos, Pearl looks very distressed. She appears unkempt and in low spirits. From the moment I saw the pictures, I knew something was not right with my nana. By now she had spent a full year on Maatsuyker and had not had a break from being her daughters' main caretaker. She's hurt here. There's no ignoring it.

The logbooks continue.

January 27, 1958: (Holiday)

Mail boat arrived 1845-1125.

Light keeper Bennet and family embarked.

Started half-watches with Skipper and Armstrong.

Harrison, Pearl, and the Four Ks went on a holiday for approximately thirty-five days. They had been on Maatsuyker for an extended period and deserved a break from the environment. There is no record of where they went or what they did.

March 4, 1958: *Cape York* arrived 0816.

Light keepers Bennet and family landed.

0900 hours light keeper Bennet resumed duty.

Morse code practice.

May 4, 1958: Light keeper Bennet duty 1200 hours had attack of dysentery.

May 5, 1958: Light keeper Bennet improving but stomach very sore still.

June 17, 1958: Light keeper Bennet cut index finger of left hand while cutting open bushel of sheep 1130 hours.

Cut across finger between hand joined to end of finger.

August 21, 1958: Head Keeper J Barrett commences duties.

J Barrett commences writing in the logbooks and presumably has the final say as the Bennet family departs.

August 27, 1958: Light keeper Bennet attending department of works for men 0830-0930.

September 13, 1958: Regulations 112-113 attended to and light keeper Bennet painting.

November 4, 1958: Bennet packing effects.

November 5-12, 1958: Bennet is packing effects.

November 13, 1958: Bennet transporting effects from number 2 quarters to whim shed 1500-1630.

November 14-30, 1958: Bennet packing and transporting effects to whim shed to landing.

December 2, 1958: Cape York arrived. Landed Head Keeper Barrett and light keeper Hay and family disembark.

Mechanic Flude fitted changed wireless.

> Half watches ceased.
>
> Light keeper Bennet and family departed 'forever we hope.'
>
> Cape York completed work 1650.
>
> Departed for Tasman 1730.

I assume this entry was written by the head keeper at the time, Mr. J. Barrett. Upon viewing these official documents, I saw that a remark in reference to Mr. Barrett is written on the cover of the logbook A. The entry lists the keepers' arrival dates and departure dates, and at the departure date of the Barrett entry, is has been written "to hell I hope." This suggests that the keeper Barrett was not approved of by everyone. There is no indication of who inserted the words after the departure date.

That timeline places the Bennet family on the hostile environment of Maatsuyker Island for a period of over two years with only one break for Harrison and the family of thirty-five days. Their tenure was from August 18, 1956 to December 2, 1958—a total of 834 days on an isolated, windy, barren and lonely island.

And to end it all they are slapped with a 'forever we hope' remark. After all that service, they get a kick in the back.

Let's assume they were detrimental people. Why would the governing body allow the family to remain on an island for so long? Where was the duty of care if the Bennet family was being difficult? I don't think it worked that way, but it could be argued it did. Perhaps turning a blind eye and the other cheek were behaviors employed by the department. The logbooks only tell of a hard-working Harrison and how he was dutiful at work. And Kendall would be the first to tell you Harrison was great at his job. It was with his de facto wife he wasn't. That's a point to be noted.

The embattled family made their tiresome way to their destination.

TASMAN ISLAND
Arrive December 3, 1958.

At this stage, Phillip has been on Tasman Island since March 16, 1957.

The only logbook reference to Phillip Harper is of his arrival on said date. There is no reference to him leaving Tasman permanently. The only other reference I have is January 25, 1959:

> Attending mail boat 1015 to 1330 hours.
>
> Head Keeper Jackson and family embark.
>
> Light keeper Harper disembarked.

This entry means Phillip left Tasman Island January 25, 1959, but he returned. There's just no entry of this in the logbook. I have no explanation for this, but that he escaped with Pearl and the Four Ks on July 12, 1959.

At this stage I should declare there are numerous pages ripped from the Tasman Island logbook manual that I do not have access to. Nor do I have an explanation for why the pages are missing. Are we to assume Phillip was an interchangeable keeper on Tasman Island from March 16, 1957 until his meticulously planned departure on July 12, 1959? That's two years, three and a half months Phillip was associated with Tasman Island.

From the time Harrison, Pearl, and the Four Ks arrived, they were on Tasman Island along with Phillip for just a little over seven months. This was plenty of time for love to blossom; plenty of time for men to get to know each other and more than ample time to scheme and hide.

From the logbooks, the head keeper of Tasman Island—Jackson—arrived August 24, 1958, which was prior to

NIGHT KEEPING

Harrison and Pearl's arrival. The previous head keeper—Mansfield, and his family—departed Tasman Island this day. This is important information because it is Head Keeper Jackson who had access to communication between Tasman and Bruny Island, where George Jarmin, the head keeper, was involved in radio communications aimed at getting Harper and Pearl off the island.

It wasn't under-organized; it was meticulously calculated by more than just Pearl and Phillip. The other point of note is with regard to the only unofficial way to leave Tasman Island. It is not via the usual flying fox option at the wharf, where the pulley system hoists you onto land. It is the backdoor option known as The Zig Zag Track or Goat Track. It's a series of cliff plunges everywhere else on the island.

There is an example of its use in the following.

On September 11, 1958, a Commander Williams landed at The Zig Zag track at approximately 2210 hours. He arrived by dinghy and made his way to the top of Tasman Island by walking the steep land ascent.

He stayed in the quarters overnight, then the following morning—September 12, 1958, at 0830 hours—he descended the weaving land track, boarded his dinghy, and left the island.

This was how Phillip and Pearl Harper, with the four girls, left Tasman Island on July 12, 1959.

If it is accurate that Phillip had been on Tasman since March 14, 1957, then Phillip would have known about Commander Williams' arrival and his method of transportation.

After that specific entry in the logbook about Commander Williams, I have only five further entries until they cease.

December 3, 1958: *Cape York anchored 0430*

Commenced work 0600

L/K Bennet and family

L/K Dillion and wife

Mrs. Jackson and child

Disembarked 0745

L/K Williams embarked 0950 hrs

Mechanic Flude station

December 4, 1958: Unpacking effects

December 15, 1958: Showing L/K Bennet how to work flying fox

L/K Dillion drives Jellbout engines

January 25, 1959: Attending mail boat

1015 to 1330 hrs

H/K Jackson family embarked

L/K Harper disembarked

This entry and the next is important. Phillip gets off Tasman. Near to a month later, it is recorded that Harrison and family arrived on Tasman Island. However, I have not been able to locate the entry where Harrison and his family disembarked Tasman prior to their return on February 22, 1959.

February 22, 1959: Mail landed 0905

H/K Jackson and family disembarked

0925 received and dispatched mail

L/K Bennet and family

Mrs. McGuiness embarked 1000hrs

There are no more entries in the logbook; they have been torn out, and the available information ceases. These are big pages too, in old government property stored in government buildings.

What I have been told is that Harrison, Pearl, the Four Ks, and Phillip went on a holiday with the Joyces. They all met up with Eleanor, Pearl's niece. That's right, they were in Launceston together, and that was by choice. I was told this by Eleanor herself. She looked me straight in the eye as she told me. Seeing my shock, she added with a slight wake-up-to-yourself-girl scoff, "Oh Melissa, they were friends. They hung out all the time."

Okay, I say to myself, *I am not about to debate that; I am in no position to.* This has me conclude that I was in no position to argue another point—the one of Phillip at his sister Lilly's wedding. It is alleged he was overheard saying he was going to marry Pearl. If accurate, it took this whirlwind desire back to December 1956. There is no foundation available for me to agree or disagree.

But how long had Phillip and Pearl known each other? Was the spark lit in the George Town days? Because it's only about to explode. A fire it is, their love. And there's some burning about to go down.

LIGHTHOUSE KEEPING—WHO SAID ISOLATION IS ONLY FOR THE INCARCERATED?

We don't much care to know about professions other than our own. I couldn't write the number of times I've heard individuals say they weren't interested until it happened to them. I dare say, lighthouse keeping would wail at the bottom echelon of selection based on interest. It's not like a McDonald's franchise, with visibility on every other corner. Knowledge about funeral parlor preparations and management is more sought after than tower watches of night.

The truth is, being a lighthouse keeper in duty and responsibility was not light at all. The seas surrounding our shores act as a beautiful oasis, but they are equally treacherous and a threat.

The ocean has demonstrated its fierceness. It has taken men to its depths and not released them. It has unanswered mysteries and is vast beyond regular understanding. It can be as cutting as the rock edges it aligns. The vessels in its territory are dependent on not only their own navigation methods, but also on the responsibility of the keeper of a lighthouse.

It is thought that over a thousand ships have been taken by the seas around the island state of Tasmania. The loss of lives is not pleasant. The *Cataraqui* that sunk off King Island in 1945 is the worst peacetime disaster, with four hundred and two people having lost their lives. The words 'Olim percilum—nunc salus' ('Once a danger—now safe') are etched into the glass doors of the Norah Head Lighthouse in New South Wales. That says it all. The duty of the lighthouses and the men who manned them was fundamental.

The trade shipped from the English and Indian ports was vital to the Australian economy and civilization. With the waters surrounding Tasmania being dotted with islands, uncharted rock formations, reefs, shoals, and swirling seas, the first lighthouse built in Tasmania was erected in 1848. With Tasmania being the 'convict isle,' it should be noted that despite the character of the folk shipped to the Australian shores, the Admiralty of London forbade transports carrying convicts and troops to use Bass Strait until lighthouses had been built.

Today, Bass Strait holds the biggest annual sailing event of the Australian water-vessel calendar. The Sydney to Hobart yacht race launches every December 26th. It attracts international competitors and global coverage and is known for its perilous conditions.

The seas around Tasmania have long been risky and precarious. There is no question the various lighthouses established throughout Tasmanian shores were done to improve safety at sea. Vessels and their captains and crew would look toward the numerous beacons of light to guide them in their passage. You could call them stars on land, as that is how they appeared when viewed from a distance.

It wasn't just about a bright light beaming from a cylinder, it was much more synchronized. Each lighthouse has its own special sequence of flashes, and their signal activity was coordinated by the lighthouse keeper that informed navigators where their vessels were located. As the keeper of each island knows the waters surrounding the islands, they are able to warn of rocks and land that need to be avoided. They do this with diligent accuracy.

The main task of the lighthouse keeper is to pump the pressure tank of fuel to keep the lights ablaze. The central source of fuel was kerosene of sheltie, and the pumping would be required three to four times per evening shift. The keeper would have to run up and down the spiral stairs and manually pump a lever system to generate flow into the holding tanks to service the lights.

The next action, which was coordinated by a rotating mechanism, was the sweeping left to right and back again of the light's ray, so that it was visible. It's all good and well to have a beacon glowing, but it also needs to move to be visible and communicative.

The engineering is similar to a clock mechanism powered by weights that moved down the center of the tower. This required rewinding several times throughout the night. Not only did the light need to be ablaze, but also continually rotating—every night, year-round. The lights also had their own rotation rate. The longer the shaft in the tower the less the weights had to be rewound for rotation. Either way the keeper would be up and down the tower stairwell numerous times each watch.

The lamp to the lighthouse was masked to send intermittent signals identifiable as coming from a specific island. The captains or navigators on the ships had documents displaying which styles and signal patterns belonged to each lighthouse. The seamen could identify where the signals were coming from and thus determine their position.

At daybreak, the keeper would close the drapes to the tower, turn the lamp off, and cover it to protect the mantle from harm. If the natural sunlight penetrated the powerful lens, the mantle in the lights could be damaged.

With this done and all the logbooks filled for filing, the last duty night keeper would return to his designated home and sleep. The other keepers would tend to the maintenance of the tower. Their duties included cleaning and oiling the metal wheels that worked the lamp's rotations to ensure they ran smoothly. All the glass in the tower was cleaned daily, as was the lens of the lamp. The kerosene and oil supplies were restocked each day and the rotation system was wound. General cleaning duties were also part of maintaining a working tower.

The other duty of the keeper was to watch for suspicious vessels entering our waters. The etiquette of the sea was taken seriously in the developing stages of the use of the world's waters. Seamen and the lighthouse network took pride in their duty to protect the country's waters, and it was encouraged and supported by the government's standing orders. The instructions to light keepers by the Commonwealth Lighthouse Service in 1917 issued that:

The ensign is to be hoisted at the signal staff, between the hours of 0800 hours and sunset (weather permitting), on Sundays and the following occasions:

- The birthday of the reigning Sovereign;
- The passing of British men of war, of Government vessels, or of vessels flying the flag of the Governor General or of State Governors;
- The customary compliments are to be paid to each vessel by 'dipping.'

There was a lot of comradery in the men of the sea. There was also an element that betrayed them: the incarcerating feeling of isolation. The logistics of their situated positions contributed to the decline of many who stepped foot far away from others. The impact of living in such withdrawn and removed posts, especially with the added compression of the weather and environmental conditions, cannot be underestimated. "You don't know wind unless you've been on a lighthouse post in the southernmost tip of any country," I have been told, and "you haven't heard a sea's scream unless you've been there too."

There's no way I could live in true isolation even though I like being alone. It's a sentence I wouldn't impose on myself.

There are, of course, levels of isolation. In its true definition, to live in genuine isolation is to live without the contact of others, to live without the stimulation of or interaction with others—meaning groups, individuals, and whole societies. This is not exactly the case with lighthouse posts, as more often than not, there are other families on the islands as well as interaction with supply vessels.

The lighthouse keepers had full-time responsibilities and shared their duties in shifts. The women and children had smaller duties for the running of the island. There were usually three houses per island with their respective occupants to interact with. This is unmistakably limited, yet not completely isolated.

Much has been said about how a child growing up in such an environment can create numerous issues. Our nature is nurtured by our environment as well as our natural disposition, which is equally important. Social interactions are one of the developing factors in how a human finds their position in life and in the world. Some people like being by themselves, and those are quite suited to the environment of isolation, but it would come with consequences.

The official guideline for employees on the lighthouses in permanent posts was that the man and woman be married. The couple would either have children prior to their posting or during. Therefore, the islands were occupied by small family groups. Maatsuyker Island, for example, had three lighthouse keepers and their families in residence. Tasman Island also had dwellings to house three lighthouse keepers and their families.

The women who were legally expected to be married to their husbands, tended to keep the house and family duties organized. This was as imperative as you could not simply cross a bridge to fetch a loaf of bread. The women had to ration and calculate survival.

The supply ship dropped off a rationed amount of food and supplies every couple of months, and it was the duty of the families on the island to see they lasted—there was no runabout or dingy available if you ran short. By those parameters, it could be likened to prison conditions. It was the women who prepared all the meals and made bread and jams and spreads and cakes etc., as part of the staple diet for their families.

On top of that, the families had to police themselves and would often charge one another for various discretions.

Truly.

I saw documentation that a family had brought forward a charge against one of the children of another family for stealing a biscuit from a jar on the kitchen bench. This was a legitimate point of contention brought to the marine governing body of authority. There was bickering and quarrelling, which needed to be further addressed, but it first needs to be stated that alcohol was officially not permitted. The government was firm on its position of denying access to alcohol to the families on all the islands. It was clear you were to be charged with the highest end of a sharp law if

NIGHT KEEPING

you were found to be consuming or harboring alcohol on a lighthouse post.

As with any prohibited substance, it found its way to the people of the islands. The code names established by the lighthouse keepers varied, but two of the most popular were: 'blue kerosene' and 'red lemonade.' There was a code amongst the lighthouse community that you were not get too inebriated as the lights were to be kept blazing, and the maintenance of weather records and reading weather instruments accurately.

This is at odds with being told Harrison was roaring drunk all the time. His service record as a lighthouse keeper was maintained, as were the logbooks that he delivered in his duty as a lighthouse keeper. However, drink was a friend to many keepers and keepers' wives.

To be standing at the most southern tip of Australia, you would be standing in the lighthouse on Maatsuyker Island. The island itself is relatively small, spanning nineteen kilometers (5.6 miles) of mountainous terrain, and it is surrounded by long swells created by the southern Tasmanian seas. The gale force winds that come off the Southern Ocean are so significant they are referred to as the Roaring Forties.

Life on the island wasn't easy. The southern side of the land mass is sheer cliff face. It is covered in bushy terrain with smaller grassy areas around the three lighthouse keepers' homes. Narrow grass trails lead from the houses to the lighthouse. It's not a free land space; it's dangerous and confining. It's steep and the land is mostly on a slant. The access was on the other side of the sheer cliff faces, where a trolley pulled by a horse and winch system was used to bring the supplies to the top of the island from the supply ship every three months. Provisions included oils, kerosene, and other materials for maintaining and running the lights. The required clothing and personal items were gathered when the families were given permission to leave the islands and visit the city of Hobart or Launceston in Tasmania.

Tasman Island is sheer cliff faces surrounded by treacherous waters. It's massive and imposing. It's not just man that is repelled, ships, too, could not venture near the cliffs; they had to anchor at a reasonable distance. A large basket and pulley system was designed and built to transport people and supplies onto the island from the vessels in safer waters.

It took three men to lower the basket from the man-made platform near the base of the island to the waiting boat. Supplies, family members, workers, relief workers or whoever else had reason to board the island would enter the basket and be hauled up to the landing by the wire cable. It was a very uneasy scenario. The waters would swirl and move the boat about and the ever-present winds made for an apprehensive transaction.

Once on the island, you can see it is a bigger land mass and seemingly flatter than Maatsuyker Island, but not at all flat. There are varying slants all over the top of the island, and certain death awaited those who neared its edges. Every night, the wind would echo the edges' threat: 'Come near me; I'll kill you.'

"Stay near the houses," were the directions given to the children, and the animals were tethered for safety. The wind was strong enough to snatch sheets from the line and send them sailing across the waves, never to be laid on again. The gale-force winds would scream on the worst days. That alone would have me place an 'unoccupied' sign on the doors, never to return.

To live in an environment that is windy, and hostile is a challenge in and of itself. Despite these challenges, the lighthouse keepers and their families never failed their duties in protecting those at sea.

And what of the isolation, what is true of this? Unless we've lived it, we can't really know what it's like. I can only gauge as much based on what I've been told. I have seen depression in the eyes of lighthouse keepers and their family members, but I see it in all professions of society. I have seen elation at being removed from the common goings on of society and I have heard phrases such as "No, it wasn't hard; it was good to get away from all that rubbish" (the daily, regular community network).

They set their own expectations; they formed their own bonds and friendships. Knowing others were around meant they were never totally alone. Interaction was a daily experience and, more often than not, there were numerous children per keeper. The community was small, but it did exist, and they did interact.

My last thought is that if you are imbalanced or perhaps have a few personal problems, the silence would talk to you. And if you don't like what is being said in these ever-present amounts, then it's a battle ground. How do you handle that? You make friends, and that's exactly what Pearl did.

So, while the keepers were watching out for passersby, who was watching out for them?

MAN LEFT BEHIND

THE STARTING CLOCK

The story has now moved to the islands. What will these treacherous days hold?

We can call the characters 'alledgers'; we can also call them at their first act of it—liars. The initial indication that this is true is with regards to Pearl and Harrison holding permanent positions as lighthouse employees. According to the Australian Government, they did not meet the official criteria, they were never married.

Harrison didn't divorce Margaret Barnes until 1960, and Pearl married Phillip Harper in 1959. How this was either overlooked or not picked up on is a mystery. They must not have had to show a marriage certificate, or they falsified one to meet regulations.

There's the first lie, albeit a white one, before they'd even stepped on sand with a tower at its command.

The major point Pearl has is allegations of abuse and severe violence perpetrated by Harrison. I am going to suggest that knowing Harrison's heritage and of his death, I will cautiously side with these accounts. He beat her, hit her, menaced her, and he was an aggressive attacker.

What I want to know is, what the other families on the islands did or didn't do about it. I haven't heard the authorities were informed, or that such and such was administered to prevent it. I understand the difficulty of the times, which are similar to the difficulties and frustrations in preventing domestic violence today. But lighthouse families saw each other every day, they spoke and they listened to each other. You can't hide a black eye or a fat lip.

In my research, I have not come across documentation of Harrison acting violently. This is a community that charged each other with all sorts and levels of discrepancies. Behavior that inflicted harm and concern to the safety, stability, and order of the island were reported. The theft of a cookie was reported. Yet no documents have been able to illustrate that Harrison hit his children or beat Pearl.

What happened? And how did he get away with it?

I can't come up with verified explanations, but I can tell of one story.

As a senior lighthouse keeper, Harrison was bound in the lighthouse tower attending to his duties, which gave Phillip and Pearl ample time to spend together, both intimately and recreationally. It has been said by other keepers of the Tasmania Island community that Pearl and Phillip kept Harrison's bed warm for him while he was watching the ships and sky in the pitch of night.

When did he find out?

Everyone seemed to know about it except Harrison.

Is that true? Is that fair?

Perhaps it is.

Pearl and Phillip were doing what many feared or dared.

They were sneaking around with hostility's air, and doing it well because he can't tell, and that's how it's kept. But it's also how they began the orchestration of hell. There'd been debate about this for years. How did they do it? This is the first question amongst the interested, the fellow keepers, the lighthouse community, and the

NIGHT KEEPING

families involved. How did they get away with it? They didn't, they left.

So just how did Pearl and Phillip get off Tasman Island with the Four Ks? I've pieced together information from several members of the lighthouse community, from the Harpers and the Joyces, and from the words of the eldest K—Kendall.

The official bookkeeping of Tasman Island, which was documented by the light keepers and held in the tower of the island, is now held in the Tasmania National Archives government historical records. And it is compromised. The last entry before the pages have been ripped out is February 22, 1959. The book commences its entries from 1949, and details a daily record of the events on the island. They are meticulously kept, and form part of the legally-bound requirements by the Lighthouse and Navigation Tasmania Marine Branch, who were the governing authority at the time.

The entries of the island and its inhabitants would have been recorded past February 22, 1959, but someone has seen reason to tear those pages out. They are most possibly long gone. It has been suggested they were removed to protect the authorities of the time; to protect the keepers of the time, or just to remove a part of history that would rather be forgotten.

We know Harrison, Pearl, and Phillip were on Tasman from February 22, 1959, and were together until Phillip and Pearl and the Four Ks escaped on July 12, 1959. That's one hundred and forty days of unaccounted logbook entries.

These pages no doubt would have provided me with a clear account, but I was made to look along every other avenue. I sought clarification from those who were there, or had been told by those who were. There have been numerous accounts as to how two adults and four children could escape an isolated island.

When I first asked, I was told the following tale by someone who wholeheartedly believed it.

At the top of Tasman Island was a flag pole that also served as a means of communication. In the event the inhabitants required assistance, a sequence of flags was hoisted to communicate to sea vessels. A vessel passing by chance, that is.

A sequence of five flags meant assistance was required—an SOS call out to sea. By mainland law and rule of sea, this flag sequence was not to be ignored. Each vessel and its crew knew the various sequences of flags and their corresponding messages.

This theory posits that after Phillip knocked Harrison unconscious, Phillip hoisted a distress signal.

Harrison had, according to Pearl's witness statement, "come into the house very drunk. He grabbed me by the throat and threatened my life. Harper, who was present, knocked him to the ground. Harper took me into the next-door house and Bennet came in again and struck me on the side of the head. Harper again knocked Bennet down."

According to this account, Harrison was knocked unconscious and this is how Pearl, Phillip, and the Four Ks were able to escape the island. Miraculously, a shipping vessel happened to be passing, saw the flags, obeyed sea law, and made its way to the island. With no time to do anything but run, Phillip and Pearl grabbed the girls and made their way to the other end of the island, scaled down the cliffs of The Zig Zag track, and waited for the shipping vessel's dinghy.

As the island is so laden with rocks and swirling rips, a dinghy is the only means of safe transport to and from the island's shores. However, the waters around the island must be calm. This is not an everyday occurrence. In fact, it is rare. For the escapees to have boarded the dinghy, the waters would have had to have been calm for the vessel to even consider being launched from the ship as the waves of Tasman Island are deadly.

Pearl's witness statement sinks this theory. "Harper and I decided we would leave the island the next day." When you hoist flags, you must wait for a ship to pass by the island, and that is as predictable as a leaf falling from a tree. This may not happen for weeks, and certainly not in the time frame Phillip and Pearl needed to leave the island.

There is another point. Mabel Jackson, the wife of the Head Keeper, Bill, liked Pearl a lot and considered her a lovely woman. They were good friends. If she knew Harrison was mistreating Pearl, she would have agreed to help her friend escape. Perhaps the flag theory was a need to fantasize and dramatize the actions of a man a woman wanted to call Dad.

It didn't go down that way; it went this way.

Phillip and Pearl had been romantically involved with each other for many months, if not years. They put in for a marriage request six weeks prior to their departure on July 12, 1959.

When they actually fell in love is only for them to know. But they did. To be together, they had to leave.

Pearl's statement was accurate in that it was a weekend. July 11, 1959 was a Saturday; the 12th a Sunday.

From her account, Harrison came into their home quarters where he grabbed her by the throat and threatened her life.

It placed Phillip and Pearl together at this exact moment, possibly conversing or sharing a beer over isolated boredom. Harrison had just returned from being on another island, as suggested by the memory of a member of the lighthouse community. Upon his arrival, he was informed by one of his daughters that she had seen her mum with another man. It was suggested this daughter was Kate, who told her father she saw Pearl and Phillip together while he was away. If this is true, then it lends truth to Harrison's behavior.

I do not condone the behavior; I would prefer clarity over silence.

Something triggered Harrison's violence. I do not have documented evidence of Harrison having to relieve on another island, nor that in Pearl's statement Harrison attacked her when he was very drunk. Although, I cannot see him being on a shipping vessel drinking to a stupor. I suggest he was already on the island, where perhaps Kate told him she had seen something. He was drunk; drinking went on in Harrison's life, and amongst the lighthouse island lifestyle.

Either way, Harrison was furious, and motivated to act in such an unashamed manner with another person present. It may have seemed to Harrison that he was acting in a manly fashion, that he had the right to behave the way he did because his manhood was compromised, that he was humiliated. That's never acceptable or excusable.

It is fair to say without any reasoning or analysis, Harrison did have his own anger about him. However, the available evidence to support this—at this point in his life and at this time—is from statements from his intimate family. His daughters have insisted he was an awful man whose inflictions surpassed cruel.

These intimate accounts are to be respected despite their solitary nature, as it is these voices that were closest to the man trapped inside his own world.

Given that Harrison was from such a troubled background, he equally brought a field of trouble with him, and it was in this that Pearl, Phillip, and the Four Ks grazed. Thus, it is plausible that nothing but Harrison's mind sparked his rage towards Pearl. Possible, yes, but highly unlikely. Truth also lies in the behavior of others, and often paints a complete picture which, in this case, we cannot see.

Pearl and Phillip left the day after the assault, and the reason, I believe, is that the jig was up—their love had been discovered.

It's simple. Harrison found out; Phillip and Pearl took off. In most cases, there is a cause-and-effect relationship to behavior, and this was the case for the connection and interaction of the triangle that was Harrison, Pearl, and Phillip—it went beyond the Tasman Island incident. It lasted longer than July 11, 1959.

They were not done with each other just yet.

PLAN KEEPER PLAN: TICK TOCK

Harrison's threatening manner had come to the attention of all on the island, and no longer could anyone turn a blind eye. Harrison's predictability had become unpredictable. By island rule, a person's safety had to be protected, and when life was at risk, it was the duty of the head keeper to protect.

The standing orders by the government are clear and they state:

Station Management and Duties Standing Orders 1-1

> 1-1-1 Subject to any orders or instructions received from the Regional Controller, the Head Keeper is responsible for the efficient management of the station, for the observance by station staff of these and any other instructions, and for the completion and forwarding and prescribed forms and reports. He is in full charge of the station and of all personnel residing at it.
>
> 1-1-4 Light keepers are subject to the control of the Head keeper and must obey without question, all lawful orders issued by him in performance of their duties. If a light keeper

considers he has grounds of complaint arising out of any official instruction, or from any other cause he may appeal to the Regional Controller through his immediate superior, but in the meantime, he must obey the instructions as far as possible.

There is close to nothing on the islands of which the head keeper had no knowledge. Getting off an island, especially, falls into this category. Simply put, Phillip and Pearl had help—Harrison's behavior ensured it.

Usually the provisions to leave the island were on the accruement of recreational leave, sickness, or special leave. This situation was very much a special-circumstances provision.

There's something else different about this situation. It is true that by July 11, 1959, Pearl and Phillip had harbored their romance for close to six months. Phillip was blindly in love with a woman who had always had his heart, and Pearl stared back at Phillip knowing she was going to be safe in this man's arms, which she had already been in more than a few times. Phillip was different, and she really loved him.

She knew the connection with Harrison had run its course and at the age of thirty-five, was looking for a kind life. She had survived the harsh existence of an isolated life and was yearning for a softer way of living. They saw in each other what they both wanted for themselves.

While I cannot be absolutely certain that Harrison assaulted Pearl on the island. I do believe he had the capacity, Pearl's witness statement matches that of the inquisition, and she swore on oath that Phillip had lived with her and Harrison on Tasman Island since January 1959, with Harrison's consent.

This dynamic is interesting and one that pertains to asking: After being beaten, and after Harrison was knocked down, how were they able to control Harrison? It's a mystery. If he was as volatile as Pearl stated, how did Harrison calm down? Or how was he calmed down? How was the situation appeased?

This would be where Head Keeper Bill Jackson stepped in. Bill Jackson was an honorable man and had fairness about him—he was not a dictator. Whilst he, his wife Mabel, and their children were at their quarters in Quarters One, which was approximately two hundred meters from Quarters Two and Three, Phillip and Pearl would have apprised them of the events.

After Harrison came at Pearl in Quarters Three, Phillip and Pearl took cover in Quarters Two, with Harrison following them. Even if we assume Harrison was unconscious in Quarters Two, Phillip would not have left Pearl alone and in harm's way. They both would have gone to Bill.

Then Bill and Mabel would have seen how unsettled Phillip and Pearl were, how anxious. Considering the immediate situation, and their experience of Harrison, Pearl and Phillip were believed. They were now able to illustrate how he was capable of inflicting serious injury. This was alluded to in Pearl's witness statement, wherein she claims that during the time Phillip had lived with her and Harrison, he had to take Harrison's rifle to pieces and hide the parts. He had also hidden all the large knives they had for butchering sheep, so Harrison could not find them during his drunken lapses. Whether Phillip stopped and did this before they fled to Quarters One is unknown.

There was a small level of safety being in the company of Bill and Mabel. If and when Harrison looked for Phillip and Pearl again, he wouldn't see them. But it wouldn't have taken much to figure out where they were—it's not a well-designed hide and seek environment.

Once awake, Harrison may have assumed they were with Bill. He may have asked the Four Ks, if they were still there, but they may have fled as well—either with Phillip and Pearl or to other parts of the island.

Sitting inside Quarters One, Phillip and Pearl were safe. Whilst Harrison was unashamed to hit a woman in front of Phillip, he would not display the same weakness of behavior in front of Bill Jackson.

Bill saw the potential for grave harm, and knew he had to protect this newly-made couple from the man they had deceived. A woman had already been attacked; she should not be harmed again.

How do Phillip, Pearl, Bill, and Mabel survive the night with Harrison still on the island with them?

Mabel had to be involved—she and Pearl were best friends It was suggested that Bill locked Harrison in a shed and told him it was for his own good, but I have been advised by a Jackson family member that this did not happen, which means Harrison was free to interact.

Immediate action, though, was required. They had to get Pearl and Phillip off the island without so much as Harrison even being slightly aware of anything, nor the Four Ks. They knew nothing either.

It's happening; they are getting what they want. Pearl and Phillip are under the guise of Pearl's safety. How though? They tell the truth and stretch it? They come up with a story and because of that, it's agreed to make plans to get the resources to get off the island. Or blunter than that—he did it; now get them off.

There was a lot to do in the very short hours they had to get the job done. There were two major components to this logistical move: transport and safety. They had to get a shipping vessel to come to Tasman Island to collect Phillip, Pearl, and the Four Ks. The safety was in managing Harrison, so he was unable to cause harm—unable to prevent Pearl and Phillip from getting onto the shipping vessel, and incapable of inflicting harm on those left behind.

Pearl couldn't have this be anything but successful. Not only was she pivotal in the plan, she was its linchpin. The safety of all involved was paramount. A lot of lying and not much truth was about to haze Tasman Island.

The plan was set. It was time for action. Bill agreed to speak with Harrison, and upon finding him, told the man to settle himself and not act in such a way on his island. It was a command, not a discussion. A legitimate and legal one.

Bill then told Harrison that the situation with Phillip and Pearl was unfounded, that what he'd been told by one of his daughters was simply untrue. There was no affair between Pearl and Phillip; the little girl had a moment of make-believe. He could have suggested he needed Harrison to work on the island as per his required duties and to not fuss with the occupants of the island. That he would not stand for such insubordinate behavior. Perhaps he threatened to lock him up but would not want to go that far. The two may have come to an agreement regarding the working manner they had established in the past six months.

A shift in the lighthouse was paramount, and any other matter could be sorted in time. Bill would have made it clear that he and Mabel knew nothing of any untoward behavior on the island, and if it came to light that there were misgivings, they would be attended to at once, and he would get to the bottom it. This was more than likely agreed to by Harrison, as he was diligent with his work and as per standing orders had to obey the head keeper's requests.

Now Bill had to cover his and his family's wellbeing, because hell was about to be unleashed on his island.

Bill returned to his quarters and explained to Phillip and Pearl that he had dealt with Harrison. Maybe Bill stamped his authority over all of them.

Bill would have stated that working the needs of the sea was more vital than the differences between a husband and wife.

To reach the next part of the plan, a kiss-and-make-up approach had to be run with.

Dinner was served. Bill and Mabel dined with their children before he took the first shift while Phillip, Pearl, and Harrison ate their prepared meals and the Four Ks. The men may not have been in the same house as each other, but Harrison would have been with his family before the Four Ks retired to their beds.

Bill headed for the tower as the sun began to dip below the horizon, turning the lights on for those at sea. He was their Night Keeper. Tonight, he would make a call to a man of equal standing on another island. From chief to chief, boss to boss, man to man, head keeper to head keeper to organize the second part of the plan—a shipping vessel. The radio call to Bruny Island's tower was to George Jarmin.

The ordering of the shipping vessel had to be had to be done between Bill and George. As Head Keepers, they were the only ones to rightfully do so. There was no way Phillip could call a ship in secret—not on the islands. Harrison would most definitely have found out had Phillip tried.

The Head Keeper generally took the first watch from dusk until 2200 hours. The second shift was from 2200 till 0200 hours. The third shift, which was usually taken by a relief keeper, was from 0200 until daybreak. The radio weather skids were sent to the mother communication station—at Bruny Island—every three hours beginning at 2400. Any time from Harrison's second shift (2200 until 0200), he could have been informed of the ordered ship.

The only secure way to get the ship ordered is through George Jarmin's telephone in his quarters, to which only he and his family had access.

Bill would have spoken with George at length about the situation as this was about to put a mark in the history of the lighthouse era. And it was not a small request. The effects of doing so were about to break a man, and that is not a decision to be taken lightly.

The truth was being told in the Tower of Tasman Island while the lies continued to be played out amongst the grounds. It was agreed a ship was to be ordered from Port Arthur, and it was at George Jarmin's discretion.

How Bill told Phillip or Pearl may be that he told them directly under the guise of popping in to say goodnight—Bill was no threat to Harrison. Or, there may have be a pre-arranged signal. Either way, Bill must have let Phillip and Pearl know a ship was coming for them. And as he settled into his family's nest, knowing strife was ever-closer, he may not have slept.

With Harrison in the tower at Night Keeper, he watched the sea and the houses below. He must have still been furious from the day's events, but as a man of professional honor, he would protect the night's seamen and their vessels.

At ground level under a well-fastened tin roof, Pearl was crushing her knock-out pills into powder form. She had long been on anti-anxiety or calming medication. As such, she was often tranquil. Now they were to be called on to tranquilize.

Pearl's idea was to drug Harrison and render him unconscious. She knew it was a big risk. Phillip may have been with her or he may have been preparing for his shift. Pearl could not alter anything about the house in case Harrison became suspicious. She had to maintain that normalcy. She would have gone to bed, stressing.

It was now Phillip's turn to take the third and last watch for the night. As he made his way up the tower stairwell, he crossed paths with Harrison, and the two possibly exchanged subdued pleasantries as he took his post. Harrison was on his way to his quarters to lie next to Pearl.

Phillip could have been living in the Dillons' Quarters Three next to the tower while Bennet and family lived in Quarters Two. Phillip could see all movement below.

It was Phillip's time to be keeper of the night. He knew of the powder destined for Harrison, but his need was to ensure his plan was executed meticulously, and he and his loved ones could flee without detection or harm.

During the shift, Phillip may or may not have made radio contact with the mother communication station on Bruny Island. He may have been told by Bill that all had been taken care of. "Keep a low profile," Bill would have said. "The fewer that know, the better. Don't concern yourself, a ship—a brand new fishing trawler—was readying herself with her crew."

With the rising of the sun the day began, and Phillip signed out for his final night of keeping. He closed the light shutter and left the tower immaculate, as was required. He took one last look out to sea and scanned for the trawler, which was not yet visible.

Phillip would have been wired yet controlled. This was a big moment in his life, and he was ready to give Harrison what he saw as a deserving blow. There would be no more hitting his secret beloved; he wouldn't watch her being throttled ever again.

In Phillip's mind, Harrison was getting what he deserved: nothing. With his menacing behavior, he forfeited the right to be the father of his four daughters and partner to his de facto wife.

It has been mentioned that Phillip was partly innocent in this deceitful triangle, but despite his perceived innocence he is also accountable. As he raced down the steps, he would have scanned the grounds to see if Harrison or anyone was around. His plans depended on it. He was as involved as any, and a stance of innocence is not a sturdy one.

What is clear is that he had been sitting in this lighthouse tower for the past four months and was familiar with its mechanics and all the requirements of living and working a lighthouse. As we know, Phillip grew up as a child and young teenager on numerous lighthouse stations, and thus was proficient at surviving on the islands and their communities. This included a well-established network of friends, and knowledge of those within the community. He knew what each could do, and who was able to assist in various situations and how. With these smarts, he knew how to organize a plan like the one he and Pearl had been concocting.

Pearl, on the other hand, had the cunningness required to manipulate, placate, and deceive. She also knew how to act swiftly and with intent. At this stage, she may have been so badly downtrodden that she was taking nerve pills to get through every day, but she was also a survivor, and she knew how to make her moves.

She saw Phillip the minute he landed on the island and pegged him as her next sure thing. Harrison had been treacherous and unforgiving in his behavior toward her and the Four Ks, and she wanted out. Pearl's ideas of how she wanted to live included a man in her life, and that man was an innocent, none-the-wiser Phillip Harper. It is presumed he didn't know Pearl had a name for herself as being on the game; didn't know she and Harrison had a tumultuous relationship. Phillip walked willingly into a seducer's web.

Or maybe he did know and cared none for it. He found Pearl all-consuming and utterly desirable. She also knew he did not have the violently cruel composure Harrison had. Whilst she stated that she'd had enough, she also felt like she deserved better. And to be frank, she absolutely did.

As an astute seaman, Phillip saw at daybreak that the seas were in a lull. Their calm nature was the sign that opportunity was upon them. It was time to execute the plan.

Calm seas were what they needed to get off the island but leaving via the 'front door' with the basket was out of the question. As previously established, too many men were needed to operate it for safety, and Harrison would not have assisted with the escape of his de facto wife and daughters.

It was the 'back door' approach they were taking—down the Zig Zag track. Whoever had organized the ship for their departure would have instructed the vessel to anchor as close as possible to that back door then send a dinghy to the shore.

If there were communications between the captain of the fishing trawler and Bruny, it is not known, but there may have been some questions asked. The fishing vessel was a brand-new ship that had all the latest equipment and sailed fast through the seas of the south. This was all recalled by a relative of Pearl's: "[it was a] brand new boat with all the trimmings and flash stuff on it."

The captain of such a vessel may have wanted to know why they were coming and if there was any danger to him and his crew and, of course, the new ship. Whatever was said, the ship came, and it knew where to anchor.

With everything in place, it was Pearl's turn to see her first glimpse of freedom flourish into full action. She was about to turn on the care and love—she needed Harrison to drink her potion. It was she who had to make sure Harrison was disabled so he could not stop them or kill them. She probably knew the repercussions but did not care. She was hurting. All she wanted was out, and more to the point—off.

While the Four Ks went about their usual morning habits, Pearl was concentrating on Harrison. Was he awake yet? What mood was he in? How could she get him to drink this insurance policy for her freedom? He needed to drink it. Every single drop.

The Four Ks were eating their breakfast at the table. They may have been thinking about what they were going to do on the island that day, possibly leisurely swinging their feet under the table and harassing each other with nudges and the odd pulling of a face. The kitchen was where it was at for Pearl, and she may have taken moments to stare out the window to escape her reality; deep breaths to settle her nerves. Maybe Harrison was at the kitchen table with them. Maybe not.

But Phillip was up to something.

Once Phillip checked that Harrison was safely occupied, he located Harrison's gun and removed the bolt to disengage its capacity to fire—he didn't want a bullet in his back as he made his way down the island towards their escape route. He may have done this with all the guns situated at Quarters Two and Three, and he could not be discovered doing so. He had to replace the guns as he found them.

It was a waiting game. Act normal. Appear normal. No suspicion could be raised, and that meant no changes in appearances or demeanor.

Everything was in position. They were just waiting for the ship.

Bill Jackson has been told Pearl was set to drug Harrison but that the man would be all right when he woke; and that they needed to do this because Harrison was a mad bastard, and he'd kill them. Bill has also been told the rifle had been disabled. Perhaps Bill has been told that Pearl had written a note telling Harrison they were gone and that everything would be all right.

Pearl now had three things to do: write the note to Harrison telling him they had gone, prepare and administer the potion and watch Harrison as the drugs took effect, then grab the Four Ks and bolt toward Quarters One.

The pressure was on because timing was everything. If she gave Harrison the knock-out drink too early, he would wake; if she administered it too late, he would be awake during their escape. How did she know when to slip the drink to Harrison? It all hinged on an estimated time of arrival. It couldn't be predicted if the ship left port on time or if it ran into problems en route. Pearl had to sight the ship in the distance before she could act, but if Harrison saw the ship, all was lost.

Someone had to have had binoculars and kept watch, and that person had to have been Bill. If Bill was in the tower pretending to attend to the usual maintenance duties from 0900 to 1200, he could have kept watch and been able to signal to Phillip or Pearl that the ship has been sighted and was near. He would have known from which direction the vessel was coming, and had access to the radio to Bruny Island where confirmation that the 'special order was on its way' might have been made. Or Bill may have spoken directly to the ship's captain and asked for an estimated time of arrival. At this stage, there was no concern Harrison was aware of what was afoot. Bill would have ensured Harrison had no need to come near the tower, but that he was close to Pearl's cup.

Pearl needed poise and discretion for the whole wait.

Another reason this plan had to work was if the boat arrived and Harrison prevented its boarding, the cost of the ship's service would have to borne by someone. Who that person would be is anyone's guess. Would it have been Phillip's or Pearl's responsibility? Or perhaps it was an organization, such as the governing department at the time, who paid for the services of the ship and its crew.

The answer is unknown, but somewhere along the line, the cost of this specially ordered ship was going to need to be covered... unless the ship was already in the seas near Tasman and not much effort was required to dock and collect a few extra passengers. This may well have been the case, and the ship would have answered the distress call after it finished hauling in the catch of the day.

To cover all suggestions, I have had put to me that I am obliged to mention that Phillip knocked Harrison out and they then fled down to the escape route. This is as ill-considered as the flag concept. The planning of this entire situation would not rest on a punch to the head. An unstated aspect of this entire situation is secrecy. Secrecy takes planning, and planning of this nature comes from calculation and deliberation. Harrison didn't have a chance or a choice in the sequence of events of that weekend in July of 1959. It was that well-planned and calculated, and the secret was guarded by two of the best secret-keepers going around at the time. A knock to the head wasn't Phillip's true style either. He was not a violent man.

Had it been approached in any other way, it would have been disastrous for all residents, as Harrison would have wrecked the island in a rage. Hence, it all resides on his incapacitation.

There was also talk of Bill Jackson locking Harrison in the lighthouse tower, but this is false. Harrison was never locked up; he was too smart and strong for that to have ever been an option. The one voice that can tell you is Kendall, and she thinks she walked in on Pearl that morning when she was mixing Harrison's drug-laced tea. She recalled entering the kitchen and her mum and Phillip were being weird around the bench where they were making the tea, and she sensed something was different. She said we always drank tea and she, meaning Pearl, took an awful long time making the tea that morning. Kendall also confirmed that Phillip and Pearl were on the island together that day.

Kendall suggested Pearl would have been proficient—or at least familiar with the idea—at drugging men, given she was a well-adapted professional in the sexual liaisons industry. It is not a consideration that is easily disregarded. Pearl had the idea and the capacity to not only grind up the drugs, but also put the required amount in the cup and hand it to the intended victim then sit calmly, watching as they drank.

I cannot imagine the scene should Harrison have been awake at the time of departure—the pulling and fighting over the Four Ks. The thought of the Four Ks being tormented any more is distressing. A scene full of fighting, screaming, thrashing of bodies and violence amongst the anger would have been horrific for all. It was best he was unconscious, although the shock when he awoke would have been excruciating.

As Kendall recounted the odd behavior of Pearl and Phillip in the kitchen she didn't stay around, but went outside to tend to her duties, leaving Harrison, Pearl, and Phillip inside.

Pearl would have placed the hot tea in front of Harrison, continuing her guise of normalcy. Perhaps she sat and drank with him; possibly Phillip did as well.

I can't imagine the need for this to work burning inside Pearl as she watched Harrison drink her potion. Was there a chant in her head? *Go to sleep, Harry,* or was it more, *Go to sleep, you bastard. This is my time now.*

Maybe she did labor over it for a long time, or maybe she didn't give it a second thought. Either way, this route led to less destruction—a form of damage control. She aimed to prevent a greater loss or harm, and in part to protect Harrison from having to watch their escape.

The cup was empty, and Harrison had no more to do from here on in. He played his part perfectly. All that was needed was for his head to drop as he fell asleep.

A moment passed. Then another. Another. Then bang! His head hit the table—asleep.

Now, panic.

RUN CHILDREN RUN: TIME'S UP

Phillip and Pearl were in a fluster. They gathered Kristen, Kate, and Kylie, but no one knew where Kendall was. Did it cross Pearl's mind to leave her? There was no time to find her; she could have been anywhere. With this summed up in Pearl's mind, they began to exit the house without Kendall.

Then in she walked.

Had she not, she would have been left behind on Tasman with Harrison.

Pearl was just placing the note she had chosen to pen—which was written with alacrity—on the kitchen table. It was brief and to the point. "We have gone, we have the girls, and I have had enough."

That was Harrison's wake-up announcement.

When Kendall entered via the back door, she immediately realized something was very wrong. She was down at the chicken shed feeding the animals and was unaware that her mum and sisters were about to flee the island. She panicked when she realized she could have been left behind. As quickly as she walked through the back door, they all left together through the front. Kendall was saved by as little as a second. The second she appeared, the second later she was gone.

The urgency clicked over with a crack. There was no turning back. The head keepers had played their part; the ship was docking. Harrison was out cold. It was time to run. Time to go.

Phillip and Pearl grabbed the smallest handful of belongings, and with the Four Ks, ran at a leg-thrashing, heart-pounding pace. Get down that sheer cliff face. Forget about the fear. Just run. Run for your life. Run.

Pearl led, with Kendall, Kristen, and Kate running behind her in formation. Phillip had their backs, protecting his loved ones. He had Kylie on his hip.

They ran, hair flying in the wind. The Four Ks didn't know what was happening; only that it was intense. Their dad was asleep in the quarters. Mum and Phillip were in a panic. They just ran with them. It was cold, the wind pushing their bodies as they forced themselves through the natural blasts that captured the island's habitat. With their coats on, they were slightly protected, but it was not Mother Nature that was causing harm, it was parents—both parents.

The Four Ks were being removed from one parent by another, and they never reconciled with their father. They were running to escape, but they could never free themselves from the loss of a dad. What worked for the benefit of one parent savaged the other. There were no winners here.

According to Kendall, the Four Ks were happy to leave; they wanted to leave. Their father was a menace. All I can say is that Kendall was clear that her father was a violent, cruel man. But with every step they took, they widened the hole in their souls, and it has stayed with them. Even now. But they could not know this; they were young, innocent girls.

They passed the relief keeper's shack and then Quarters One. Bill and Mabel may have watched from inside the quarters as a means of protecting themselves, for they had to endure the remnants of this escape. Phillip and Pearl were fleeing to their happy abyss, but Bill and Mabel would prepare for the coming storm.

Alternatively, Bill may have still been in the tower to watch over the proceedings and see the dinghy loaded off the ship, rowing toward the island's shoreline. He also had to ensure Harrison didn't prevent the plan coming to fruition. He needed to stay close to Harrison.

In either scenario, once past Quarters One, Pearl, Phillip, and the Four Ks headed straight down the cliff face and took the Zig Zag track to the bottom of the island. They did not speak to or see anyone except the man rowing toward them.

The track was laden with rocks on both the path and climbing its sides. So easy it would have been to fall to one's death or come to serious harm. Concentration and sure-footing was a must. This was not achievable for the small and young Ks. As Kendall put it, they had to "bum it down" the track.

They were all working toward getting to the bottom of the track, and while steeped in terror, there was also an eerie calm about them. Their life literally depended on that calmness.

"Hurry," Phillip and Pearl urged. The Four Ks did what was asked of them. They could see the dinghy and the ship; knew they were escaping off the island.

According to them, they didn't feel too sad about leaving their dad behind. In their words, they preferred to not feel this man's pain being inflicted on them or their mum. Apparently, they weren't displaying anxiety or concern. However, no one knew if Harrison remained asleep or if he was awake. They were not yet out of danger.

The dinghy rowed ever closer; the Four Ks knew they were to board this boat and never return. The apprehension of the situation, though, was palpable.

At the base of the Zig Zag track was a formation of various rocks and a small accessible landing for a dinghy to dock.

It had a very short amount of time to stay before heading out to sea again. Too long at the dock and the sea would push and smash the dinghy into the shoreline's rocks. It is common sea knowledge that every seventh wave is a big one. The crew member who rowed the dinghy to the island's shore would have been an experienced seaman, and would have known this. As much as he was there to collect Phillip, Pearl, and the Four Ks, he also had to protect himself and the ship's dinghy.

As he neared the shoreline, the seaman would have circled and backed as close to the island's edge as possible.

Speed was off the essence—the waves stop for no one and would have broken across the bow. It was not an easy or simple task to execute.

Phillip, Pearl, and the Four Ks didn't need any real encouragement. They wanted on that dinghy as much as the captain of the ship wanted the dinghy back.

It would have been a quick loading onto the dinghy, which would have pleased everyone, including the captain, and Bill, if he was watching from the top of the Zig Zag track.

The seaman would have been aware that it was unusual for occupants on these islands to leave under such circumstances, and was probably briefed as to why they were boarding. This is not known, but somewhat clear in supposition. All they knew was the threat was the sea, not the unsuspecting human just waking up above them.

The seaman may have given Phillip a nod hello, or the kind of nod that says, 'You're all right, mate. We've got you covered.' He may have smiled or even said hello to Pearl and the Four Ks, and quipped, "Now, let's get you on this ship so we can get back to dock and unload our catch of the day." Whatever was going on, he rowed away as quickly and powerfully as he could.

I imagine silence from Phillip, Pearl, and the Four Ks while on the dinghy. Whilst it was acceptable to them, it may not have been agreeable to others. People may not have wanted to be involved in such an escape.

Aside from the intensity and the anxiety of the situation itself, there would have had a mixture of fear, desperation, excitement, and relief running through Phillip, Pearl and the Four Ks. You would have heard it in their breath, seen it in their eyes, and felt it in the energy pulsing from them.

I'm assuming that as they sat in the dinghy together, they glanced at each other a number of times, stared into each other's eyes. Each oar stroke brought them closer to freedom. Phillip knew he couldn't be shot, even if the trigger was pulled. Pearl knew that even if Harrison woke, he wouldn't be able react quickly enough now to stop anything. Harrison couldn't get to them, and as the ship loomed, Phillip and Pearl's hearts would have been pounding, their smiles widening.

Gotcha, Harrison, you can't hit her now, Phillip may have been thinking. As he stared at Pearl, looking weather-blown and distressed from a recent beating, he would have wanted to give her everything he could. He was never going to hit her, and he was never going to hit the Four Ks, who were now, in his opinion, his daughters. He had probably begun loving the Four Ks long before now. He had been in their lives for many months. There was plenty of time and space to bond with four innocent, young girls.

As they climbed the ropes of the fishing vessel, they may have been nervous about falling into the ocean, but the adults would have ensured the young Ks boarded safely.

All now seated, and the dinghy secured, they sailed toward Port Arthur. Phillip and Pearl were perhaps still anxious as they were not entirely free just yet. They were not on dry land, and Tasman was still visible.

The Four Ks were used to this mode of transport. They had been embarking and disembarking ships for years now, and they knew the drill. They may have spoken to the crew or been offered a warm drink. I assume they huddled together, anxious, but don't be fooled—they were watching. They were well apt at watching and observing but not involving themselves. As they looked up at Tasman one last time, they saw a man engulfed in fury screaming and running as best he could on top of the cliffs. Although the edge of the island was treacherous, with gulfs and holes along it, this man was doing a good job of running along its line.

Harrison had awoken.

From a drugged daze, he would have raised his head from the table, opened his eyes, and tried to shake awareness into himself. Then he'd have seen the note. Confused, he would have looked around. Heard the silence. He was used to silence, but not this kind. There'd have been a profound emptiness to it.

Harrison would have snatched the note from the table. The only reaction racing its way from his boots was an explosion of rage.

The sound forced from his very soul would have been distressing to hear. He'd have barged through the front door, eyes darting to detect any form of life, then made his way to his gun. Wild with hate, pain, rejection and suffering, fueled by loss, ownership and betrayal, he'd have raced toward the island's main track—an inferno burning within. Yelling Pearl's name, calling for the Four Ks, hope would have warred with his fury, but fury would always win. He knew they were gone.

He didn't find them in the quarters or anywhere near the dwellings, but he kept searching. Further along the track where he could see out across the edge of Tasman Island's boundaries, confirmation of his rude awakening. There was the vessel stealing his family away. There was his family.

Harrison raced at them without any care for the terrain he was sweeping through. Pain and vehemence pumping through his blood. "My family! My daughters! My Pearl! Mine!"

He knew not to go over the edge—that was certain death. Windblown, it was hard to keep his footing amongst the pitfalls and crevices. He stumbled. Appeared out of control. His appearance matched his desperation. Gun in hand, he stopped and raged. "Pearl! Pearl! Pearl! Come back! Come back!" He raged, drowning in sorrow until he lost sight of the fishing trawler. "Pearl, you're all I have!"

It must have been shocking to watch, but Pearl and Phillip did not allow the trawler's captain to even consider turning the ship around.

They sat in silence and huddled for comfort. Pearl didn't flinch; she knew only the pain inflicted by the man she once loved. Was she secretly pleased watching Harrison's distress? Perhaps it was her time to watch him in pain. There would be no remorse nor regret or sadness. He had beaten any care away. Here she was as cold as she was at her father's death bed.

Phillip and Pearl's elation would have grown with every progressive movement from Tasman. The excitement of their escape would have banished that nervous fear and been replaced with joyous relief.

Good riddance, Harrison. Good riddance, you cowardly bastard, may have been Pearl's thoughts.

Kendall recalled being relieved. According to her, it was she who bore the brunt of most of the Harrison's beatings. It is only she who may remember the true sense of the day they left their father behind. She says she and her sisters were doing what they were told and were content with this—Pearl was their mother. Any shortcomings she may have had as a mum did not compare to their father's. They were also very happy to accept Phillip as their friend at this stage—they knew him well.

Harrison would have watched them disappear, not knowing where they were going, only that that were gone. That they had left him. Overwhelmed by loss, pain became his shroud, loneliness his tomb. After a short time, Harrison picked himself up and headed to Bill and Mabel Jackson' home. He walked this time. No urgency in his step. His anger was still apparent, but his loss was stronger, deeper. He was a man distraught.

Bill Jackson had watched Harrison and his reaction the entire time. Now he watched Harrison head toward his quarters and knew the man's questions required worthy answers.

Harrison's anger surged as brandished questions. It was a lengthy visit, and Harrison was restrained enough for Bill to not raise any alarm. But I'm told that didn't last.

Harrison was the man of his family, the head of his family. From his perspective, he had just been bitterly betrayed. I must make assumptions here, and proffer supposition from my understanding: if Harrison was the controlling, menacing type or the caring type who loved his family—I have evidence of both—his reaction would be the same. He was going to be furious and hurt.

Or was he? That depends on who you talk to. Either way, his behavior after this event was the indicator.

Right now, he fired question upon question at Bill and as he did, he calculated how this all came about. Who knew what, and what needed to be done by whom for it to reach this place.

He soon realized that George Jarmin on Bruny Island had assisted the escape. He was furious about the concept of another man aiding and abetting the loss of his family. It has been recounted that he threatened to find Head Keeper Jarmin and kill him. It was vengeance in speech only; nothing ever came of the threat. Jarmin was safe.

I was able to locate Bill and Mabel Jackson's children in Tasmania. With much gratitude on my part, they shared their memories. It was Bill's memory of which they spoke, and how their father had assisted Pearl and Phillip to flee the island. Reassuring confirmation of my thoughts.

It is true, when Harrison returned from watching his life disappear, he was furious and volatile. This was a cause for concern, and Bill forcibly locked Harrison up. The family does not know where or what in, they just remember that Bill locked Harrison up. It did happen.

Harrison would have been unpredictably hysterical—Bill Jackson locked Harrison up to protect those still residing on the island.

How he got him in a confined space is anyone's guess. Bill may have had help.

Once imprisoned, Harrison would have punched the walls, kicked and thrown himself about. He may also have yelled, sworn, and threatened to harm people. He most certainly would have demanded to be let out.

There are two pressing considerations as I search for how this came to be. Where and what did Bill lock Harrison in? Was this organized prior to Pearl and Phillip fleeing?

Bill Jackson would not have intentionally hurt Harrison, but he was smart enough to be prepared for the fallout. Harrison was a man on an island who had just been made aware that his de facto wife of nine years was having an affair, and his children had been taken. The holding pen had to have been a strong one.

How did Harrison allow this? I doubt he'd have agreed. He had just suffered what he would consider the ultimate betrayal, during which he was forcibly rendered unconscious.

Was he tricked by Bill? And if so, what repercussions would there be once Harrison was released? Was there a physical altercation that resulted in Bill knocking Harrison unconscious? Harrison would still have been affected by Pearl's concoction, hampering his true physical ability.

If Harrison was locked up, would Bill have remained to speak with him? Bill's utmost priority was the safety of his island and those who dwelled on its shores, for his part he is serving his code, and being an honorable man.

If we agree with the Jackson children that Harrison was locked up, we can assume that either Bill or Mable or perhaps both spoke to Harrison while this was happening.

Harrison may have calmed with Bill's words, or he may have been left to rage and finally calm himself. If Bill did talk to him, I imagine he would have said, "They've gone, mate. She's left you." Then perhaps followed with, "There's nothing you can do now."

There was no scenario or response available to Harrison that would have changed anything. He was stuck on an island in the middle of nowhere with no clues as to where his family had gone.

Bill Jackson was right; there was nothing Harrison could have done.

The head keeper may have then moved to a supportive role, telling Harrison things such as, "We'll sort this out, but tonight I need you to get it together and work with me. We still have a light to work tonight and I need you." Harrison had the afternoon (approximately six-plus hours) to get himself together emotionally to work with Bill in a split-shift to man the tower.

I'm not sure if Harrison did, as the pages of the logbooks have been torn away.

This was a good move by Bill, as to treat a man with continued brutality is to expect brutality back, especially someone of Harrison's composition.

It is assumed Harrison was released on agreement he remain calm and not take out his anger and frustration on Bill or his family. Harrison never sought revenge upon the Jackson family. It is assumed both men worked the tower that evening.

Upon release, Harrison would have been exhausted and suffering an abundance of aches. Given what I have heard from the Jackson daughters, he was "deeply, deeply hurt." This knowledge could only come from their parents. They were very clear that Harrison was seriously and deeply hurt by the events that took place on Tasman Island in July 1959.

There is sincerity in these women's voices, truth The Jackson family was supportive of Harrison, and looked upon him with fondness. They had spent much time together and had adopted him as part of their own. The children referred to him as Uncle Harry, and they, too, felt his sorrow.

They reassured and supported him with a warm home. They also assisted with his mindset. And they could see, too, that he was focusing on getting off the island.

Harrison had shifted into survival mode.

But it was duty first. Dusk was on her way, and Harrison and Bill had found common ground.

Harrison did his job and would continue to do so. For now.

His real focus was to get off the island and find his family. This, I believe, gave him reason to keep breathing. He would honor his head keeper and man the tower, but in return Bill needed to get him off the island.

I cannot imagine the loneliness Harrison felt if he did man the tower that night. Isolation would have held a whole new meaning within his new existence.

As anticipated and naturally expected, Harrison immediately requested leave from his duties, and Bill got on the radio to organize Harrison's departure.

With his new purpose, all Harrison could think about was finding his family—he wouldn't stop until he did. He no doubt made a list of where they would go, where they would be welcome—Pearl's network. Pearl's family would have been top of the list, but he needed to get off this island first.

How quickly Harrison got off Tasman is unknown, but I am assuming that with a situation such as this, the Tasmanian authorities would have acted fast.

Leslie, the eldest daughter of Bill and Mabel Jackson, informed me further of this situation. One of the first things she said to me was that her mum and Pearl were best friends. Mabel really liked Pearl. She then went on to say that Pearl was a lovely woman. About Harrison, well, she just said that he idolized Pearl and adored his girls. That says a lot. Leslie mentioned that Harrison wasn't on the island when the affair between Phillip and Pearl began; he had been sent to another island for more experience. Phillip relieved him.

This cannot be substantiated due to the removal of those logbook pages. All I can say is at this stage is that we know they were all on the island together. If Harrison did disembark Tasman without his family for some reason, it is not documented. However, we should not discount it. According to Leslie, upon Harrison's return, he was informed by one of his daughters that Pearl was sleeping with Phillip.

While she didn't know which child had informed Harrison, she did say that the kid was just doing what kids do: telling her dad what she had seen. If this is true, then it provides an insight into why Harrison grabbed Pearl by the throat. The timing of the incident is relevant, as Pearl stated it happened in July, and they all departed that same month. Just as Harrison discovered what was going on. It also may explain why Pearl stated that Phillip was living with them. If Harrison was relieving at another lighthouse under unusual circumstances, then this may be very plausible.

Having said this, I am not convinced Harrison had been truly locked in anything other than Pearl's lies. I think she told him she was sorry and that it was Phillip who had to leave, that she would stay with him and the Four Ks and everything would be okay. At this stage, Harrison is depicted as a gun-toting, menacing time bomb. Why hadn't he shot Phillip and Pearl there and then? He was angry enough; he was grabbing her by the throat and threatening her life. What or who stopped him from pulling that trigger? How did he allow Pearl to sleep on the island that night? Something is very unclear about this situation.

All I can gather from the logbooks is on February 22, 1959, Bill and Mabel Jackson returned from their holiday and Harrison and Pearl left for theirs. Phillip moved from Bill and Mabel Jackson's home to Pearl and Harrison's home, which was Quarters Two. Phillip continued his relief duties and presumably, as this is the last available entry of the Tasman Island logbooks, Harrison and Pearl took leave for the delegated twenty-eight days. This has them returning to Tasman on March 22, 1959, weather and conditions permitting.

It is assumed that light keeper R. Dillon and his wife then took their leave, as they arrived December 3, 1958, along with Harrison and Pearl, and thus would have taken their delegated twenty-eight days.

This would have Phillip moving from Harrison and Pearl's home of to the Dillon's home in Quarters Three. Phillip would have lived there for the twenty-eight days of holiday leave. This would see Dillon and his wife returning April 19, 1959. Assuming Dillon returned to duty, this would complete the vacation period of the keepers, and thus cease the relief keeper's services as the three keepers—

Jackson, Bennet and Dillon—returned to normal duties. There was no need for Phillip to remain on Tasman if the above occurred. If this is not what happened, Phillip may have been required, as he was the relief keeper, not a permanent lighthouse keeper. Therefore, from April 19 until the July 12, 1959, there is no evidence that informs me of what Phillip was doing and where he was. This is a period of eighty-four days, and there is no documentation that states Phillip was on Tasman.

It is a very gray area, as a number of people have Phillip on the island. Kendall recalled that he was carrying Kylie down the Zig Zag, and Pearl mentioned in her statement that Phillip was living with them on Tasman at the time. But upon asking Kendall if Phillip lived, ate, and slept with them in the same house on Tasman, she stated, "No, I don't recall he slept in the house, but he did eat with us a lot."

The Tasmanian Maritime Authorities would not have allowed a permanent resident on any of the islands unless they were working or part of the family of the working father/husband. Therefore, for Phillip to still be on Tasman Island on July 12, there had to be a reason. Was he relief keeping? This would indicate that Dillon was not on Tasman. He either did not return to his duties from leave March 22, 1959, or he did return then left again prior to July 12, 1959. This is but open conjecture.

What we do know is there was communication between Pearl and Phillip as they organized their marriage certificate in late May or early June 1959. There was a six-week waiting period for the certificate to be ready by July 14, 1959. This is pure calculation and should not be overlooked.

It is to be noted that when Pearl was examined by the police over her witness statement, she was taken to task on these details as they were of the opinion she knew a lot more and had a lot more to do with the events than she let on. She would not have gotten away with lying about Phillip being on the island.

That said, I would not rest my case on Pearl's word, as there are aspects of this story that do not add up. There have been numerous times where I have realized something is amiss about what has been said. However, it is the sequence I am not clear on. For a start, it was mid-July 1959, not late July 1959, as she was already in Launceston by July 14, 1959. Second, she and Phillip could not just decide to leave the island when the notion took them. The weather decided for them, but it had to be planned months in advance. Was she throttled that night? Or, did it happen weeks ago? Did Phillip hit Harrison the night she says? If so, it would have made the living arrangements very hostile.

I still don't understand why Phillip was on the island and why he was said to be living with Harrison and Pearl in Quarters Two. I wonder why the logbook for Tasman Island has been partially destroyed. Is it possible the authoritative decision makers of the time accessed the log and thought it best to have its contents withheld from public knowledge? Or, was it simply lost over time?

Did the authorities allow Phillip to live on the island as part of the Bennet family, and once matters went awry they thought it best to cover themselves from accusations or protection of self-interest? Or was it none of the above? Is it common practice for a single male to live on the island with a family?

Leslie and I continued speaking, and she told me Harrison was severely damaged when he was left on the island. She told me that he did wake up as Phillip and Pearl left on the fishing trawler, and it had come from Port Arthur. She mentioned that her dad, Bill, helped organize the boat to get them off the island. She agreed that Phillip could have got on the radio and organized the boat during his watch.

She told me Harrison remained on the island until relief was organized by the authorities, and when he eventually left the island, the Bennet family belongings returned with him... except for the sheep.

It was recalled that Harrison would always wear a cap and that she never saw or heard any abuse. She said Harrison adored his daughters, and as they misbehaved he would reprimand them, but she never saw him mistreat them. She stated clearly that she never saw any signs of violence. If Harrison was ever violent, it was behind closed doors, and she never heard a thing. She never saw any nastiness from Harrison and said that her mum, Mabel, never said different.

She told me that growing up with the Four Ks was fine, and that they were just normal kids that played croquet, had a horse, went for picnics on the landing, and put the dinghy in the water to go and catch fish together. She told me of a time she took all the kids camping overnight to give the adults a break and heard nothing negative from them. She only said that she knew how shattered Harrison was, and you could hear the sadness in her voice as she remembered.

This is interesting, as this memory tells me how he behaved toward Bill and Mabel Jackson and their children. It was amicable, and they liked him; if there was any difference in this it wasn't mentioned.

That night when he was left though, would have been anything but amicable inside; he would be reeling whether it is visible or not. The silence in Quarters Two would just about shatter Harrison—no noise, no girls, no smoke out of the chimney, no food cooking on the stove, no warm beds, no boiling teapots or chatting at the table, nothing.

Harrison's wait in solitary confinement would have only fueled his drive to survive, to find his own and be with them again. The day-in, day-out duties and ticking clock would have continued until he was free. *Tick, tick, tick...*

    The ship arrived, and this was Harrison's day for action. He bounced onto that ship like he had a new lease on life. It's got to be truly stated, until the ship's arrival, he'd been surviving in a crypt of terror. The reminders would have been everywhere. He continued to live and breathe in his own burial ground. Every time he walked the track, he heard them. Every door he passed, he saw his family's belongings. The sweets jar that contained the hard-boiled lollies he always made sure were brought with every supply ship wasn't going down in volume because no little-one's mouths were around to eat them. There was no washing flapping in the wild wind, no stories of the horse pulling the tent down, no company that would keep his cold soul warm. The emptiness grew as his days alone moved from one to the next. The memories and experiences didn't free him from pain; they entombed him.

    Harrison took all the belongings he could, firm in his intent to get to either Port Arthur or Hobart's Constitution Dock. He didn't care which, he just needed to reach the mainland.

    Upon arriving at the mainland, he took his and his family's belongings and headed straight to Pearl's family in Launceston. His first call was to Pearl's niece and her husband, Maureen and Daniel Ogilvy, and asked if they had seen his family. They told him they did not know where the girls were and knew nothing of Pearl or her movements. They lied.

    Harrison was distressed and appeared genuine in his need to find his family. But Harrison was a smart man, and he possibly knew he was being lied to. Without causing any concern, he left, but he wasn't about to give up.

    Next, he made his way to where he began his life with Pearl: Beaconsfield. He walked to the home he built and sat and talked with Joseph and Carol Joyce. They, too, told him nothing. Joseph was a very kind-hearted man and spent many years with Harrison, but he was silenced by the rule of the women. No one in the Joyce family was to speak a word to Harrison about Pearl. And that's what Harrison got again: a bag full of nothing. Carol and Pearl had put a blanket of silence on where Pearl and the Four Ks had gone, and no one from the Joyce family helped Harrison.

The wall of silence was inordinately strong, and Harrison was fed empty clue after empty clue. He was given no indication of where his family had gone. Even though they knew where his daughters were, a father's love was not honored at this time.

They had their reasons. Some of the Joyce family disliked Harrison's nature, but not all; they just kept their word as per the matriarch's order.

Despite this, he did not give up. He continued searching Tasmania from August until November of 1959.

He was as lost on the mainland of Tasmania as he was on Tasman Island. This loss and its effect on his spirit were weighing him down. Where were they?

From having them in his life daily, he now has nothing. His is a hurt that encompasses both day and night. They are all he thinks about. Then out of the blue he gets a letter from Pearl asking to send some clothes over as the girls had nothing. He obliged, and made his way to Melbourne, Victoria, to see the Four Ks, where he spent a part of November 1959 visiting with them.

Phillip, Pearl and the Four Ks story begins when they docked at Port Arthur July 12, 1959. It was a Sunday afternoon. In their minds, they were all very safe. According to them, Harrison was long gone. He couldn't get to them. And even if he could get off Tasman Island, there was much sea and much time between them.

Phillip and Pearl cared not for the traumatized Harrison. They felt nothing but relief as they walked toward dry land to continue the execution of their plan.

The only pain Pearl had was from bruising from the blows Harrison had rained down on her head. She may have had swelling around her neck from being throttled. She was slight of frame, and it would not have taken much to harm her.

She would also have been in psychological turmoil. She was flying with excitement at getting married to Phillip. That's right; they were about to get married. She was beside herself with exuberance and relief that she was finally going to live a happy life, but she was hurting, too. She had just drugged a man she once loved, and I assume she was feeling guilty and her self-esteem was low.

Even though she was a woman of little expression, hiding from the effects of life events was not in her skill set. It was clear as the blue sky, she was a mess, yet she was also a woman with a plan.

The Commonwealth Coffee Palace at 20 Tamar Street, Launceston, was the place of residence Pearl and Phillip listed as their current address on the marriage certificate. From Hobart, Phillip and Pearl and the Four Ks caught the train up to Launceston guesthouse, still in the clothes they fled the island in.

Pearl went straight to her family in Launceston and organized for the Four Ks to be cared for by her sister Nelly. This is interesting, as although Pearl and Nelly had attended the same Catholic school in Beaconsfield, and were said to be fond of each other, they knew how to get each other's back up. The story goes that whenever the two were bickering, all Nelly had to say was, "Midnight." It was a reference to a man with whom Pearl had intimate relations, and it was clearly a sore point for Pearl, because she would clam up instantly.

For understanding, the Joyce family assumed the man they called Midnight was of darker skin color, and a secret lover of Pearl's. He was not a discussion point and it was a story well-remembered for upsetting Pearl. Nonetheless, the sisters did stick together.

The Four Ks arrived at Nelly's home on Monday, July 13, 1959, where they were presumably bathed and fed and given a warm night's rest. They had met their Aunty Nelly on previous occasions and were reasonably comfortable waiting for their mum's return.

Pearl and Phillip were spending their first official night alone together. They were child-free, Harrison-free, and generally free to their love. They returned to the guesthouse to spend their last night unlawfully together. After a restful evening, they awoke and dressed as best they could then made their way to the registry office in Launceston on the Tuesday morning.

The occasion would not have been about bridal waltzes, with a flowing white gown and black suits accompanied with top hats with applause and cheers all round. Not at all. It was standing with love and the formality of "I do."

Phillip and Pearl didn't care that they weren't decked out in the finest clothes. They just wanted to be together.

With the marriage certificate stamped and authenticated, Pearl Joyce became Pearl Harper on July 14, 1959. The Four Ks remained Bennet until Pearl had their names changed by deed poll. Phillip did not officially adopt them, but they adopted his surname.

I am not aware if Phillip and Pearl spent another evening alone together. I do, however, suspect they did not, as they had a state to leave and four daughters to introduce to their new family. Pearl and Phillip picked up the Four Ks from Nelly's and headed for their new home.

The newly crowned family left Tasmania and, according to Kendall, flew to Melbourne. Phillip and Pearl were now completely free, and Harrison was none the wiser.

The Four Ks were excited; their mum was happy, and they had their best friend with them—Phillip, who was about to be called 'Dad.' He was also about to give them a life free of violence.

But as life often dictates, that didn't last forever.

ARRIVAL FROM A DEPARTURE

The newly-married couple touched down at Essendon airport. They hired a car and drove toward the south beachside area, stopping at Frankston, where they spent their first night in Victoria sleeping on the beach. It was the end of spring, and the weather allowed for a night of comfort... despite sleeping on sand. Waking to the rising of the sun, the family stuck together, and though they appeared disheveled, they ventured into the town of Frankston and organized a stay at the Grand Hotel for a few nights. Having secured a roof to sleep under and facilities to shower and groom, they took the courage to find a friendly face, they hoped.

They made their way to Wells Road, Seaford, where Phillip's parents—William and Agnes Harper—now lived after retiring from the light-keeping lifestyle.

Phillip loved his new life and wanted to share that with his parents. Phillip's behavior showed me that Pearl was right—Phillip was a perfect choice. He was 'it' for Pearl; they were 'it' for each other. Now they were standing at the Harper's door, with Phillip's parents unaware of the destruction in Tasmania. It had only been days.

Going about their daily rituals, the Harpers must have been happily sipping their cups of tea or coffee, eating breakfast, washing up dishes and morning faces. They were unaware their lives were about to be altered forever.

At the front door, Phillip held Pearl's hand to reassure her then knocked.

Agnes Harper opened the door.

"Hello, Mum," Phillip said.

"Phil," she said with surprise. She may have then enquired, "What is going on, Phil? What are you doing here? Why aren't you working the lights?" She then called out for Phillip's sister, who was living with her parents at the time. "Lilly, come! Phil's at the door."

I sat with Lilly and watched her return to the moment. Lilly remembered well the time she first met Pearl. "Oh, it was only a day or two after the pair had married, and only three or four days since leaving Tasman Island," she recalled.

Lilly was living in a bungalow at the back of her parents' home with her husband and their first child, Lindy. They stood at the front door looking at Phillip and his new wife, who was standing slightly behind him.

"I can still see her standing there," she said. "Phil was telling Mum that this was his new wife and they were now here to live." Lilly was silent, hearing her brother declare his marriage to a woman who looked like a "shipwreck", Lilly said, "We were both standing there listening to Phillip, stunned."

Nothing was flattering about the woman, she said as she began to describe what she had seen. She repeated the statement again "I can still see Pearl standing there. She had a long coat on and very, very scraggy hair with not a spot of makeup on. She looked very unkempt." She was in a bad way and had literally just stepped off the island, and whilst Lilly said that she went on to look better, she would never forget how unkempt she was on the day they met.

This is in keeping with the time of events. Pearl had nothing. She had been nowhere to get anything, and she was still experiencing the trauma of recent events. It is visible, she was still feeling and reeling from its effects. She may well have had the sweeping winds from Tasman Island still swirling in her bones—it didn't pass through you; it ripped and tugged as it strangled.

After Lilly reflected on how Pearl presented herself upon their first meeting, she moved very quickly to a point she wanted to make clear to me.

"There was no mention of leaving Harrison back on the island, no mention of him at all. Mum knew none of that. She didn't know he had stolen another man's children, we knew none of that."

This I believe. The Harpers didn't know what had transpired in Tasmania.

She said Agnes got a big shock when Phillip brought Pearl home. It was the first any of them knew of it. "Mum couldn't quite believe it. She kept saying to me as we stood staring back at the pair, 'Just tell me, Lilly, it can't be true, it can't be true.' And I said, 'Well, if he is saying it, it must be true'."

It wasn't just the shock of her son turning up unannounced—that would be a pleasant surprise. Agnes was bewildered; she hadn't known any of this was transpiring in her son's life. By saying, 'Tell me this is not true,' it was her denial of what was happening. She didn't want this. She wasn't pleased about it, and she wasn't approving of it either. Not at first.

Agnes's shock at her son turning up at her door with a wife is an indication to Lilly that the coupling of Pearl and Phillip was unknown to anyone but Phillip and Pearl. Agnes was left speechless and disgruntled, which she made known.

I mentioned to Lilly the rumor circling about Phillip boasting at her wedding on December 15, 1956, that he was going to marry Pearl. This presented evidence that Phillip and Pearl conspired for years to be together and had known each other for some time previous to their marriage on July 14, 1959.

Lilly asked me where I had received this information, and I informed her that Kate, who had met with Lilly early this year, had told people of this. This was in April 2009, and Kate had been informed by a Harper family member.

Lilly immediately refuted this and said that she never heard anything. Whilst she agreed Phillip was at her wedding, he was not heard to be boasting to marry a woman named Pearl. If that was the case, why had her mum got such a shock when he presented Pearl?

I do not have an answer, and I'm not sure whether there is truth in the rumor. I do question how the rumor came to be. The specific content had to come from somewhere, and whether Phillip did or did not boast of wanting to marry Pearl is a question that will remain unanswered.

Lilly added support to her position by stating that her husband, Don, and Phillip spent much time together and got along quite well. If anyone knew of Phillip's feelings, it would have been Don. Although she was quick to add that if Phillip did have feelings, he would have kept those to himself.

Back to Agnes. The shock she displayed may not have been so much about Phillip turning up unannounced and married, but rather more about who he had married. If Agnes knew of Pearl and her reputation, Agnes, being an upstanding Catholic woman, would not approve of Pearl and her past. It must be said that Pearl had a well-set reputation, to the point whenever I have mentioned her name to the folk in Tasmania, her behavior is still vivid today. Back then it would have been written in lights. The reality is, it matters not how they met. That was not going to change the reaction of the matriarch of the family. Here she was saying, 'No way' to a woman her son had married. I am intrigued by and understand this reaction. How would Agnes have reacted if Phillip was standing at her front door with a pretty beauty on his arm?

It is credible what Lilly suggests about Phillip keeping secrets, and his ability to contain his feelings. He did this with perfection on Tasman. His ability to hide his true self needs to be taken into consideration, because not once did he break his silence on his and Pearl's intentions. However, it also needs to be said that he was a man of good times, and at a wedding where the emotions of love and the union of two people were in the forefront of everyone's mind, it would have encouraged him to express his own position.

We do enjoy boasting of being loved and in love. If ever there was a safe space to embrace the love he felt, Lilly's wedding would have been it. But I don't think that's what happened.

The other reason he was secretive of his feelings was because he had established a trusting mateship with Harrison. Phillip knew the etiquette of the time, which remains the same today: do not sleep with your mate's wife. It is viewed as a 'dog' act, and Phillip would have had to conceal his feelings for his friend's de facto wife, even if she was unbearably miserable.

That is often used as the excuse to support the initial betrayal, but it doesn't cover the fact that the truth wasn't presented up front. This exemplifies the expression that two wrongs do not form a right. This entire situation revolved around lying.

Dishonesty shatters a person's trust and betrayal shreds what's left. If that is taken, a person's belief fades and with that, their reason to breathe. All three of the triangle members were stealing each other's breath away, and what made it worse was that they were friends.

When I found out that Phillip, Pearl, and Harrison were friends, I was surprised yet...not. The three of them would go on holidays together; were seen as a happy together by the Joyce family. Some members told me clearly, "They hung out together. They were friends. Going on holidays together, you know, like mates do. They'd come off the islands together and do stuff together." This supports Pearl's statement that Phillip was permitted to live with Harrison and Pearl on Tasman, as they were friends.

Back to Lilly's memory: "She didn't waste any time," she said, referring to Pearl marrying Phillip and leaving not only one island but two.

In barely four days she was standing at the door of a stranger's house, had just drugged a man, and had spent months conspiring and organizing the marriage and escape plans with precision. She had packed the slightest number of personal belongings, run down a cliff face on one of the most treacherous islands of their kind, and boarded a dinghy to a fisherman's vessel, then sailed to a port to make her and her children's way to safety.

Prior to this, she had been throttled and smashed about the head so much that she still would have been hurting. She had travelled from Port Arthur to Hobart to Launceston and then on to Melbourne. And here she was standing in Seaford, and not once would she have relayed that information to anyone. So, when Agnes and Lilly were staring at Pearl, they would have known nothing of the lengths the woman before them had gone to and through to be with their son and brother.

There was a window of insight into the Harper's admitting that at the time of Phillip introducing his new wife, "they knew none of that." Her reference and the way she said that were convincing. If the Harpers knew Pearl prior to them meeting each other on Tasman, they would have known Pearl had daughters. It's not something you can easily hide or forget. They were four girls, and all their names started with K. I believed Lilly when she told me they knew nothing about what Phillip and Pearl had just done as there was a strong sense of disdain in her voice and facial expression. Trust had been established between us—she would not lie.

Intent on seeing their union take the path they had paved, Phillip and Pearl searched for proper accommodation, finally setting up a home in Mornington, Victoria. It was now some time past July 16, 1959, and the family was starting its new life in a new home.

Phillip returned to his carpentry-building trade and was well-liked and well-known in the beachside peninsula. He quickly established a healthy source of income, and his building skills provided a living for his family. Pearl and the Four Ks were proficient at living on the bare essentials, thus they did not ask for much. The reality was that they had no clothes, no toys, and their favorite play items were presumably still on Tasman where they had left them.

It was expected that Pearl had by now met William, her father-in-law and Phillip's remaining siblings, or at the very least, they had all heard of her arrival into their brother's life. I am not aware if Pearl was well-received or not. As she was not by Agnes, I can only assume this theme was carried through with the rest of Phillip's family. Kendall recalled the family was quite rude to them all at first; however, once it was established that this new couple was the real deal, the Harper brothers—Morris and Tony, and maybe their father, William—welcomed the union. They helped Phillip not only establish his business, but also move to a new house.

What they moved, I do not know, as Phillip and Pearl had no belongings, no furniture, nothing. They had literally just stepped off the boat. Furniture and household goods may have been loaned to them.

What I do know is that Pearl was dependent on her husband and husband's family, and so were the Four Ks. Pearl and Phillip were finally accepted by the Harper clan as it was clear they were almost inseparable. But at this point I believe Pearl acted with desperation for survival. Her children had no clothes, but she knew where some were. She was about to make another mistake.

"Don't Pearl, for god's sake, don't."

But she did.

She was thinking of her girls. Some might suggest she wasn't thinking at all. For all she knew, her ex de facto could have killed himself. She hadn't a clue, and that's exactly what could have been playing on her mind. This may have affected her thought process, and if so, she went the wrong way down the fork in the road.

Pearl was a woman with a plan, but what brought about her next move is unclear, but it unraveled everything.

This is the point where Pearl wrote to Harrison and requested he send the children's belongings. She sat in her home in Mornington and penned a letter to Harrison. This was a hand out.

No one is sure if Phillip was aware of this, as he may not have approved of the disclosure of their whereabouts, especially to Harrison. But that is what she did. Where Pearl sent the letter and how it arrived is unknown, as is the when. She sent it either via her family or via the lighthouse network. This was a period from August to November 1959. Kendall remembers it well.

Harrison now had direct confirmation that his family was safe and well. He also knew exactly where they were. He found them... or they found him. I imagine he expressed a mixture of emotions that ranged from jubilation to anger and then looped back and returned to hope.

This is his first confirmation of his daughter's well-being. The questions and answers that had been swirling in his mind would have been almost driving him crazy. He hadn't spent a minute without them in his thoughts. They were his daughters, his love, and his entirety. And this needs to stop being dismissed; it's the axis of his existence...them.

Did Pearl really need to request that he send the clothes to her? Could they not have made new ones, bought new ones, had new belongings given to them by the Harper family or the Salvation Army? Or, did a part of Pearl need to know if Harrison was all right? Were the clothes and belongings approach a cover for this?

This was a woman who still cared for the man who had hurt her; it was just she loved another man more now. She stated her life with Harrison was a misery, and this may be absolutely true to her recollection, but she spent nine years with him, and not all those times were bad. She and Harrison and the Four Ks did have laughter and happiness in their lives together. There was love.

There is much contradiction and confusion to take in. She had a reputation for taking back men that hurt her. She was also a woman who needed a man regardless the type. She demonstrated her capacity to put herself before any other, as demonstrated by what she had just done to Harrison. She acted selfishly. She also committed the most intolerable betrayal. For my way of thinking, she committed the worst act a mother can, and this was utterly unfathomable or forgivable. What are you doing escaping a man's wrath, only to put your children back in harm's way?

Upon Harrison reading this letter, he obliged. He bundled belongings together and had them delivered.

Kendall recalled the belongings he sent were old and next to useless, but a parcel had been sent nonetheless. I imagine as he was putting them together he was completely unaware that his de facto wife was now legally married. She no longer answered to Mrs. Bennet. She was Mrs. Pearl Harper, and she would be the first to say "my husband" when she referred to Phillip. There was no way Harrison was aware of any of that.

I suspect that Pearl's motive behind reaching out to Harrison was manifold, but the three presenting reasons are related to guilt, need, and infliction.

She felt guilt for the suffering she conspired and acted upon, and because she played her part in the life with Harrison—she had her own misgivings, her own weaknesses. Harrison knew this and accepted her entertaining ways. She, too, drank with him. She, too, had a violent streak. But the magnitude of betrayal she inflicted rests its weight on her. She could be as cold and calculating as they come, but she also loved.

She needed to know if Harrison was alive. It may have had nothing to do with care and all to do with knowing if a search warrant was out for her arrest, for his possible murder. Having said that, Pearl may have been in contact with her family and they would have informed her Harrison came looking. I suggest she knew he was alive and had decided to inflict further harm on Harrison. She too easily took an opportunity when she saw it.

Harrison had been presented an opening. He hadn't changed his mind, he wanted his family back. His rage and sadness had settled since the initial rampant shock, and now that he had escaped isolation's rock, he could travel interstate to see his daughters.

I wonder and amuse myself in thought: how did he feel? At any stage throughout his trip did he happen to mention to a stranger, "Hello, my name is Harry, and my de facto wife just drugged me and escaped down a sheer cliff face with our four daughters and the man she's having an affair with. I was stuck on the island as I watched them sail away. But now I know where they are, and I really can't wait to see them again. Such fun."

I think not. But if you were told this by a stranger, you might think they needed a bit of help with their mental health.

At this point, he was not a threat to anyone, and Pearl knew this as she had provided him a point of contact. People have wondered what Pearl was thinking, but there was no fear or panic in her, nor was there any need for further fleeing. Why? Has anyone processed any of that?

I don't know how to reconcile this, as according to Pearl, Harrison was a psychopathic monster, yet she voluntarily welcomed him into her house.

Considering the lengths they had taken to leave him behind on the island—the planning, the treachery, the web of lies and all the distress consumed by everyone that was near—yes, I concur, what exactly was she thinking?

Was she not the least bit anxious that Harrison had worked out that she had drugged him? Or was she well at ease and confident of her capacity to lie and manipulate Harrison to the point where she would deny any wrongdoings? Pearl could duck and weave with the best of them.

Would she point out to him that he had done wrong by taking to her with his fists?

I'm not sure if Harrison made his plans to visit known to Pearl. He may have put a note in the clothing parcel advising her he was coming to see his children. I cannot see Harrison sending just a parcel without a note.

Who knows? It all gets very tiring, doesn't it?

I wonder if any of the Four Ks had asked about him in the months since coming off the island. Did they miss their father? Or, had they been told not to talk of him at all? Were they having so much fun with Phillip as their new father that they did not give Harrison a second thought? Did anyone ask if Harrison was okay? Had anyone spoken his name?

Or did they loathe him so completely that they didn't care? I have been told over and again he was cruel, and it was more relief and good riddance that was on the new family's mind, so perhaps they couldn't care less.

A menace is a menace, and if Harrison was one then I wouldn't care for him either. I, too, would immerse myself in the happiness surrounding me. Writing to Harrison has no basis in rationality. But much of this story doesn't make sense.

Harrison found his way to Victoria and went straight to see his daughters and Pearl. He had been much like a bloodhound, foraging over lands to find his family. Although he had been fed red herrings, he had never given up. He knew they were out there, he just didn't know where. He had no clues. The biggest clue he probably needed was that Pearl was no longer his. Quite possibly he had romantic thoughts of asking her to come back to him. He also had the capacity to take back those who had hurt him, and while he pined for his daughters he really did love Pearl in his own way.

Did Harrison knock on the family's door and say, "Hello, Daddy's home?" Likely not. Whether or not the Four Ks came running to him or not is unknown, but you would think they may have been a little relieved to see their father. Or is that just me hoping?

On this visit he asked Pearl if he could take his daughters on an outing. She agreed, and possibly told him to return on Sunday as that is what she states in her coroner's statement. He had two meetings with Pearl in Mornington. On the first, he appeared and requested time to be with his daughters. On the second, he returned on the Sunday he had been granted by Pearl.

"We lived in Mornington from July 1959 to November 1959. During this time, Bennet came to see me and asked to take the children out. I granted this request and he took the children out one Sunday."

The Sunday Pearl could be referring to is in November, and in 1959 there were five of those. It could have been earlier, as collectively from August to November there were thirteen Sundays. My guess is that the Sunday outing did occur in November, because it's what Pearl and Phillip did after Harrison had left their home for the second time that gave me the clue.

On this first visit, he was welcomed into the house by Pearl. Once through the front door, did he sit for a cup of tea, or did he refuse to drink anything Pearl made from now on? What an awkward moment for them both if it presented itself.

Does it go like this: "Here, Harrison, do you want me to make you a drink, more of the same will it be?"

Harrison would be feeling the fury, but he would remain calm as he wanted something, and it was not in a cup

The two exchanged pleasant-enough words and Pearl the Almighty granted Harrison time with his own daughters. It was agreed upon that he would return Sunday. His girls may have been home, and he may have gotten a cuddle or caught a moment he was able to share with them. That's why he was there—not to harm anyone or cause pain to others, he just wanted time with his family. He didn't hit anyone; he had no intention of doing anything of the sort.

Perhaps he himself has had a wake-up call and realized that his bastard behavior was less than serviceable for a healthy family life, and he may have reflected at some point that half the blame lay with him. He was, in part, sorry. Either way, he left amicably and there was no cause for concern.

After all this he possibly returned to his temporary accommodation. He may have called in for a visit with his sister April and stayed the night with them in Richmond, or he may not have informed them of his visit at all and stayed in cheap accommodation in the city of Melbourne. He was familiar with Melbourne; knew his way around. I suggest he sat in his room, happy as he could be. He'd seen his girls, and he was going to take them out on Sunday. That was all he needed. It was all he really wanted.

Back at the Mornington home, upon Phillip's return from work, Pearl informed him they'd had had a visitor. Yes, it went all right, and nothing untoward occurred.

Phillip may not have felt at ease, but he may have been pleased knowing nothing bad had happened. We'll never know at what point Phillip became aware that Pearl had disclosed to Harrison their address, but he'd have noticed the Four Ks wearing familiar clothing. Phillip may well have been open to disclosing their address, and thus wasn't bothered. The night found itself safely asleep for all.

The Sunday Harrison had been waiting for, arrived. A day with his daughters. Wake up everybody, let's go!

Pearl had no concerns, and went with Phillip for a social visit to her in-laws, in Seaford. That's right, they went out. It is difficult to comprehend, but it is correct. Pearl and Phillip went out for lunch after they allowed Harrison to take the Four Ks out for the day. Unsupervised, he took them to the pier at Mordialloc where they had ice cream together and walked about.

Kendall recalls that it was fine, just like normal. "He took us out for the day. We had ice cream, walked about, and it was all good."

Harrison had his daughters all to himself. He took them to another part of the peninsula and honored his word—the Four Ks were not in jeopardy at all.

But why weren't Pearl and Phillip worried?

Because there was no need to worry.

Not everything about this entire situation adds up, does it?

What mother puts not one but four daughters in harm's way? Not Pearl, because Harrison was not 'harm's way'. They were safe; she was sipping on a cup of tea with that in mind.

The other thing is that the Four Ks went willingly with him and had a good time with the monster. Why did the Four Ks feel comfortable with him? Why weren't they scared? They were old enough to voice their concerns: Kendall was nearly ten, Kristen was seven, Kate was nearly six, and Kylie was four. They could speak. From my point of view, it's clear the Four Ks, who were quite adept at surviving, probably hoped the 'good Harrison' took them out.

In Kendall's memory he was Jekyll and Hyde, so perhaps the forgiving little Ks wanted a day with their good dad. They would have also wanted to see that Dad was okay. Love for a parent is strong, and it remains inside you—in some capacity—possibly forever. Not for everyone, but most definitely for those young girls that day.

I've asked Kendall what he and the girls spoke about during their outing. Understandably, she could not remember much, just that they had a good day.

For Harrison, it would have been both painful and joyous for him this day. The relief of being able to see his girls would have been almost suffocating, even for a man who showed very little emotion. He adored his daughters, had turned his back on his entire family and disappeared to the wilderness of Tasmania with the tribe he built with the woman he loved. How do you think he felt when he was once again with his girls?

As agreed, Harrison returned the Four Ks safely home without issue or volatile altercations. He'd proved he could be trusted with his daughters. Some would say this was Harrison's charming side, that he was able to hide his violent side. Nonetheless, that day, Harrison showed much love and care. He was grateful to Pearl for allowing him to see them again. Even knowing that Pearl and Phillip were living in a new home, and were clearly together, Harrison still wanted his family back. As he had returned his daughters safely to their new home, he spoke of this.

Pearl and Harrison had a conversation at this time, and it is not reasonable to suggest Harrison wanted to leave as quickly as he could. He had just spent the worst weeks of his life not knowing where his family was; worse than the war he served in, worse than the isolation of living on the islands and even worse than the beatings he endured at the hands of his father. Harrison had spent the day with the ones he loved, and he was not ready to leave.

He possibly voiced regret for his behavior. He may even have used the words "I'm sorry" … or perhaps not. He had not moved on from or let go of being the family he had worked so hard to create. He'd built their first home, worked tirelessly to provide for them the entire time they were a family. They were clothed, fed, cared for, and shown aspects of a good life. In his mind, he was doing a much better job than his father had done for him and his brothers and sisters.

Put simply, he wanted the love he created that he had never had as a child.

It was no surprise he asked Pearl to take the Four Ks back to Tasmania with him. He wanted them, no doubt, and he was prepared to be a single father to achieve that.

Pearl's statement said, "He had asked to take the children with him." He asked Pearl; he did not just take them and flee as she had done to him. He sought her approval, and had she said, "Yes, if you like," he would have taken them back to Tasmania and raised them.

In her statement, she said no he could not have them because she was now married.

Was that all that was preventing Harrison from having access to his daughters? If that was the case, then it provided a very dubious second reason for Pearl marrying Phillip so quickly. It was also cuttingly cruel. As cruel as any beating Harrison delivered to Pearl. Taking a man's children from him hurts as deeply as it can, especially when that man loves them and wants to be their dad.

Pearl would have been so very cold and distant when speaking with Harrison. Just as cold as when she turned her back on Tasman. Again, it was her time for infliction. Now I have seen the cold manner Pearl had at her disposal. We are talking bitterly cold, here. It was used as a weapon to emotionally hurt others. It was no different in its intent than a punch to the head. Coldness shut the intended victim out, freezing them, nullifying their own sense of rational thinking. The adopted the 'I am right, and you are wrong' mentality. And also, 'See how cold I have had to become because of what you did to me.'

It's torturous.

But this technique lacks the full picture. Pearl desensitized herself to wrongdoings, held it at bay. She put all her effort into being cold and distant. She never once admitted fault. Never once said, "I did the wrong thing a number of times, and I am as much a cause of all this pain as Harrison."

Never did she remove her cold, distant armor. So, when she stated without love and care that Harrison could not have access to his daughters, she did so with a sharp blade. She was gloating; glad that Harrison was suffering. She didn't need him anymore; he had been replaced.

Unlike Harrison, she was not in the least bit remorseful that she had deceived him as much as she had. And she could tell the world she did it because he was such a violent, psychopathic nutcase who had guns and knives and drank to excess—and yet this is the same person she allowed her four daughters to spend the entire day with.

When she gloated about being married to Phillip, Harrison did not believe her—he knew her to be one of the best liars he had ever met. She had to get the certificate, which was equal to a trophy, to show him. He may not have believed they had time to get married. But they did. Because of the planning.

Harrison was a clever man, and upon reading the certificate, was able to calculate how quickly they married once off Tasman, and obviously how long it had been calibrated. With the dawning realization that his hopes of his family returning were over, anger began to fester. He was also dealing with the brutal emotional slaps Pearl was serving—one remark after another. His once happy day was getting sadder and sadder, and his already present pain was surfacing above the joy he felt at seeing his daughters. He could only take so much. He was angry when Pearl delivered another blow, telling him she would have left him regardless of Phillip coming into her life.

The message he heard was that he was not wanted—a blatant rejection. It is an emotional trigger, as he had a need to belong given he was discarded as a child by his parents.

The relationship he had with Pearl was the longest, most significant union he had ever had in his entire life. Now she was treating him with such hostility and brashness that his only defense was anger, and that anger mixed with the anger at his past—his childhood, his father's beatings, the guilt of his own abusive behavior, the humiliation of being drugged and deceived as methodically as he had been, the mental instability from the war service, the effects of a hard living and isolated lighthouse lifestyle, the fact that his de facto wife had been sleeping with another man he called friend (or multiple men), the frustration of not being able to fix the situation, and the sadness of his loss. He was carrying a lot of baggage, and I'm not sure I've met anyone who could cope with all of the above.

Harrison was damaged, and Pearl was not helping. In fact, she was twisting the knife. It was she who had brought him here.

Harrison spoke harshly to her but did not strike her as Pearl would have eagerly said this in her statement. He'd searched for his family, flown interstate when he'd found them, and was now learning of his de facto wife's new life.

He had also seen Phillip again, the man who'd slept with his de facto wife and who he had trusted and welcomed into his home. This man who was part of the plan that took his daughters and partner from him and left him behind on an island. He did not attempt to abuse or kill Phillip at this time, nor did he cause any concern or place people under any threat that would give Pearl reason to tell us so in her witness statement. All he wanted was his girls. When Pearl said, "No, and by the way, I'm married", he just went away.

He didn't sit in his car and stew with loathing, seeking revenge; he returned to Tasmania, defeated.

Of course, he didn't want to walk away, but he was given no choice. He was pushed away. Pearl was brilliant at pushing people away and shutting people out. She made very clear there was no room for him; he was not wanted. To them he was a cruel, abusive thug who hurt them. 'Go away Harrison, and stay away', was the message he received.

People hurt people every day, and I just can't help but consider how different life would have been had Pearl allowed Harrison to see his children. Even had it been one Sunday a month, just to give him something—how different may things have been? If she had asked him to move to Victoria, he would have in a heartbeat. But she gave him nothing but a backhand. They may not have wanted Harrison anywhere near their new life, but that was not a choice for them to make. He was entitled to see his children, but Pearl played her selfish card, and when it was put on the table, it took out the players in the game.

Harrison knew he had been abusive, knew he had not done the right thing by his children and Pearl all the time. He understood his cruelty was partly to blame for his family's demise. So, he walked away, returning to Tasmania and by all reports, suffered a nervous breakdown. As Gwen Jackson said, he was "very, very, very hurt."

Harrison was shattered. He lost his battle with hope and happiness, and this loss rendered him incapacitated. Anger no longer fueled his body to keep him going. He was embarrassed as well as hurt. No doubt he didn't go to his biological family because he didn't want to be a burden. He was broken. All he could do was retreat.

Harrison was admitted into a psychiatric ward with acute emotional and psychological collapse. This admission would be by consent. He was not certified by the Mental Hygiene Authorities; instead, his presenting condition was expressed under the following euphemism: 'in the need of a rest,' as he had succumbed temporarily to the strains and rigors imposed on his life.

The catalyst was his experience in Mornington, and all that stemmed from the event on Tasman Island. He had lost his loved ones, and the anxiety, stress, loss of self-esteem, and severe sadness manifested as acute depression. As the trauma of his past was never addressed, his condition deteriorated further.

It was understandable that he was extremely tired and weak, that he had episodes of uncontrollable crying. He lost weight and was quite drawn in appearance. It is thought that one of the contributing factors associated with those who experience a breakdown may be a result of unpleasant emotions resulting from poor relationships. Harrison most definitely had his share of those. His father was an intolerable man who ruled with his fists. His mother was not protective, and possibly unable to nurture. He watched his older brother ousted and blatantly rejected from the family. It was only when his sister April stepped into his life to raise him that he was touched by genuine care.

His sister was the woman who would be a role model for Harrison to love women.

It is evident he hadn't mastered the skill of love for his first relationship, and it was clearly not his intention to commit to it. Thus, when he married his first wife, Margaret, out of instruction, it was not a valuable means of drawing understanding. Pearl was Harrison's first and only love. Yes, I have heard and am agreeable to him being charming and liking the ladies himself, but he loved Pearl. This was his serious relationship.

He had one healthy role model, and he didn't have much faith in himself, but he found Pearl, and they—in their own weaknesses—clicked. His peace, though, had been snapped and hence the reference—broken.

DOES A BROKEN MAN MEND?

Who did Harrison Bennet have to turn to? How was he to fulfill his loss? Who was there to comfort him or to fill the void of his once ever-present family?

Fair questions I think many—both living and gone—have also asked.

Harrison had no one in Tasmania; his family lived in Melbourne. Therefore, I am not sure how he ended up being admitted to hospital, but someone saw a man wrecked, and he was taken into care by the state. I am uncertain whether this committal was instigated by the police, a government agency, or by the maritime officials he was working for as a lighthouse keeper... or even whether it was self-admittance. The Joyce family did not hear from him again—they had made it clear they no longer wanted him in their lives, even though he had spent a lot of time with them in the last nine years. They quite possibly had nothing to give that would have helped Harrison. They did not see him again. Ever.

He was in Tasmania from November 1959 and was about to face his first Christmas alone since 1950. I don't know exactly where and with whom he spent this time. What I do know, is he was cared for by nursing staff until he returned to Melbourne in October 1960.

He returned for a reason: to die one way or another.

During his time within the Tasmanian health services, he may have been diagnosed with depression or other psychological conditions, and he may or may not have received shock therapy as part of his rehabilitation. He may even have attended group sessions to rebuild himself. Whatever he did, he rebuilt his strength to be part of society again, but he was also diagnosed with cancer of the liver.

Harrison was advised he didn't have long to live, and that the cancer was an aggressive form already in its advanced stage. The only contributing factor to my considerations that Harrison received medical treatment for this cancer, or that it was having devastating effects, was because when Kendall saw him again on November 28, 1960, she was struck by how much weight he had lost, and his sallow complexion. He may have had chemotherapy or some other form of treatment, but to no avail. A time limit was given, and that set off another state of sorrow within him.

Phillip had pressure of his own to carry, and he knew it was his to bear. When he said, "I do," he became responsible for Pearl and the Four Ks. He was the new man in their lives and had to provide for them. He knew and accepted this. Therefore, he took to building their dreams. Literally.

With his determined approach to hard work, Phillip soon acquired enough money to purchase a block of land in Eden Road, Seaford. Eden Road ran into Wells Road, which was where William and Agnes lived. It was also the road where Beatrice owned the property with the tenuous shack on it. It was essentially a little Harper-hub, and that was where the new family was going to nestle in and call home.

The land owned by Phillip and Pearl sat waiting for a short while as the family continued to build their new existence. They departed the Mornington home almost immediately after Harrison left on that Sunday in November 1959. Apparently, Harrison made a verbal threat to harm

Pearl on his departure. Whether this forced an early departure from Mornington or not, I cannot be sure. Pearl had almost certainly been told to not contact Harrison under any circumstances. This was their fresh start and there was nothing she needed to say to him.

Pearl would have been comfortable with this as she had inflicted the pain she wanted by parading her marriage certificate, and letting Harrison know he had been replaced by a better man who loved her. The terms of her safety and privacy have been agreed upon, and the new family moved to where they thought they would be untraceable.

They organized to rent the asbestos shack from Phillip's sister, Beatrice. It was the most modest and rudimentary of dwellings, but it was home to the two Ps and Four Ks.

The shack was raw in its finishings and wasn't a true home, but it was a tin roof and walls that they were able to fill with second-hand furniture and lots of reasons to come together. It had an outside toilet and one bedroom the Four Ks slept in, and another area with a bed that Pearl and Phillip shared. There was no stove, but instead an electric frying pan in the small kitchen near the back door. The kitchen had a fridge and a table with six chairs around it for the family to be together during meal times. It was basic and less than attractive. It was set back into the block with a long driveway at the side which you would use to reach the back door. Upon entering you walked through the laundry then into the kitchen. The front door was rarely used.

For Pearl, Philip, and the Four Ks, life was going along incredibly well. Eden Road and its offerings—even the rented shack—seemed to be suiting the family well. Christmas came and went as did birthdays. A new year turned over, and 1960 began its time in history. With it came a new school term, and the dream of living next door once Phillip finished building the new home he had just started.

This was not a fantasy. With the block of land purchased, the stumps in the ground and the framework nearing construction, the Four Ks were watching their home become a reality, and in turn smiling. Pearl had settled down, and Phillip was creating a prosperous business with his carpentry skills that would have seen them set for life. They were enjoying the fresh air, the void of violence—or the threat of such—and it was this eighteen months they spent together that provided them with an abundance of joy.

The Four Ks attended the local state primary school at Seaford, and this was a first for all of them as they had been homeschooled to this point. The three older girls suited up and took to being in a socially-interactive learning environment. Here, they experienced their first lessons of social integration in an educational environment. They had seen more than any of their fellow pupils, but they were not about to tell them any of it. Nothing of where they came from would be made known to the teachers or their classmates. Not even their dog Buster was told of the things the Four Ks had seen. They integrated unassumingly well. They were competent in personal-interaction skills, yet they rarely parted company. They had their issues, but they were sisters and they looked out for each other.

From the start of December 1959 to the end of November 1960, the Four Ks and the two Ps lived none the wiser of Harrison. He was not given a second thought. To them he had vanished into the void.

At the start of 1960, it was a lovely summer and with the beach just a few minutes away. Seaford made for a fun-filled child's playground. They were well-experienced with life near the sea, more acquainted with the ocean than a bay's sea but they were at home nonetheless.

The Harper family now welcomed them into their lives, and Agnes was fondly remembered for her acceptance and warmth for the girls. They walked past their grandparent's home every morning en route to another day of learning. William could often be seen out in the garden with either a wave or nod to say, "Have a good day, girls." The family saw nearly all of 1960 together without so much as a hint of aggression: no violence, no alcohol abuse as they had known it, and no smacks to the back of the head or guns pointed at faces. They embraced the social interaction of school and the comfort of stability.

Happiness was theirs.

Harrison had last hugged his daughters at least eleven to twelve months ago, but he hadn't stopped thinking about them. He suffered under the weight of trying to hide his unpleasant emotions, but their enormity overwhelmed him. I do not believe he recovered from this moment, as his alienation from his friends and family he could not fix, but he was able to return to society, be it on borrowed time.

He had been given a death warrant, yet he knew he needed to present himself well and adjusted enough to leave the Mental Hygiene Institution. Melancholic, self-worth shattered, he had even lost the ability to self-love, which I would argue was never authentically there to begin with. The only thing keeping him going was the need to say goodbye to his son and four daughters.

He left the hospital and made his way to Victoria to say his farewells. He removed himself from the support and care of the hospital network and landed in Melbourne in October 1960.

What stood in his way was that he didn't know where to find his children, and in his desperation, he put himself once again on the radar.

No, he was far from mended.

FIRST TRY—
STRANGER DENIED

Harrison's body had been dealt the hand to host a killer; cancer was taking him out for sure—or was it? That depended on something that wasn't his choice, initially. But right at this moment, he was well aware he was dying of liver cancer. For now, his mind was not hosting a killer, it was hosting a father who wanted to say goodbye to his children before cancer took him away.

No one knew this. The only people he told of his condition were April and Thomas, and a woman named Jill Reed, who was a nurse whom he had met in Benalla way back in 1945.

Upon his arrival on the mainland in October 1960, he stayed at a hotel in the city of Melbourne for several days. He had an agenda, an honorable one, and accompanying him was the melancholia he had been unable to shift after collapsing under the weight of his emotional distress. It had only been ten months since he fell into this pain, but it was nowhere near enough time for recovery. His emotional instability was well-housed within. He only had one more important task to see done; and it was just too bad the emotional baggage had to come along for the ride.

From the hotel, he decided he needed to see his sister again. After nearly ten years of isolation from his family, he walked back into April's life. He shared with both April and

Thomas the loss and pain of the last years. The reason he offered for not keeping in touch was that he didn't want to be a burden to anyone.

He was still independent and informed them he was not staying in Melbourne long but was bound back to Tasmania as soon as he said his goodbyes. I am not sure if Harrison speaking of a return to Tasmania is truth. What did he have to return to? But that is what his side of the family recalled.

Harrison told April and Thomas he was dying of cancer and did not want to bother anyone. He just wanted to say goodbye and disappear again. This was a man who was messed up. He could not think rationally, he was struggling with his nervous breakdown, and his common sense had disengaged. Harrison was full of self-blame, self-loathing, and riddled with as much sorrow as he was cancer.

Fiercely independent, he was a survivalist who could look after himself. That suited his two needs: to not be a burden on anyone, and to not rely on anyone. It meant he wouldn't be hurt or rejected.

After seeing April and Thomas, his next step was to find his children.

He had not heard from Pearl since she psychologically backhanded him into a totally different stratosphere at their Mornington address. She had kept her promise and not made any attempt to contact him again. She had no need. All Harrison had was his memory of their last home. In his efforts to find the Four Ks, he more than likely returned to the same address. They were long gone—a theme of his it seems.

His loss, while standing at the Mornington address would have cut deep, like losing them all over again. He'd traveled across an ocean to find them, yet all he had was their echo.

He was alone.

Loneliness shredded his hope.

The following is an account from a woman who was once Harrison's sister-in-law. I met with her in her nursing home, and she was a delightful woman to sit with, a character with her wits about her.

Her name was Shirley, and she had once been Cameron Bennet' wife. Her clear recount was that Harrison had stolen the car in which he was driving on his search around Melbourne; however, other reports have him owning the car. Either way, Harrison took himself down to the Frankston region, looking for his daughters. Shirley said it hurt him deeply, and he couldn't take it anymore. It was all he came over to do—find his daughters—and he'd had had enough. Life had dealt him another blow, and somewhere around this time, he resolved that he just couldn't get past this pain. He wanted out. He *literally* wanted out.

Pain overrode every other emotion he had; he was sick of himself and how he was living. He parked the car at the side of the road. He may have sat there for a short time and had a bout of uncontrollable crying, or he may have been completely numb and void of any emotion.

Something inside him had snapped. He just didn't care anymore. The one thing he yearned for he couldn't have. This occurred October 12, 1960, which was a Wednesday. Harrison had not been in Victoria for long.

According to Shirley Britter, his car was parked to the side of the road close to the Frankston police station. He had exited the car and rigged it with intent: there was a hose attached from the exhaust through the back window. He had fitted everything securely—no mistakes.

Harrison returned to the driver's seat and sat there with the engine running. How would it feel to just sit there, waiting to be taken out by toxic fumes? How desperate would you have to be? He just sat and waited to be overcome with the carbon monoxide, hoping to never wake up.

He was rendered unconscious, and his plan would have worked if not for a stranger.

A passerby became suspicious as they drove past the running car and stopped to assist. They could see the pipe coming from the exhaust and into the window and the unconscious man in the driver's seat. It was an obvious picture, with no need for further interpretation. The stranger opened the door, pulling Harrison free before beginning to revive him. He was given mouth-to-mouth resuscitation and Harrison was awoken, his life returned.

The police, given they were not far from this, were in attendance, and an ambulance had also arrived. Harrison was taken to Frankston Hospital, and placed under twenty-four-hour observation. This would be October 13, 1960—a Thursday.

From constant watch at the hospital, officers took Harrison to Frankston police station to be charged. He was taken to the cells where he waited to represent himself at his trial for attempting to take his life.

I do not think Harrison would have thanked his savior. He may not have recovered enough to see him at the scene. The stranger may have returned Harrison's breath, but not his awareness. Maybe he did not regain full consciousness until he was in hospital, but his functioning returned, and he was now in the care of the authorities, who had genuine concern for him.

They located his next of kin while Harrison was recovering in hospital, contacting Cameron Bennet. It was Cameron who informed April and Thomas of the happenings and Harrison's condition.

Harrison was a shattered man. He had not recovered from being unable to find his daughters. This was the last straw for him. He was not violent or aggressive in any way, and he gave the police no cause for alarm, nor did they charge him with anything relating to assault or theft of a motor vehicle. The car wasn't stolen, and he wasn't violent.

On October 14, 1960—a Friday—Harrison stood before the magistrate and represented himself. He was comfortable with this proceeding as he had had experience in courts with two court martials. Harrison had endured the humiliation of being found in his most vulnerable state, and he was now standing in a witness box owning his behavior as he did at his court martials.

The shame and complexity of being punished for being so desperate was an extraordinary event on top of what he had already endured. The proceedings were very formal, and the magistrate was compassionate yet firm. Upon Harrison's guilty plea, he found at the Court of Petty Sessions at Frankston that on October 12 1960, the defendant—Harrison Jake Bennet—did commit a breach of attempt to commit self-murder. The decision upon the hearing was that Harrison was to be tried at the Supreme Court at Melbourne commencing November 7, 1960.

Bailed out at the Petty Sessions, he was fined in the sum of fifty pounds, which was presumably paid by Thomas Hagen who had by now attended to Harrison's needs and was present to support him. It was Thomas and April who answered the call from Cameron.

I cannot imagine the pain the two men were feeling, or the conversation.

"Tried to kill yourself, mate?"

"Yeah, I've had a gutful. Sorry about this, Thomas."

The intensity as they peered at each other would have been horrific, as it was mixed with Harrison's shame, anger, embarrassment, and loathing. Thomas would have seen this as he was a clever man; he would have reached out to try to help any way he could in Harrison's wretched life.

Thomas watched the proceedings at Frankston—the only person who had his back. Once again Harrison had a source of support that wasn't government provided, and that was this reliable man who had married his lovely sister—the sister who raised him.

During the brief hearing, the men shared glances, and for the first time in a long time, Harrison saw a friendly and familiar face. The magistrate saw this, and at the end of the session, agreed to release Harrison into Thomas' care. Harrison accepted the terms the magistrate handed down and swore an oath that he would attend his coming trial. He also agreed to stay with Thomas and April. His fighting spirit was gone. Utterly lost, Harrison was almost infantile in his identity. All he wanted was for his life to end.

The two men left the court and headed to Richmond. Did they speak on the drive? What was said? Or, did silence fill the car?

Harrison was exhausted, no doubt still feeling the effects of carbon monoxide poisoning along with the emotional and psychological debilitation. Drained is a vision I have of him. He tried to kill himself, was saved by a stranger, caught by the police, taken to hospital, and put under surveillance. He was then charged with attempted self-murder, stood trial, fined, was found out by his family because the authorities called them, and now he was on the way to face his sister. I think silence travelled with the men.

Thomas brought Harrison home to Richmond to live with them, where he was among the love of those he trusted. April and Thomas held Harrison's heart with tenderness.

His sister—who had always loved him—didn't make much of a fuss. Instead, Harrison may have been offered a warm meal and shown to his bedroom. Maybe some small talk was had and a mention of, "We will talk of this later. Get some rest and we'll have breakfast together. Good night."

Harrison would have gone to sleep, and Thomas and April would have gone to bed and talked amongst themselves—April would have wanted to hear all about the day and Thomas would have wanted to tell her. They communicated well together and had just taken on the responsibility and care of another. April would have been concerned for her brother, but also aware she had her own family—their son, Gary, who was thirteen at the time.

Harrison took some time to recover. He was legitimately fragile. Quiet and withdrawn, he sat silently in the chair in the lounge room quite often. Thomas and April did not push him, but they did try to lift his spirits.

They knew Harrison well, and were aware that throughout his life he had a pattern of simply vanishing. It was a survival mechanism, and whilst April and Thomas knew he had gone to serve in the Army in the Middle East when he returned they could barely keep track of him. They did know he had gone to Tasmania and become a lighthouse keeper, but little else.

On previous occasions when he returned from any of his numerous absences, he acted as if nothing had happened. This occasion was different. The ever-reliable April and Thomas hadn't changed, and Harrison fell back into the welcoming arms of his non-judgmental sister and brother-in-law. Whilst they were not completely settled with his manner, they accepted Harrison unconditionally.

They knew Pearl, as Harrison had introduced her to Thomas and April in 1950, and they had spent some time together. They were even part of the discussions about the move to Tasmania, but they had not seen him for ten years. Thus, when I was researching and meeting Harrison's nieces and nephews, there were large parts of Harrison's life the family members know little about.

They told me: "He comes and goes, we don't see much of him, and he simply vanishes." To them—and they were young children at the time—he vanished in 1950 and they didn't really know or care to discover where he had gone. This was the same for Harrison. He had no calling to keep in contact with any one because he had what he wanted: the love of his life. Until, of course, she left him.

It was true that Harrison was considered the no-hoper who was unbalanced and cruel by loved ones of his. Those still living have told me Harrison was abusive and intolerable and could snap in a second. But he himself couldn't see it. In his mind, all he wanted was to love and belong.

To be fair and equal and as removed from bias as possible, Harrison did contribute to his fate and he did act mercilessly as he beat Pearl and Kendall. He was not innocent of wrongdoing. He had hurt the ones he was so desperately wanted to be with, and the damage was long lasting.

It was not too complex a situation to grasp. Put simply, his rejection issues were being fueled and he was, in part, fueling them. He was rejected by his parents, who set up his poor personal relationship skills. Harrison possibly didn't even understand he had helped create this situation. He was used to being rejected; expected it from those around him. So, he sought it in his unconscious behavior, and in his conscious behavior—much like a mouse on a wheel. He wouldn't connect that he attracted his pain. His biological family was now a mirror of his own family; he had brought his past to his present.

Back to April and Thomas's care. The mornings started, and the days passed. Harrison was encouraged to return to society and embrace life.

April, and especially Thomas, were very caring and supportive people—they helped Harrison immensely with his recovery. They not only provided him with a warm safe home, they also talked to him and listened to him; it was their company that healed, too. They did not belittle him nor torment his insecurities. There was no flashing of marriage certificates or telling him he could not see his children because they had married someone else. No controlling, manipulative behavior. No hurting here. This was exactly what he needed, and he gained the confidence and esteem necessary to return to the workforce. Whilst he was a damaged man, he was, in part, a decent man. Harrison was not as criminally minded as some would have you believe.

It's hard for a handful of people to acknowledge that Harrison had goodness about him; and those who could not see that, couldn't give him an ounce of credit, not a single grain of credit. They had him pegged as a torturous, murdering bastard, where talking about him was done with a poisonous palate. Anger boiled in those who felt this way about him. Allow me to be the devil's advocate: part of this anger felt by these individuals is their own guilt.

I think it was forgotten, and while I'm not at all suggesting it was excusable, his experiences in the war in the Middle East and Papua New Guinea never left him. He had smelt blood from the dying and the dead, heard the screams of men—their flesh pierced with knives, guts spilling, and all to the accompaniment of exploding grenades and tank fire. In his nightmares, sirens wailed, and the whistle of incoming bombs played havoc behind his wall of silence.

Drink, drink, drink, drink and it will all go away.

So often he had sat in a tower as the Night Keeper, just him and his memories. How often had he replayed the death of his brother Jack? Or the beatings from his father. Tears may have been shed, anger may have festered, but he didn't have the resources to overcome his psychological misgivings, and he wasn't about to seek advice. Not during the 1950s.

Harrison had issues before he met Pearl. Now he had more. Conversely, Pearl had issues before she met Harrison and now, as part of Harrison's growing pile, he could add her personal issues. It was her issues that were in part contributing to his present behavior.

For now, Harrison was hired by the electrical company Ring Grip, which was based in Abbotsford, Victoria, the suburb where Harrison grew up. He was responsible for inspecting products, and took his duties seriously. He attended his employed position daily. If we assume that Harrison arrived in Melbourne on or around October 10, 1960, and we know he then attempted suicide on October

12, 1960; he commenced his employment from October 17, 1960 and maintained his position until he surrendered responsibility of everything.

His trial commenced November 7, 1960, where he pled guilty to the charge of 'attempt to commit self-murder,' and was recorded with a conviction to serve two years' probation with strict bail conditions. He was to report to a person of the law daily and be in the care of April and Thomas at Jameson Street, Richmond, by 1800 hours each night. His car had been confiscated since the suicide attempt, yet he was never charged with vehicle theft.

He upheld his bail conditions from approximately October 17, 1960, until December 2, 1960. Again, he displayed the capacity to integrate with society and walk in the socially accepted way—no wrath or vengeance or menace. He even revealed his true feelings and psychological angst to the magistrate at the Supreme Court in Melbourne. While in the witness dock, he told the judge that he just wanted to see his daughters. He missed them terribly. "That is all I want, your honor," Harrison said, and the judge could see he was visibly distraught. The magistrate advised that it was a terribly sad state of affairs, but he had not the power to assist Harrison as he and Pearl were not married.

This was the true Harrison. He was not a killer or a madman; he was a man who missed his daughters.

He wasn't angry; he was sad, very sad. At the trial for his attempted self-murder, he begged for help but was offered nothing but the sympathy of a high man of the law. Harrison received a nod of support and slight acknowledgement from the magistrate, accompanied by a few slaps on the wrist and strict conditions. Nothing to genuinely help Harrison.

There is little doubt Harrison left court feeling let down by a system that could not help him. His frustration may have extended his sorrow, the weight of it all may have just gotten heavier as he walked out of the building with Thomas by his side. Nothing could really help Harrison's exasperated disillusionment or predicament.

They returned home to the Jameson Street address where Harrison retired to his room while Thomas informed April of all that had transpired. It was another somber night in Richmond. How did hope live for a new day? The universe was about to have its say.

UNIVERSE PLAYS A HAND

What's happened now?
         Isn't it settled yet?
Aren't we all exhausted?

You can't explain the unexplainable. This ripple of cause and effect. A demonstration of what will be will be. It was certainly the final slaying of a man that was both responsible—and not—for the harm that came by way of his hand.

It's well documented that since July 12, 1959, when he drained the last of Pearl's concoction, Harrison's life had been relentlessly crippling. Whether this was a form of karma or an option for satisfaction to those Harrison had hurt, is worth a thought. Whatever form of absolution you seek, since that cup of tea a man's soul had been in torment. By December 1960, Harrison was just hanging on. How he got to December is mystifying in and of itself.

On the face of it, Harrison had no avenues to help find his daughters. He had not told the authorities that he was dying of cancer, and he had no special favors to call in. He just got on with life the best he could.

He was charming enough to catch the interest of a woman called Jill Mead. I am not clear about where they were able to reconnect since meeting in Benalla at the Tarax bar in 1945. Perhaps they reconnected accidentally, or through Harrison contacting her. Or perhaps Jill Mead was a nurse who crossed Harrison's path in the hospital he spent some time at in Tasmania, or more plausibly in the Frankston hospital during his suicide attempt. Either way, Harrison had a woman who was in love with him, and it matters not how these two adults rekindled their care, only that they did.

If they'd met when Harrison returned to Melbourne, then it was a short period of time they had together. If they rekindled their union while in Tasmania, much longer were they together. Whenever their desires were founded, Harrison was sound in mind enough for Jill to agree to marry him.

What?

It's true; Jill and Harrison had spent enough time together that for the rest of this life, Harrison had a woman by his side.

In fact, it's exactly by his side that she played a crucial role in the events that followed. She was smitten with Harrison and him with her. This is supported by Harrison's actions. He finally applied for a divorce from Margaret Barnes. He'd had no need to divorce Margaret previously, as he'd long left her life. Any thought of her was well behind him. He had last spoken of her at his second court martial on June 19, 1945—eleven days after he had married her.

He filed for divorce in October 1960

Evidence that Harrison left matters as they were, which in hindsight may have returned to haunt him. Had he been married to Pearl, he may have had more legal standing for access to his daughters.

Cause and effect and its impact.

I'm not sure if Jill Mead knew of Harrison's past, if she saw the violent man his previous family had seen, or if she saw a man who had none of that within him. What she did know is that he would die of cancer within two months or so.

This was confirmed by April, who stated it was one of the reasons Harrison and Jill were to marry. Jill was to nurse Harrison in his days of need. This woman cared enough to sit by his bedside as he lost the battle with the 'taker.' The cancer was going to take him out; Jill would hold his hand and change his bed pan.

April's son, Gary Hagen, remembered a woman around Harrison at this time, and he agreed he met and saw her at the Richmond home. According to Gary, Harrison did not have trouble attracting the interest or affections of women. He was charming. How he managed to be charming enough in his poor psychological and physical health is a question for which I have no answer.

Life was looking up, and in late October, Harrison was working and falling in love—or falling in need—with Jill, and she was falling in love or care for him. He appeared to be moving forward, and for the month of November he was working on living a decent life. He attended work, and he abided by his probation conditions. He had April, Thomas, Jill, and Cameron around him as much as possible to keep his spirits up. It was all okay.

There was one thing that kept tripping him up, though: he was desperate to see his daughters. That was what really consumed him. What this man really wanted was to put things right with himself and those who didn't call him Dad. For this, he had to see all five of them to say goodbye.

He took the easiest option open to him to quell one of his urgencies. Locating Margaret Barnes was easy; he knew that she and her family were from the country town of Benalla. He may well have assumed she was still there, and that was his first move. What he didn't know was that his son Joshua had kept his surname—Bennet.

Harrison hired a car and drove through familiar country towns. He passed Euroa, Glenrowan, and Violet Town. He was amidst Ned Kelly country, which was a beautiful serene part of the Australian countryside. While he was surrounded by landscape beauty, a family had no indication their day was about to be interrupted by a ghost from the past.

Standing of the stoop of Margaret's home, any moment now she would appear. He had not seen this woman's face since he last spoke to her, but he had no shame or guilt for having left her. He had his own need to feed now, and that was far more important and powerful than owning his neglect.

It was easier for Harrison to say to his son: "I'm dying, I just want to say goodbye" than taking responsibility and telling Joshua, "I did the wrong thing."

He was unmistakable. He had aged but had not changed enough for Margaret not to know exactly who was at her front door. Harrison no doubt used his pleasantries and charm when speaking with Margaret, because whatever he said worked. She welcomed him, and he sat with her for a brief moment enjoying a cup of tea. She knew Harrison enough to know he was not violent and could be trusted. When his son entered the room, Harrison stood and introduced himself. Joshua was not six months old when Harrison last saw him, and now before him was a teenager—a young man himself.

Harrison sought Margaret's permission to take Joshua out for a drive; he wanted the two of them to spend some time together. She granted his wish. All were highly agreeable, and with a jovial manner the three of them spoke with trust.

The two men drove to Shepparton, where they spent the day talking about the time Harrison had been away and what Joshua had been doing with his life. They took a stroll and offered some genuine gestures to each other. Harrison may have apologized for his absence and explained why his parenting role had not been fulfilled, why he had been a void in his son's life. He may have informed his son that he had four half-sisters, but this was not pursued by Joshua in his lifetime. In their lifetime, the Four Ks didn't even know they had not one, but two half-brothers until I come across these facts in my research. The other son was Pearl's firstborn.

Like he did with the Four Ks in Mornington, Harrison bought ice cream, and he and Joshua walked the grounds of the rural town, reflecting on this moment. By day's end, he returned Joshua to Margaret safely and without any harm, no physical or psychological menacing, just an overdue day finally spent between a young man and an old man—father and son.

With goodbyes said, Harrison left them again. He did not share with either of them too much of his condition or his past experiences, and he did not promise to return. He simply came, made his peace, and went.

He returned to Melbourne that same day and made his probation conditions. He also now had the signed divorce papers and could proceed with his new marriage.

His ending of this estranged marriage happened around November 7, 1960, although this was a Monday, so it is more likely that it was on the weekend of the 5th and 6th, as Joshua was not at school nor was Harrison working. Harrison never saw Joshua or Margaret again. Neither party needed to. Margaret had a new man in her life and had had children with him. This man became Joshua's stepfather, and he was the role model for Harrison's firstborn.

The next Margaret was to hear word of her first husband was in the newspapers, then six months later when April's letter arrived to tell her the truth.

Harrison felt good about the visit with Joshua and was pleased he had done it. It fed his need and he achieved one of his goals.

However, he was more fueled by the experience to find the ones he really wanted to say goodbye to.

That night in Richmond, the mood in the house was lighter because of the day's events. Harrison told April of his day, and both April and Thomas enjoyed the moment, albeit with sadness, as they knew he was preparing to leave in peace. That had been the true intent behind the day. An honorable intent with a sad reality attached.

Harrison's daily routine returned November 7, 1960—he went to work and came home. He did this all week and spent time with Jill. He continued this routine the second week and even the third week of November. In fact, November was but a harboring for the finale of December. Life appeared normal, duties were met, and probation restrictions adhered to. The house was heavy in spirit but livable, love was blossoming, cancer was progressing, and a man's anguish was intensifying.

Tick tock.

Harrison watched a month pass without as much as a hint of his daughters' home. 'Where are they?' was the unanswered question tearing him apart.

Jill helped where she could. She could see his heaviness and the effort Thomas and April were also putting in. She asked him to assist her father with moving his furniture from Frankston to Essendon. Her father only too happy to receive Harrison's expert helping hand. This Harrison did without hesitation, and he spent the weekend moving Mr. Mead's belongings. He was well and truly experienced in moving furniture items, as he has done so ample times on the islands of Tasmania, both his own family's belongings and those of the other families in the community network.

The logbooks are a credit to his ability to work hard, as they are full of statements like: 'Bennet and Skipper moving effects up haulage,' etc.

Well-accustomed to hard work, Harrison delivered Mr. Mead a hand on Sunday, November 27, 1960. It gave him a break from monotony. It made Harrison feel needed, and he was also helping his future father-in-law. What more could he want?

The last week of November was about to give Harrison more than he had ever expected. Whilst he and Jill were travelling in the removalists' truck, Harrison was chatting with the driver—a complete stranger. The two hit it off really well, chatting as if they'd known each other since birth. This stranger would return life to a dead man walking.

The conversation eventuated in Harrison telling the driver that he had four daughters he could not find, that he just wanted to say goodbye before he went that way himself. He was desperate to find them, had driven up and down streets, talked to whomever he thought might know where they were, but he kept coming up short-handed.

The driver turned to him. "Harrison," he said, "I know where your girls are, mate. I moved them last year."

Bang! Take a photo of that!

Did Harrison yell in jubilation? Could the smile not be wiped from his face? Was it pure elation? Did the truck driver feel that ride of exuberance?

Was it sheer luck Harrison had come across a stranger with whom he felt comfortable enough to confide? Or, was life playing out its game of coincidence? I am not a believer in coincidence of this nature, and therefore I lean on the option of believing this encounter was set in both men's fates.

The truck driver gave Harrison the address where he could find his girls. His body and mind were released from the torturous enslaved hell in which they'd been confined.

What Harrison didn't know quite yet, was that he was only a few streets away from the Four Ks when he attempted suicide. On this day, they were not five minutes away from him.

He stayed with Jill until all his work was complete. The two of them discussed the findings of the day and were both overjoyed. With all his chores completed, he returned to April and Thomas to spread his good news.

The old Harrison burst through the door and announced to his sister, "I found them! I found them," he repeated, smiling wider than he had in years. Hope surged, and nothing could deny his stupendous display. April was perplexed but excited for her brother, and the two shared the jubilation. Those in the Richmond house slept well that night.

The next morning was all happiness. Harrison wore a large smile to work, thanking the heavens for delivering his dream. He went to work and either left early or his shift finished early, as he was at Eden Road, Seaford, by 3pm that day. He travelled from Abbotsford, where his company was located, or he took the day off to prepare. I am not convinced of this, as he would have made his way to Seaford earlier had he the chance.

As he was making his way to their address and the unsuspecting happy family, I wonder if Harrison was aware it had only taken forty to fifty days from his initial arrival in Melbourne to be now minutes away from standing in their driveway.

Did nervousness accompany him? I suspect it did.

He had not seen his family for over twelve months. He had been emotionally throttled by Pearl, told to get lost and leave them alone. Despite his abusive hand in why Pearl and the Four Ks did not want him around, he was not convinced he was such a threat. He absolutely adored them. For him, that connection would never go away. His intention was as pure as it was in Mornington a year ago, except this time he had knowledge. The time spent since seeing them last had been a very emotionally challenging one.

It was a big move for Harrison to make. He was going unannounced and did not know how he would be received. All he was doing was seeing to his own needs, his own self-fueling requirements. His desire to see the Four Ks was stronger than any other thoughts that could influence his arrival at their doorstep unannounced.

Here I come, ready or not.

He drove along the dirt road, stopping when he saw the mailbox marked '31.' Harrison cut the engine to the hired car, and out of the vehicle he got. He may have been looking around to see if any of his daughters were coming up the road, as they were due home from school at this time. He may also have hoped that Phillip was not home, so he could go about doing what he wanted without interruption or confrontation. But he knew no one's routine or location. He was simply winging it. He had absolutely nothing to lose at this point.

He walked down the dirt driveway under the boughs of various trees. The cement-sheeting shack sat in all its modesty at the back of the block. He may have gone to the front door and knocked, then realized it was not frequented and walked around to the back door. He may have followed the driveway all the way to the back of the dwelling and seen that was the entrance.

When he arrived at the doorway, I suspect he was seen by Pearl, as the Four Ks were all at primary school. She more than likely received the fright of her life, as she had no idea that Harrison was in Victoria, let alone knew where she lived.

Pearl claimed he arrived at 3.15pm, and he had been drinking. I wonder if she thought to mention in her statement that she used to drink with Harrison. Was it such a bad thing that he had been drinking? Given Pearl was a drinker herself and that every Friday night she and Phillip had a bottle of beer together. I do take issue with this point of Pearl's, as she herself was a massive drinker, and she and Harrison were known to drink beer together while they lived in Tasmania— both on and off the island.

Now, it was used against him when once it had been a thing that drew them together. The two of them were what we'd now call alcoholics.

He had more than likely been drinking, as he would have been very nervous about going to the door and saying hello again. A glass or two, yes, I concur, but not a dozen or more. If he took to drink before his arrival, it wasn't a form of abuse on his part, more comfort or his own way of Dutch courage. He was scared, too.

He wasn't coming to the home to hurt anyone; he was coming to the home to say goodbye to his daughters. This would have been made very clear to Pearl very quickly, because despite her resolve, she had a heart too and the shock she had just been served needed to be managed instantly.

Would Pearl have been wide-eyed, her mouth possibly hanging open? Or had she been shocked to silence?

Before she had any words to present to the situation, Harrison may have cut in, "Hello, Pearl. I'm not here to cause harm. I just want to see my girls."

She may have known he was not there to cause harm and wasn't frightened at all. Just shocked at the sight of a man that just wouldn't go away. Perhaps she may have been annoyed.

Like last time, Harrison was permitted to enter the family home, where the two sat at the kitchen table.

What must have Pearl been thinking?

She may have offered him a beer and had one with him, or she may have sat rigidly, not giving him anything. They had spent nine years together, and there was no audience to seek attention from. It was just them and their own truths, the last moment of 'real' they had.

They had previously shared laughter, had worked together as a team, and while Harrison was violent at the end of their relationship and Pearl had caused a lot of hurt, the two sat talking without the intent to cause further harm.

Perhaps they were able to have a clear discussion where matters were somewhat aired, and questions asked and answered.

Whatever was said, they no doubt discussed many things including why Pearl left Harrison, and how Harrison felt about this, and Pearl surely airing her grievances.

He told her that he blamed Phillip for taking her away. He had to blame Phillip, as he still loved her, and it was easier to blame another party than look at his own behavior, to possibly hate the one he loved.

All the betrayal and deceit inflicted on Harrison by Pearl was intense, and for Harrison to face this reality was a very big ask of an already unadjusted man. He loved Pearl for who she was, and that included her shortcomings, which suited his. He could not blame her, as that would be to blame himself. It was easier to blame the other man, but this was not the right target. Phillip was not at fault in the decline of Harrison and Pearl's relationship.

Harrison had taken the shallow option. If he and Pearl blamed a third party, there may have been a scapegoat who could cover the real causes and thus present a path for the two of them to get back together. But that wasn't going to be the case. Pearl loved Phillip.

She'd had enough of Harrison and his disgusting behavior; she was clear on this and told him so again. She wasn't as cutting as she had been at Mornington but took a more explanatory approach. The time she spent apart from Harrison and the lighthouse community way of life helped rebuild her. The happiness she felt with Phillip and her daughters together as a new family had brought love into her heart and her daughters' hearts. She was not as psychologically brittle as she had been.

The last time Pearl and Harrison were together, the ink from their marriage certificate was barely dry. She was still reeling from everything that had brought her to her desperate state. The isolation of the lighthouse communities and their mere habitat could undo the most centered of souls. This lifestyle was truly detrimental to both Harrison and Pearl.

She may have not liked Harrison, but she was still ending a relationship, and that takes time to heal, regardless of the situational variables surrounding its demise. She was also suffocating in her own guilt and her loss. She had much to hurt over in 1959, even if she did get married and start a new life.

By year's end, she had secured her feet on the mainland and reintegrated herself into a society that was welcoming of her, and she did not have to concern herself with physical threats or the overconsumption of alcohol. She had also had no reason to fight for a living, so to speak. On the island, you had to kill the meat you ate, make all the food, and store it in accordance with what was available on the island. The washing didn't fly off the clothes line and disappear into a crevice or the ocean, and you could walk down the street without the wind threatening to swirl you away. The children were being schooled by a teacher, and if you wanted to go to the shops or speak to a neighbor, you could.

She was on dry land again and all the small things that didn't figure as much on their own, amounted to a good way of life that brought a smile to her face.

Across from Harrison now, she was wary and protective, but she was not fearful. The house being built next door would give her more than she dreamed of. I wonder if she remembered it was Harrison who last built her a house.

Upon hearing Pearl's words, Harrison was not going to take it too well. It hurt psychologically, not so much on its own, but because it was rejection, and confirmation that his behavior caused his relationship to breakdown.

Although Harrison was set to marry Jill Mead, he still sought interaction with Pearl.

Pearl looked well, as she had new clothes and was taking care of her appearance. But as the time lengthened, so did a feeling of awkwardness, and then they ran out of things to say. Between 3.30pm and 4pm, they both waited for the footsteps of the Four Ks heading up the driveway to the back door.

The Four Ks were again to receive the fright of their lives—they had no idea their real father was inside with their mother. To them it was just another day at school. Their dad was a man called Phillip, who loved them very much and was at work building someone else's house.

The moment arrived as the Four Ks did. They entered the shack as they had done all year.

Harrison was there. They were there. He opened the silence with a huge smile. The Four Ks all stood wide-eyed, stunned. No talking.

He got to his knees and instantly put his arms out. "Come and give your dad a kiss and a hug."

He hugged them all.

Not able to get enough of them, he told them he missed them and how happy he was to see them. The truth of this would have shone bright from him; his happiness clearly visible. The Four Ks would also have been smiling; their dad was being lovely. Pearl may have been sitting in silence, thinking that for the moment this situation was okay, but that Harrison had best be off soon as Phillip wouldn't be too far away.

I wonder if it was all one sided, the love. Did anyone else have care in that room aside from Harrison? Kendall says they really do not care. If this was the case, I understand that for them he equaled hurt, being hurt, inflicting hurt, and causing hurt. But what of their inner feelings? Of a daughter wanting to be accepted and loved by a father. What about those ties? I question how the Four Ks were processing their love and connection with their dad.

They knew who he was. He'd been with them day in and out for nearly ten years. Then he was gone, and a new man took his place. To them, a better man—absolutely, yes—but not their biological father. Despite being aware Harrison was associated with pain, I'm going to assume the Four Ks were still young enough to have love in their hearts for this man who knelt before them.

For now, the cuddles continued and 'daddy dearest' loved them wholly and completely. There was excitement in the kitchen. It couldn't be helped. Harrison's energy and devotion at seeing them again was infectious. His return told them—indirectly and directly—that he loved them and wanted them in his life. They were wanted; their father had come for them. If he hadn't, what message would that have sent?

It's not been considered from this angle, but perhaps it is time it was. He did not have to come searching for them; he didn't have to treat them with care and respect when he found them. He could have walked away as he had with Joshua. He kept coming to see them; he even asked to raise them. No one has ever whispered this.

After the happiness swept through the shack, Harrison left around 4pm, before Phillip arrived home from work. Pearl didn't require any protection from Harrison in the slightest, and there was no mention of him being aggressive or hostile during this visit.

However, Pearl's witness testimony stated that as Harrison left, he turned to her and said, "I will get even with you, and make you pay dearly."

I'm confused and unclear as to whether this was something he said back at the Mornington visit or if it happened at the Seaford visit. It sounds more in tune with the atmosphere of the Mornington visit. The statement is something I believe needs to be known, as I do not wish to withhold anything I have uncovered while researching this story. I am as unbiased as I can be, and presenting everything is an indication that I, as the storyteller, want *all* to be known.

This scenario perplexes me. Like most aspects of this story, it doesn't fit the profile or the moment. I wasn't there, and I do not know what the facts are; I don't know if Pearl is telling the truth or lying. Once again, I will draw information from their behavior after the event, and at this particular moment—Pearl was still alive and in no way harmed.

On the face of it there was no cause provided by Harrison to have said this, and she had not informed anyone if she had provoked this retaliation of words.

Harrison was a very happy man right now—his dreams had just come true. I see no reason for his demeanor to shift when he was so fulfilled, unless his Jekyll and Hyde character reared its head, which it may well have done. It was a statement made in anger, not part of normal goodbyes. You don't say goodbye in a cheerful manner then threaten the next.

If he did make such an intolerable threat, then Pearl may well have thrown another barb Harrison's way, hence the threat. Or, did he actually say this at all? Pearl's statement, of course, was very one-sided; the other side of the story was not given. With the knowledge there are always two sides to any story, we must be mindful to not swallow only the one line being fed us. That principle that can be applied to every aspect of our lives. Thus, we will never know how, why, or even *if* Harrison threatened Pearl the way she claimed.

She did not mention in her statement that the children were happy to see their father, and that they hugged and kissed him as he held his arms out.

She didn't tell the court he hadn't caused her any harm and in no way was she fearful for herself. But they did talk for an hour, and what is represented in her statement falls very short of the full picture of this afternoon. It is another example of how Harrison was set up. Pearl gave him just about nothing, and it would have pained her to give him the truth.

This is a stance the Four Ks went on to uphold, that is still slightly around today. They know so very little of the actual events and rely heavily on their young, faded memories, but they are adamant about their conviction to stand by their mum. Even when you can see the guilt and loss is eating at them. They argue between themselves because they all carry anger and disappointment inside, some less than others, but anger all the same. I wonder if they know their past is always present, and if they will ever talk of this calmly.

Conversations were more than likely had that were not represented in Pearl's statement. Did he tell her that he missed his family? Did he tell her that he only had two months to live? Did he express that being left on the island unconscious to wake without his family caused him much pain? Did he tell her that he had tried to commit suicide forty-seven days earlier, and that was why his car was confiscated? Did he tell her how he found them in Eden Road? Did he tell her he was going to marry Jill Mead after Christmas, and she was going to nurse him until the cancer took him? That he was employed as the inspector of products at the electrical company Ring Grip? Did he tell her he had met his first son, Joshua, and travelled to Benalla to say goodbye? That he had taken his son out for the day to Shepparton, and that he just wanted to say goodbye to his daughters as he had his son? Did he tell her that he loved his girls? Did he tell her anything more than what she stated?

Like the anger-infused statement Pearl alleged he made in Mornington about 'getting even' with her (he never acted on that allegation), she stated that he told her again before he left, "I will make you pay dearly", at Seaford; more angry words with no real intent.

Was she at all fearful of her safety while Harrison was there with her alone? If this was the case, Pearl would have stated so at the inquisition, and referenced that Harrison was a very bad man. At that time, he had not intended to hurt her, or do so in the following days. He didn't blame Pearl. He blamed Phillip Harper. His anger and intent were directed at Phillip.

Did it occur to Pearl that she was protecting a man she'd known for less than two years over and above a man with whom she had spent ten years? Pearl clearly owned the reference to her "husband" in her statements when she talked of Phillip. She clearly loved him, wanted a life with him, and wanted to raise her daughters with him. She was safe in his company, but she had completely cut off someone who was not as easily terminated as she had hoped.

Granted, Harrison didn't help himself, but he equally may not have been helped by others.

Was Harrison really worth nothing to Pearl? After all that he had worked for during their time on the Tasmanian islands, he was the father of her four daughters, yet he was discarded as insignificant. Did she not think that just because she no longer wanted Harrison in her life, that Harrison didn't want his daughters in his life? What did she really think would happen when she fled the island? Did she really expect a man to forget about his children? Did she really think he did not love them? He may have displayed violent behavior, but his heart was with his children. Could she not admit that she and the children were not really in any danger from Harrison in the period of 1959 to 1960? Would she be able to admit that today, given all the evidence that has surfaced?

How would you feel if you were told you could never see your daughters again, and that another person was now their parent? Where would you go with that?

For now, he'd done it, Harrison had achieved what he wanted—he'd spent time with his daughters and was able to speak with his ex de facto wife and had some time to just be heard. His visit to Eden Road was a successful one, and as he left, everything was all okay.

The relief that came from seeing his girls again was significant. Imagine finding something you lost, the joy that embraced you as you picked it up from its hiding place. That's what Harrison was feeling, only magnified fiftyfold.

He drove home where he sat with April and Thomas and told them. He was as happy as April had ever seen him. Harrison was bursting at the seams, and according to April, he was just like his old self. She said it was like they had their Harrison back. It was a joy to see. The house was warm with spirit and nothing but vibrancy and happiness were leaping about the walls.

He told her how much the girls had grown, and who said what and how wonderful it all was. He then told April that he could see the children whenever he liked. According to Harrison, it was all sorted—nothing to change, nothing for anyone to fear.

Why Harrison stated that he could see his children whenever he liked is unknown. Had Pearl informed him that he could? Was he relaying what he had been told? Or, was Harrison assuming that because the children were his, he was entitled to see them? It seemed to him it was his legal right, although he had been told by the magistrate during his suicide hearing otherwise. He had no legal entitlements to his own children. None. He knew that.

Or was this a statement of defiance and frustration? A 'give me a break will you.' He wouldn't be bullied by Pearl any further. He'd had enough of being mustered by a woman who was controlling him to detrimental effects. He meant no harm; he had proven that a number of times.

Perhaps Pearl was annoyed that this man she wished to expel from her life just kept coming back. Remember, the first time he surfaced was because Pearl had written him. She was acting on her own needs at the time, newly-separated and grieving, wanting to inflict pain. But now she was less brittle yet still acting to fulfill her own needs. This time she just wanted him to go away. She didn't once consider that he had a right to see his daughters. She didn't care about that. To her, he was a bastard and always would be.

However, Harrison stated that he could see his children when he wanted. Thomas and April Hagen would have told you that he did not breach any boundaries after seeing them on Monday the 28th. He had no intention of doing so. Harrison did not harass them, return, or engage in stalking behavior. He left them be for the next three days even though he knew where they were. It wasn't until the solicitor's letter arrived that his fury became greater than himself. It was the solicitor's letter that signaled the end of his composure. Had this solicitor's letter not come, Harrison would have remained as happy as he had the last three days. He had boundaries, self-control, and until now, he had a plan: say goodbye and die.

From the minute this envelope was opened, it was the undoing of all his good intentions. What he did from here devastated everyone, including generations to come.

It is quite possible that Harrison's existence was about to come full circle. Just as he was introduced into this world, with an upbringing that was harsh, brutal, and full of rage and intense pain, he exited this world the same way, if only a more saddened man.

Phillip returned from work. He hadn't had much thought of his old mate, Harry, in the year that had passed. All he knew was Harrison didn't know where they were. Case closed for Phillip.

But Phillip didn't know about a chance passing with a stranger that had just given up their location.

That Monday, was it left to Pearl to be the harbinger? Did she wait in the kitchen for Phillip, then say, "Harry found us, he was here today."

How Phillip responded to this news is unknown. Did he ask a barrage of questions that demanded a response? Was he jealous? Incensed that this man just wouldn't go away? Harrison didn't tell Pearl about the removalist driver, and it was not known how he found them until I uncovered the information from reading April's letter. It was assumed that

Harrison found William and Agnes Harper's location and went to them, but this was not the case. I wonder if Phillip walked to his parents' place and demanded of his father if it was he who had told Harrison of their whereabouts.

Did the Four Ks overhear Phillip's response to Harrison's visit? One wonders whether Pearl was honest in her assessment of the visit; that it had been amicable and friendly enough given the circumstances.

We'll never know the truth of whether Pearl told Phillip that she and Harrison had agreed he could see the Four Ks when he liked, or if that was something Harrison decided for himself. Perhaps Pearl felt that letting Harrison see his daughters was the solution to their annoyances. She didn't know he was a dead man on a cancer watch. She couldn't suggest to Phillip that because of this, it wouldn't be long before it was all finished.

Imagine if that had played out. The chapter would have very well ended there, and all would have been well. But an entire new chapter was created, one filled only with sorrow, violence, and unanswered questions. Pearl introduced an entire new series of contempt that had way more than one powerful encore; it had sequel after drama and drama after sequel, which is played out even today. We don't escape what she and Phillip were about to do.

TWO SHOTS FIRED

Phillip's reaction was not a positive one. It was Lilly Harper who suggested that it was on Phillip's insistence that legal action be sought, and he was adamant about it. He was protecting his family, and that included the Four Ks. Phillip and Pearl were saying, "No, you can't have them; they are ours now. Go away and we hope this letter keeps you away."

How was this ever going to work?

Phillip just wanted his family to be his. He wanted none of Harrison's business, and neither did Pearl. They were done with the hiding from guns, knives, and beatings. They had left fear and angst well behind, and they wanted none of the past in their present. The stumps in the ground for their family home was where their future lay—the foundations of a new life.

Phillip and Pearl had grown since November 1959, and Phillip was well adjusted to life on the mainland. He had confidence and belief in his ability to provide for his new family, and he was doing the job no one thought he could. His brothers and sisters had all questioned him when he had turned up with Pearl, but he was proving them all wrong. Harrison was most definitely out of the picture Phillip had drawn for his family.

Lilly was right; Phillip told Pearl in detail that she had to go to the solicitor tomorrow and execute their legal rights.

Phillip wanted protection for him and his family, and they both knew he hadn't any standing legally. This would finally sort the situation out. Harrison would continue to come around, and there had been enough of that already. No more. Pearl was totally in agreement.

The Harper family slept with much on their minds that night, and Harrison snored with a grin on his face.

The following day began as every day does: the sun rose. It was Tuesday, November 29, 1960.

In the Harper house, they had their breakfast, got dressed, tied their shoelaces, grabbed their school books, and off to school the Four Ks went. Phillip headed to work, knowing that Pearl would follow his instructions to seek legal intervention.

Harrison awoke and smiled. The Four Ks were back in his life. He went to work a happy man.

Pearl had well-mothered the Four Ks in the last year, and after getting them ready, she arranged herself for an outing. She donned her finest clothes, did her hair and makeup as she knew how, and made her way into Frankston to seek counsel and advice from a solicitor's firm opposite the Frankston railway station. She was nervous yet resolved. This was what her husband wanted, and she would do it. The haste with which this was done tells me that both of them had not considered other options, or the repercussions of their actions. As the saying goes: for every action there is a reaction. Did they know what was coming? What exactly this reaction was going to be?

What they did know was that their days of running were over, and they now sought a means to protect themselves with an injunction against Harrison.

If Harrison went away, then they could be happy and forget the events on Tasman Island. Forget the wrongs they'd done and move on with their lives. The truth is, they didn't need protecting; they just didn't want Harrison around.

In Pearl's eyes, if Harrison went away he and his annoying behavior would not have to be endured by herself or Phillip.

We all know what it feels like to have a person in our lives that we don't want around, someone who is bothersome, especially when you have such happiness in your life. You don't want the baggage they bring with them. It's fair that Pearl and Phillip wanted to be left alone, but it was only fair to them. Pearl and Phillip were shortsighted in this, I believe.

If Harrison had really wanted to hurt Pearl and the girls, he would have. He'd had prior opportunity to inflict harm; first on the visit to Mornington around the start of November 1959—he not only sat with Pearl and talked with her, but also took the Four Ks out for the day. The second opportunity was the Eden Road visit on November 28, 1960. He could have hurt them on both these occasions if that was his intent. He had opportunity, motive, and capacity. Why didn't he? The answer is because he never intended to.

I doubt any of this was told to all of those involved with getting the injunction signed, sealed, and delivered. Sitting in the office, Pearl explained to the solicitor that she and her husband wanted protection from her ex de facto husband, Harrison. The solicitor acted within the law, and assured Mrs. Harper that she indeed could be protected and that the law was on her side. Pearl would have provided only the information she deemed necessary to the solicitor to get her desires met. Whatever she was saying as she sat across from the man behind the desk, he was listening and, with payment, was more than happy to write up the injunction stating the cause for protection and prevention as a means for granting Pearl's wish.

A letter was written in support of the Harpers and the matter was put before a court to be certified by law and then served to Harrison. Pearl was reassured, that the matter would be addressed immediately and resolved this week. She would have been advised to be sure to notify her husband on his return home and to rest with comfort that evening.

The solicitor did not lie; he drafted up his injunction and had it seen by a court of law. As it was written and was before him, the magistrate had no consideration other than to approve the request and grant it as law. He was not privy to any information supporting Harrison and his intentions; they did not factor into any of this. The big stamp was applied to the paperwork, and Harrison had just been rendered unable to see his daughters again.

I wonder if Pearl felt at ease as she made her way home. Did she truly feel so sure that she was doing the right thing even though it was only yesterday that she had watched a man feel whole again? What didn't she see when Harrison was hugging the Four Ks? Was there more reason for her guilt to grow as she stepped toward her home? Had she really done the right thing? And did she really think she was in danger?

Perhaps as she sat waiting for the Four Ks to come home, sitting in the kitchen staring at the wall or out the window with a beer and a cigarette, she contemplated what she had just done. She most certainly welcomed the end of the day as her daughters filled the home, even if it was with their usual bickering and messing about. Today she didn't mind at all. She was also very glad to not have unexpected company; and was most appreciative when Phillip and his utility rolled up behind the back door.

He entered and immediately queried Pearl about the day. "How did it go? What was said? What can be done? What has been done? Are we safe, and protected, and can we sleep well tonight? Will we be left alone?"

Pearl answered yes to all the questions.

The Four Ks knew nothing of any of this.

Wednesday, November 30, 1960, was a day of travelling for the paperwork that was about to change the lives of all in this triangle. The letter I wish had never arrived was en route to April and Thomas's Richmond address.

Harrison was blissfully working at his job at Ring Grip, still in the throes of happiness about his daughters, not even caring that he was dying. He was tired, true, and knew he had had enough of the pain, but he had achieved what he wanted, and was ready to let go. He hadn't a choice; the cancer had him.

The Four Ks presumably carried on as normal; off for another day of school, and like any other day, they walked past their grandparents' home and got to school on time.

They had all seen much by now, and seemed older than their years. Credit to them and their character must be given, as they spent many years on a lighthouse without social interaction, but they integrated well into a public school and had taken to a regular lifestyle. They were now your stock-standard school-goers, and they had a skip in their step and friends to sit with at play time.

Phillip took himself off to earn another day's living, and they all saw Wednesday as just another day.

On the other side of town, it was another happy night's sleep for Harrison and the Jameson Street home.

Thursday, December 1, 1960—the last Thursday some would see.

Phillip rose at daybreak, dressed, at breakfast and was off to work before most eyes in the house had recovered from their sleep.

This was the last time Phillip was to walk out his back door to work. The building site next door would remain forever unfinished.

With regular morning visits to the outhouse, the traffic from the back door to the toilet was constant—big feet, little feet, back and forth, hot weather, cold weather, and rain or shining sun. Even under moonlight and stars, this was a beaten path all could walk with their eyes closed. Pearl was usually the first out the door and then Phillip, followed by four impatient and possibly competing girls. The dog, Buster, perhaps remained asleep or watched the foot-traffic and its everyday occurrence. The Four Ks had their hair brushed, and with their school uniforms on, they raced up the driveway. Sadly, this was the last day these four innocent passengers skipped to school.

Pearl sat at her chair in the kitchen and thought of the tasks she had before her. She washed and cleaned the morning dishes, and I know she did washing that day and hung towels and sheets on the clothes line. They were flapping casually in the gentle breeze, and no rain took any of her hard work away. They would be dry by tomorrow, not that she was going to care for anything tomorrow.

Harrison took off to another day's work and thought nothing of the mail.

To be mentioned again, as it poignant in an untold story. He had not at any stage attempted to contact the Four Ks further. He had not threatened to kill or get even with anyone, and he had not acted inappropriately in the last three days.

This tells you everything. He had boundaries, and he had respect for the right thing to do. No stalking, no harassing, no 'I'm going to make you pay for this dearly' behavior—none. Because he wasn't a threat, there wasn't any need for protection. All would have continued to have life if someone had just stopped and thought clearly. But no one did, including Harrison.

If it was anyone who needed protecting, it was Harrison from Pearl and Phillip's psychological menacing. They were the ones who were relentless in their harm. Not once did they apologize to him, say sorry for all the deceit, pain and suffering they had caused.

When the Four Ks arrived home, they placed their school bags in their spots and raced around as usual. Pearl was sitting at the kitchen table waiting for Phillip, and after making the Four Ks some afternoon snacks, she was happy to hear his utility pull up. Phillip parked the car in the driveway and jumped out. He'd had a good day. The engine retired for the night, and it would stay that way for some time.

He entered the shack and gave Pearl a kiss on her cheek as he always did, and told her, "It will arrive today."

Pearl nodded; she knew what he was referring to. "It should make things clear then, shouldn't it?"

"Yes, it should." Phillip could see some apprehension in his wife and offered her reassurance. "It will be all right, dear, you'll see. There will be nothing of it. It will be fine."

They all sat at the table and consumed their last dinner together. Their happiness on this night would be a memory they would forever search for again.

With the last gulp polished off, they prepared for another night's rest. Friday night's regular after-dinner was a lollie bag each for the Four Ks, and two bottles of beer for Phillip and Pearl. The ritual they all loved—their Friday night dinner.

The Four Ks went to sleep in their bunks while Phillip and Pearl slept in the kitchen area.

"Good night, love," he said, cozy in his pajamas as he snuggled into the blanket.

"Good night, Phil," she said and snuggled into him.

All Harpers were sound asleep, and completely unaware of the turmoil that was ripping into a frenzy on the other side of town.

Harrison arrived home from work and sat down to read his mail. He rarely got mail, and had not seen mail like this before, but noted the Frankston address. He may have considered it a part of his suicide attempt or related to it, or he may have known it was from Pearl. Whatever it was, it was of a serious nature as it was all professional. With this he opened it with care.

Upon opening the letter, Harrison saw the letterhead insignia was evidence that the documentation was from a solicitor's office. As he read its contents, he stopped and stiffened, having to slowly read the words put to him in legalese. Fury began to rise within as he continued to read. A legal notice advising him to keep away from the children.

He'd had an injunction placed against him by a court of law, which stipulated he was not permitted to see his daughters again. He was not permitted on or near the premises of the Harper's family residence on Eden Road—now or ever. His was not permitted to speak to or contact any of the Harper family members ever again, and he was advised not to break or breach any of the said conditions. Should he consider himself above the law on this matter, breaching such would carry a sentence of incarceration. This was the wish of the Harper family, and it was supported by Victorian law.

Harrison, you have just been erased.

What a whack to the spirit, what a whack to endure for a father. What a stupid thing to do.

They had less control now than they ever had. They had just forced the hand of a father. He could not bear this whack to who he was, what he felt, and what he desired. He was a man, not a robot; he was made of blood and heart, not iron and steel. There was nothing anyone could do. Harrison's rage was about to ignite into an inferno that would only be extinguished when he was.

He was broken, and this letter was as good as a stab to his heart. It was a persecution he could not take. He was ultimately insulted, and his love was denied.

Harrison flew into a rage so intense that the young thirteen-year-old Gary Hagen, who was in the family home at the time, still remembers how vivid it was. Harrison had snapped, and his rage controlled his actions from there on.

In Thomas Hagen's statement, Thomas recalled that on November 28, 1960, the now deceased Bennet informed April that he had located his de facto wife and children.

Harrison told her he could see the children whenever he liked. On Thursday, December 1, 1960, Bennet showed his wife a letter he had received from a solicitor in Frankston asking him to keep away from the children. This letter appeared to have worried Harrison, and he seemed very depressed on Thursday night. They were watching television and the now deceased Bennet was sleeping in a chair. Thomas woke him up and told him to go to bed. Thomas went to bed. But Harrison left for a walk at about 2345 hours and came back in half an hour. Thomas heard him go out later but didn't know what time. He had never seen a rifle or a firearm in Harrison's room. It had been ten years since Thomas had seen Harrison's de facto wife. Thomas thought the whole trouble was because Pearl left Harrison.

This statement tells me that Thomas had met Pearl, and during this meeting, they would have had good relations, as after Harrison's death, Pearl offered for April and Thomas "to see the girls whenever they would like to," as described in April's letter to Margaret Barnes. This also supports the position that Harrison did have feelings, which is a face missing in reports of this story. He was depressingly sad when he read the letter. He would have felt hopeless. All he was trying to live for had been taken away. The final blow had knocked pain into his chest, and in his mind, he had given up.

That night while he had as much rage as he had sadness, he composed himself and had dinner with April and Thomas. He had shown April the letter and had voiced his concern about what it said. The two sat and read it together and April was upset by the letter as she didn't see it as necessary. She offered all the support she could to Harrison and suggested they all take to the lounge area and see what could be done the next day.

Harrison sat in the lounge room on a single chair, and as he was emotionally and physically exhausted, he fell asleep. He had quite possibly had a drink, but he was not over-intoxicated. Thomas and April knew it was best to let him rest. They also looked at each other and considered what a mess this all was. How terrible the situation was and how much despair she had for the brother she loved who hadn't hurt anyone to her knowledge. She hadn't seen the violence others had referred to, and she had raised him. They stayed in the lounge with him and sat quietly in case he awoke. When he didn't, they took themselves to bed, so Thomas woke Harrison from the chair, told him it was time to go to bed and that he and April would see what could be done tomorrow.

Harrison was calm as Thomas spoke to him,

Thomas and April and Gary retreated to bed. Harrison picked himself up from the chair and simply walked out the front door. He walked the streets, constructing his new plan. The one he had thought had been working had been derailed. It was quite possible that during this walk he decided he would kill Phillip as well as himself. He didn't quite know all the specifics of how it would play out, but a walk in the fresh air had afforded him the time and space to decide what he wanted to do.

He would hurt them back.

He wanted to kill Phillip. Then, as there would be nothing to live for, he would kill himself.

No more pain.

It is unknown where he got the .22 caliber rifle— no one had seen it prior to this event. And had he had it back in October, he may have used that instead of the exhaust pipe and running car method for his suicide attempt. I think it can be assumed that it was at this point, on that particular night, he purchased the rifle and bullets. There is a slight chance he may have had the rifle and bullets in the boot of his car prior to this, but I have no evidence that this was the case.

When Harrison returned from his first walk he put his plan into action. He knew exactly what he was doing; and did so with calm precision.

In his room he began a ritual, a ceremony, for his final act. He didn't need to speak to April or Thomas to ask them to stop him or talk him out of it. He didn't want anything to disturb his decision, and thus he took to his preparation with meticulous accord.

It was here that he comprehensively prepared himself for death. He washed his face and gave himself a neat, clean shave. He used the comb to brush and position his hair perfectly. After removing the clothes, he had been wearing all day, he dressed himself in his best suit. He took out his pressed and crisp, white shirt and did up the buttons in front of the mirror, watching himself. He tucked the shirt into his dark trousers and tightened his belt. The bow tie that matched his suit jacket was straightened so it was faultless. Then he donned his jacket. He placed the solicitor's letter in his suit pocket, and then did up the buttons. Harrison looked in the mirror one last time, straightened himself up, and he was ready. His shoes were polished, his socks fresh and on; he was done. All this grooming was done in silence. No tears, no talking, no harping on about anything, just methodical preparation.

He was as quiet as could be. So much so that in the small home, April and Thomas heard nothing except the opening and closing of the front door April and Thomas were not alarmed enough to get out of bed to see how he was.

At some stage, he must have thought to say goodbye to April and Thomas, to thank them for all their support and love. Did he stop to reflect how much he was about to hurt his sister?

He didn't stop to write a note to her saying, 'I am sorry, sister, thank you and I love you.' No, she didn't get that. She just inherited a massive mess to clean up.

He left Jameson Street, Richmond, for the last time. This was around 1a.m., as April told Margaret she heard him leave, but thought he was going for another wander. Possibly because he could not sleep with all that was on his mind, she said. The truth is that what she *thought* was on his mind was absolutely *not* what was on his mind.

In the dead of the night, Harrison drove to Seaford. He slowly moved along Eden Road, as he didn't want any of the residents to be alarmed at a car driving up at that time of the morning. Seaford was a quiet and small neighborhood, and he chose a space and parked the rented car to the side of Eden Road. This position wasn't far from the entrance.

He turned the engine off and sat. He waited close to five hours in his car. But come just after 6a.m., there was no turning back. Any form of second thought was quickly extinguished by the letter in his suit pocket that rested close to his heart.

Harrison didn't enter the house at 1a.m. as he could have done. He sat and waited. Stewed, perhaps. Did he wait for daylight, so he could see what he was doing? I wonder if any sorrow ever entered his thoughts as he waited. He knew he was going to kill himself. Did that sadden him? I wonder if his experiences during the war meant he wasn't fazed about shooting a man. Did it cross his mind at all that his life was worth more than this?

Surely, breathing was far more valuable than death. I guess not.

I know he was thinking because he had been methodical, and his intention was adamant and clear—adamant it was going to happen, and clear on the end result.

And what of the weapon of choice? Did he have the rifle sitting with him? Or, was it in the boot of his car in case a passerby noticed it? Then his plan would have been thwarted. Where exactly did he get the gun? Was it Cameron's? Was it owned by a friend? Did it belong to Jill Mead's dad? Or, did

Harrison purchase it through a gun dealer or the black market? And when exactly did he organize this? Before he received the solicitor's letter or on the night of Thursday, December 1, 1960? How accessible were firearms in 1960?

The night sky held on in silence; the new day was about to break, and when the light brightened to signal the day ahead, Hell came in. Through the back door to be exact.

It is unknown whether Harrison sat waiting in the car from the time he arrived at the Eden Road address, until just after 6a.m., or if he waited at the back door of the house the moment he arrived. More than likely he sat in the car and waited for daybreak. It was said that he waited at the side of the house amongst bushes, where he could hear movement in the house and know if people were up and about. The bushes hid him from prying eyes, and wouldn't have prevented from taking aim at the man he hated.

I would suggest he did both. Waited in the car for a period of time, and then when he saw the rise of daybreak, made his move to the side of the house, much like he would have in the trenches during World War II. He was well-trained at military-style advances, and it would suit him to wait by the side of the house, listening.

Whatever method he used when lying in wait, the following is known:

At around 0605 hours, with loaded rifle in hand, Harrison walked to the entrance of Eden Road, Seaford, and followed the driveway to the back door of the makeshift house at the end of the block. The following is an actual account from Pearl's inquisition statement:

'The next time I saw Bennet was about 0605 hours in Eden Road, Seaford, on the morning of December 2, 1960. I had just opened the back door and walked out when he appeared pointing a rifle at me. He said words to the effect "I am going to get Phil." I ran in and shouted out to my husband, but Bennet grabbed the door, pushed me aside and went into the bedroom. He looked crazy. By this time Phillip had got out of bed and was covering himself with some blankets. Bennet had the rifle pointed at Phillips head. Phillip said, "Don't be a fool, Harry." I was standing right near Bennet when he pulled the trigger of the rifle, and I saw Phillip fall to the floor. I ran out screaming and got a next-door neighbor who came in with me. He is a Mr. McVicker. I did not see Bennet, but when I went back into my house with McVicker, I heard another rifle shot ring out. Police later attended."

Along the side of the house, Harrison was listening and heard movement. He knew that the footsteps were heading toward the back door. It was the first thing the Harpers did, go to the toilet. He heard the steps and made his move. It was now.

Now was the time for death.

Harrison was coming.

He was easily exposed to the neighbors as he approached the house, but he wouldn't be around long enough for anyone to react. As quickly as he appeared, he would execute a man then himself. Rifle held at the ready, he strode with deliberation to the door. Finger on the trigger, Harrison believed the first person he'd see would be the one who would eat the bullet. Phillip Harper.

But it was not.

It was Pearl he met at the back door. If she had truly been his target, she'd have been shot there and then. He didn't give a stuff about listening to any more of her words; he didn't let her speak. He just pointed the gun in her face and told her he was there for Phil. It was an indirect order that said, 'Get out of my way, you stupid woman.'

Those words were enough for Pearl to know that she was not his target, nor were the girls. He even pushed past her to get to the man he blamed for his losses, and Pearl was standing next to him as the bullet entered Phillip's brain.

Pearl was never Harrison's target. He blamed Phillip. He did, however, according to Daniel Ogilvy, a Joyce relative, say to Pearl, "You will have to live with this for the rest of your life." Perhaps that was the punishment he dealt her—life without her husband.

Pearl did not tell the court in her statement that she pushed the barrel of the gun away from her as she was confronted by Harrison at the back door. In doing this, Pearl left her fingerprints on the metal of the gun, and this gave the police just cause to arrest her for murder in the following days. She was released without arrest, but it was a significant factor she kept out of her statement. Not the first or last omission on her behalf.

When Harrison pushed past her and walked into the kitchen, Pearl ran after him, screaming for Phillip to get up and get out, that Harrison had a gun. She was palpably hysterical.

All Phillip had as his defense were the blankets he'd slept in. He was a small man, and was holding the blankets up to screen himself from Harrison. The triangle was standing in the kitchen, and Pearl was by Harrison's side, the rifle fixed on Phillip's skull.

Phillip was pleading in the only way he knew how. "Don't be a fool, Harry."

That was his last sentence.

Bang!

The bullet made its way down the barrel, splintering through Phillip's skull and into his brain.

The barrel was pushed hard up against Phillip's head; the blanket offering no resistance to the bullet. The bullet lodged in Phillip's frontal lobe, and he slumped to the floor.

He was as good as gone.

But not completely yet.

You can't survive this, friend.

Pearl was in hell. *This can't be happening! This can't be happening!* She ran from the house, screaming in terror. Phillip had been killed. Shot.

She had lived by the principle that she would always wait for tomorrow, but all her tomorrows had been shattered. She was falling... What reason was there to see another day? The one meant to catch her had just fallen himself, and *nothing* would ever make him stand again.

I'm sorry you can't survive, Mr. Phillip Patrick Harper.

All the girls were still in bed. Kylie slept through the entire incident, but the others—still in their pajamas—had been blasted awake. First by Pearl's screaming then by the sound of gunfire.

The second shot would have confirmed chaos awaited. Something wasn't right. Kristen heard the first and second shot; Kendall watched the second shot. Kate and Kylie apparently heard nothing.

But they all saw Phillip on the kitchen floor in his last fighting moments.

Pearl left the girls as she ran from the house. Harrison was still inside. She did not think they were at risk; knew they weren't. Harrison had told her as much. He was there for Phil, no one else. She knew he loved his girls. But what standard of love for what he took from them was not their breath. No, he took something else, and sentenced them to a life of torment. Is that love, is it?

Circles and triangles of pain, selfishness and wrong.

Harrison, having seen Phillip's body fall, knew the job was done. He had said no other words except those used to tell Pearl of his intent.

Phillip didn't look down the barrel of the rifle; not looking at his killer. He did not try to run or fight him off but pleaded for his life. This does not sound like a man who was violent by nature. It has never been said that Phillip Harper was an aggressive man, because he wasn't. He was a family man, and had he fathered his own rather than taking another man's, he may not have taken a bullet to the brain. That doesn't make Harrison's actions at all right.

With Phillip lying motionless under the blankets, blood pulsating from the hole in his head, Harrison turned in silence and exited the kitchen area. He walked out the back door, leaving behind him a house filled with terror. I wonder if he saw his daughters. I wonder if he noticed that Kendall was watching him. She was the only daughter who saw the gun fired. She had just heard her dad shoot Phillip, who lay alone as Kendall continued to watch her dad.

She watched him walk out the door, stop, eject the spent cartridge, then reload his gun.

Harrison stood before Phillip's car, and prepared the gun for a second shot. Then with utter calm, chose a space toward the front of the property where he himself would die.

He sat himself down; legs outstretched, took a breath and arranged the rifle so the barrel was fixed to the center of his forehead. Without hesitation, he pulled the trigger.

Bang!

Just like Phillip's presenting execution act, the bullet whirled down the barrel, smashed through the skull, and lodged in the middle of Harrison's brain. Instant death, lights out. He fell back, and that was that.

Goodbye, Mr. Harrison Jake Bennet.

Harrison lay there for some time, alone, without anyone going to see his condition. They may have not known where he was, as it was only Kendall who held that information. But the gunshot would have been heard.

Lifeless, his body lay there until the ambulance arrived to take him to the Frankston Community Hospital, where he was pronounced dead. He died a lonely death.

How he fell is captured vividly within Kendall's memory. She says he walked to the long grass and it eventually ended.

She told of how his fall was slow; back to the earth, a fall from which he would never rise. She can still see it. "You know how it's quick in the movies when the bodies are shot and they fall down? Well, it's not. It's slow and everything happens in slow movements. I will never forget it."

The choice of rifle and the size of the bullet was a risk because the caliber was potentially not a surety for death. Harrison knew this as he was familiar with firearms. This was precisely why he put the barrel of the gun to the head of both Phillip and himself. For his plan to be successful, the gun had to be hard against the frontal lobe of the skull, so the bullet would enter the brain without the likelihood of failure. Front and center was the kill shot.

This reality was played out with what Kendall was about to face. Harrison's bullet was on target, but Phillip's bullet wasn't. Because a .22 is a small bullet, positioning is everything to affect a kill shot, and Phillip's bullet trajectory wasn't as accurate as Harrison's.

Phillip was still alive, but only barely.

Kendall returned to the kitchen area and walked to the wounded Phillip, who was with his last breaths.

She knelt beside him, put her hand on his chest, and she and Pearl covered him as best they could with the blanket. There was blood everywhere. Some had sprayed up along the wall, and there was now quite a thick pooling that had begun to spread into the laundry area. The smell was quite overpowering.

Phillip's hair was wet with blood, and his white sleeping top with the hand-sewn odd button on it was soaked crimson. His eyes were closed, his mouth open, and while he was not moving, he was still warm to the touch. He wasn't ready to die just yet. The other Ks were around, and everyone was excruciatingly upset.

Phillip lay about, moaning and groaning. Gurgling noises coming from his 'on borrowed time' throat while suction like hissing sounds were coming from the hole in his head. The police and ambulance arrived quite quickly, and he was taken by ambulance immediately. Phillip lived for a further forty-five minutes after he was shot. Kendall has stated, "was just as well, as had he lived he would have been a vegetable."

Next door was another young girl who was possibly as traumatized as Kendall. Because Kendall was not the only one to have watched the death of a man that day; an innocent, fifteen-year-old girl with no involvement with the Harper family or Harrison watched that incident play out.

She told the court what she had seen in 1960.

This young girl's name was Pricilla Brenda Griffin—a machinist at the time. She lived with her family at Eden Road, Seaford, and on this morning, she was at her kitchen window.

"Our place is next to where the deceased, Phillip Harper, and his family lived. Just after 0600 hours on December 2, 1960, I was in the kitchen of our place when our next-door neighbor, Mrs. Harper, ran in and said, 'He's shot Phil, ring the police.' My mother immediately ran out of the house to get in the car to drive to a telephone box, which is down the road from our place and I followed her out. As I got to the front of our house, I looked across toward the Harper's house, and I saw a man who I know now to be the deceased, Harrison Bennet. He was walking away from the Harper's house and he went about twenty yards when he stopped and started fiddling with a gun which he was carrying. He then walked on about another twenty yards among some bushes and long grass. I then saw him sit down and put the barrel up to his head. The next thing I heard was the noise of a gun going off and I saw him fall back in the grass. I had never seen this man before."

This is precisely what Kendall saw.

Policeman Constable Andrews stood with the dead Harrison and looked at the gun and its positioning. He left him there and went to the hospital with the barely-alive Phillip.

Interpreting the event, it goes without saying that Harrison's method of killing Phillip was his final stand over him.

It was very personal—an act of authority. Harrison was telling Phillip that he didn't have the final say; not in this. Harrison wanted to see Phillip die. I wonder, after shooting Phillip, did he feel a sense of relief and psychotic euphoria as he completed his mission? There was no turning back. Not now. But there was never going to be. Half the mission had been completed; one part of the love triangle was gone.

As he was walking to his own death, did Harrison feel at all satisfied that he'd had the last say? That he was now the one in control, that he was the man that they listened to. Did he feel like saying, "Who's laughing now?" as he stood over Phillip's wounded body? Was there anything that offered him satisfaction or righteousness? Or did he not feel at all, simply walking in robotic motion to complete the second part of his plan? He never faltered; he didn't stop to think or rethink or take a breath or even say a word to anyone. He was in a state of deliberate motion—to reload the rifle and find a place for the second shot to ring out.

Harrison was done. *Goodbye*, and *I've had enough*, were probably his last thoughts.

Then he pulled the trigger.

When the cold metal of the barrel is pressed tight against your forehead, your finger resting on the trigger… that is full on. Despite your psychological intent your physiological state is showing signs of fear, yet you still pull the trigger on your own murder weapon.

Bang!

You're dead.

Your hands still clutch the very thing that just sent you reeling backward. You have no need for that any more, yet it lays next to you—part of the cast of that brought you to your final curtain call

Sadly, for those left breathing, their shows must go on. And you, well you get put in a hole. And as the dirt is covering you, so are your truths. How is it that you felt the right to take another man's life and then your own?

Your voice is buried as deep in the ground as you are. Your voice is less heard now than it would have been had you'd just let the cancer take you. Now, no one even so much as mentions you. Your grandchildren do not know who you are; they don't even know you exist outside being called the 'bad man.' You didn't just kill the triangle; you killed your memory, too.

I now know you are not called Mr. Bad Man. Then I find out a eucalyptus tree has grown to represent your headstone, because no one cared enough to purchase a headstone for you. So, on top of a brother you are. He, who was as disappointing in life as you were. You both are left there—silent and nearly forgotten all together.

Harrison Jake Bennet, in 1960 you were silenced, and forever you are not worthy. And know this: the generations that followed will be told you were an atrocious man, and that is all.

So, to you we say: who's laughing now? No one. None of us.

Just like that Harrison was no more. But even in death, he hurt many. The aftermath delivered more pain and hostilities, and it was now time to clean up the remains of his destruction and see if anyone could rebuild their lives.

It was a murder-suicide that would blaze for many decades. What Harrison considered an act of honor and courage; to others it was selfish and gutless.

Thanks for nothing.

LIFE AFTER DEATH

By the time Pearl returned to the bloodshed, Kendall was kneeling with Phillip. Kristen and Kate were out of bed, aware of what was happening. I am not sure if Kylie was awake.

The neighbor, Mr. McVicker, was with Pearl, but there was not a lot anyone could do. Kendall was one who did what could be done. She sat with Phillip and held his head. She was ten years of age.

The police arrived and took control of the scene.

About to arrive soon was the very strong-willed Beatrice, Phillip's sister. Shortly after that, she would be supported by brothers Morris and Tony.

Pearl was in the room, but she was incapacitated. She was hurting, reeling in torture. The man she loved was dying before her, his blood splattered for all to see. She was spared a .22 bullet to the skull, but she had been shot with an emotional bullet. Make no mistake; she too took a hit that day. She wasn't bleeding, but she was hemorrhaging inside.

Phillip was still moaning, and ever so slightly twitching. For each heartbeat, blood pumped from the hole in his head. His breathing was shallow, the hole in his head making its own ungodly sound.

"Have you ever heard the sound that wheezing makes through a hole in the head?" Kendall asked me.

"No, I haven't, nor would I want to."

She was staring out, as if she was with Phillip still and said, "Good. Because I'm telling you, you don't bloody well want to. It's not nice."

I sat there with Kendall as she told me her understanding of it; I could see how much it still haunted her.

She continued, "Well, it makes a weird sound and it's like a sucking or like air is coming out of a tire and then when he breathed out, all this mess splattered out. It was absolutely horrible, just horrible."

She sat with Phillip while the ambulance and police were in transit. Frankly it was well long enough, the time she spent with him. How does a child hold the head of a man who is bleeding out? How did she do this? What a spirit.

They all waited, and as the time passed in minutes, it felt like weeks. The experience lives inside them today, it has lasted decades.

When the police arrived, it was Constable Anderson who entered the shack first and saw Phillip, and noticed he had signs of life. Anderson then walked outside where he met Harrison for the first time.

The constable noted the rifle and the spent cartridge but saw no sign of life. As he was searching the body and surrounding area, gathering evidence and information, he heard the ambulance. As it pulled up the driveway, he left Harrison and went to oversee Phillip's removal.

Kendall was still kneeling beside the injured Phillip. Without warning, she was scooped up from behind by another police officer and taken outside. That person then hosed her down, and she watched the blood roll down her legs, rippling over her knees and fading as the water diluted it and took it away. The officer wiped both her legs then got her to lift her feet up. Then he asked her to put her hands out and he wiped away what she should never have had on her innocent hands—a man's blood. The officer then decided the girls should no longer be at the scene, and it was agreed they would be sent to school.

Kendall took a moment to walk over and see her dad for herself. She stared at him without a word.

She told me that while she was sitting beside Phillip, other police officers had arrived, and she could hear the men arguing over whose jurisdiction it was. The Frankston police and the Chelsea police were both in a suburb they considered being their turf, but eventually the Frankston police took control.

I asked her who else was sitting with her, and she said no one. I then asked her who told her to sit with Phillip, and again she said, "No one, I just did it."

"That's my point," I said. "What kind of ten year old sits with a bloodied and dying man she calls Dad?" Before she could answer the rhetorical question, I said, "An amazing one, that's who."

We agreed in silence.

The trolley loaded Phillip up and into the ambulance; he leaves with sirens wailing.

Constable Anderson followed Phillip's faintly-beating heart.

At the hospital, with all the resources of modern medicine available at the time, the doctors were looking to save him. But there was only a narrow margin of success. They did not operate on Phillip; they knew he couldn't be saved. Perhaps all they could do was be with him until he lost his battle against death.

In the crime-scene photos taken of Phillip at the morgue, he was still fully clothed, and there was no sign of any medical intervention. The photos show him still wearing his pajama top. It hadn't been removed or cut off his body to access his chest for cardiac massage, and there were no medical tapes or visible incisions or tubes. They may have given him some painkillers, but this was not stated in the autopsy report.

Upon the pronouncement of death, Constable Anderson returned to the Eden Road scene by 0700 hours, and oversaw the taking of photos while he continued with his evidence gathering.

Harrison was delivered to the morgue by a second ambulance, where he was officially pronounced dead.

The two men were at the same place again, only this time in death.

It was a full day for the men as they waited to have their photos taken. The police photographer was dutifully organized, and the flash bulb lit up the room as the camera clicked into action. The last images of both men are the head shots. There's some irony in that.

It was over for Phillip and Harrison, but it was just beginning for the rest of us.

The policeman faced the daunting task of messenger—searching for the contact details for the next of kin of both men. They located Harrison's younger brother, and were soon on the phone to Cameron explaining the recent events. He was asked to come to Frankston morgue and identify Harrison.

Cameron agreed. He took a minute to recover from the shock of the information that had just been delivered. He was at his Balcombe Road service station, and he had a business to run, but this was a serious family matter. He told his wife Shirley what had happened, and asked her to take care of the customers. He then called his sister April and told her the terrible news. He then made his way to the hospital.

As he was driving to the hospital, he reflected that he hadn't had much to do with Harrison. They had served in the war together, and their older brother's death had upset them both. But after their return from the Middle East—

where all three had fought together—they separated and searched for their own life and love.

    Cam met the beautiful Shirley and they soon married and created a family. Harrison met Pearl and they took off to Tasmania. The two brothers didn't communicate until Harrison returned to Melbourne in 1960. The only reason Cam's family knew of anything to do with Harrison was because they saw an article in an Australian magazine—either the *Woman's Weekly* or *Women's Day*—documenting the story of a family living at the southernmost tip of Australia.

    I was told of this article by Cam's daughter, who remembered it vividly and said they couldn't believe it. They had known nothing about him and there he was in a photo in a magazine in the middle of nowhere. I have not been successful in locating this article, but I believe she was telling the truth, as her expression was genuine, and I was engaged in her memory when she recalled how amazing it was for them to find out where Harrison was.

    Cam had his own demons he was fighting, and he was losing the battle with alcohol. Just like Harrison, he was searching to save himself and establish a family to be loved by. He didn't have time for Harrison for the same reasons Harrison only had time for his immediate family. Both men were doing what nearly every person in life does: find a tribe to belong to. He knew April and Thomas would assist where they could, but he was closest to the hospital and the police officer was waiting.

    The policeman made the next call. It was to Phillip's older brother, Jarrod. This family was to endure great loss. Just as the policeman had had to do with Cameron, he explained the events to Jarrod and extended his sympathy, but could Jarrod please come and identify his brother.

    Jarrod was in Mt. Martha and agreed to leave, but before he did, he made a call to his mother and father. They already knew. They only lived around the corner and with all the ambulance and police sirens; they were alerted to the scene and its carnage. The police may have also walked up to William and Agnes's home once it was established that their son was the one lying in the kitchen.

Somehow the Harper's were alerted as Morris, Tony, and Beatrice were at the scene. Lilly, Agnes, and William didn't make their way down to the shack. They didn't want to.

Jarrod made his way to the hospital. He was close to his younger brother.

Now two men walked the same hospital corridors to identify their dead brothers, but each lived different nightmares. Each reacted according to their own connections with the deceased.

In discussions since Harrison had attempted suicide, April, Thomas, and Cam had become aware of Phillip. Since Harrison's arrival in Melbourne, Jarrod and his family had become aware of him.

They were quiet and reserved in their manner, and as they walked to their duty, they quite possibly crossed paths. Did they know of each other as they passed in the corridor? I suspect not. But did each man look for a member of the other family? They knew there were two men in the morgue, not one. Perhaps the police managed it so their paths would not cross.

It is chilling to think that Jarrod and Cameron passed each other at the morgue.

Each man saw his brother and said, "Yes, that's him."

With that, the white sheet was returned over the face, and the men were escorted out of the room. As the door closed behind them, another man pushed the steel panel the body was lying on and returned the dead into the stainless-steel tomb and shut the small door. That was it for Harrison and Phillip.

Phillip's family waited for Jarrod at the Wells Street home with Lilly and Lindy sitting with William and Agnes waiting for any news. We know Beatrice Harper had already made her way to her rented shack and was in the thick of it, making her presence felt.

Back at the bloodshed, Pearl was none the wiser about what to do next. She wasn't aware that Kendall had gone over and seen Harrison. She wasn't aware that the bodies weren't even cold yet and the finger of blame and distain was being pointed right at her head, much like the rifle was at Phillip's and Harrison's. Life carried on, but did living?

Somehow in the chaos the children were cared for by a family friend, perhaps the next-door neighbor. After Kendall was dry from her hosing down, all the Ks were dressed and removed from the scene. They were taken to a family friend's home for breakfast and sat huddled together, scared and confused.

On the instructions of what an officer had stated earlier the Four Ks were to get ready for school. Given no one was really thinking clearly under the circumstances, it was agreed. They were given their bags and a neighbor walked them to school. Along the way, they were in complete shock. Not much speaking was going on, just silence. They were beautiful-natured girls who all walked without so much as a tantrum or any indiscretion. They took to their classrooms and sat in the chair they had sat in yesterday. But yesterday didn't feel like today. Yesterday they were happy.

Today, that happiness was taken from them, and it didn't return for some of them. Ever. After about an hour, Kendall was still staring at an indoor plant. She hadn't stopped staring at it since she was placed in the chair. Eventually the shock hit, and she began vomiting everywhere. The teacher ran to help her, but she couldn't be helped. She vomited and vomited and vomited for over an hour until she was doing nothing but dry retching.

They stayed at school.

How so, I cannot fathom.

Back at the shack, both bodies were gone; the crime scene photos had been taken. The policemen had scribbled notes, sketches, and statements, collected evidence, removed spent cartridges and the rifle, managed the onlookers who were able to watch just about everything as there were no fences to conceal.

Pearl was asked questions and she answered them as best she could, considering the frailty she was in. She was just managing to breathe through it. As much as people despised and blamed her, she was the one who hurt the most. She was devastated, and no one stopped to hold her. Her cycle of concealment continued; she wasn't seen or looked at by anyone.

Beatrice Harper wanted only to look out for her own self-interests—which she was entitled to do—but her timing and manner were questionable. She was persistent with instructions to clean up and remove the violence smearing her property. She requested that she and her brothers be allowed to clean up the mess. And so it was, once the police had what they needed, the Harpers got to work.

Buckets, hot water, and sponges were vigorously employed. The blood was washed away, and everything removed from the kitchen. Now, nothing remained from the incident of three hours ago. It was spotless. The physical manifestation of the carnage had been erased, but the loss would always linger.

Pearl organized for Kristen and Kate to be sent over to Tasmania the next day. Once the girls returned from school, their bags were packed. Kendall was to stay at home because the police wanted to speak with her. Kylie was too young to leave her mum.

Kristen and Kate flew out, and they stayed away for no less than five days but no more than two weeks. In Tasmania, the two young family members were cared for by their nana and pop Joyce. It was done as you would expect: diligently. They were protected from the aftermath in the short term.

As Pearl returned to the shack to collect fresh clothes for herself and her daughters, she passed her husband's utility. It was still parked where he'd left it two nights before. It would only be moved when sold to help pay off some debts, and for his own funeral and headstone. Even in death, Phillip paid for himself.

The Harpers were busy organizing the funeral, and where Pearl was involved she tried to be busy, too. She had rights over Phillip and his property, but those rights were not respected by the Harper family. There were a few members who appreciated her, but that didn't protect her from the others doing whatever they liked.

The Harpers were many to the one Pearl, and thus she was disadvantaged. The fact that she was reeling in loss didn't help. She had to continue to be a mother to her traumatized daughters. The funeral details were swiftly organized on the day of his death, which was a Friday. The newspapers gave notice of these details in the Saturday edition.

The funeral notice conveyed that the late Phillip Patrick Harper would leave St. Francis Xavier Church, Frankston, on Monday after prayers, which would commence at 1530 hours at the Frankston Cemetery.

Meanwhile, Beatrice and her troupes, and perhaps the Salvation Army, were going for it. They had removed most of Phillip's belongings. His carpentry tools disappeared, as did other items, and they could do this because Pearl was gone for five days. Once they had sifted through the belongings and taken what was wanted by them, they painted the kitchen and other areas to completely remove the bloodstains. A lot was achieved in a weekend, and by Monday morning people were waking to prepare for a sending-off ceremony. All the Harpers congregated at

William and Agnes's home. Pearl was still at a friend's house, and she left Kylie with that friend while Kendall attended school. It is sad to think Kendall was left to her own devices at a time when she needed all the support she could get. She was alone.

I understand why Pearl sent Kristen and Kate away, but what it did was leave no one for Kendall to talk to. Kylie was not old enough to understand what was happening, let alone talk about it. No, Kendall only had the police to talk with, and over the weekend they had asked her over one hundred questions. Or as she put it, played "happy chats with Mr. Policemen." She wasn't in strife, she was a key witness to the situation and they wanted to know what she knew. She told them everything she could.

On Monday, she was sent to school all by herself. I wonder how she was received that day, as over the weekend the rumor mill had well and truly circulated, and the events were warped by various reports in the papers. Most of them at the time stated that a crazed, jealous man murdered his de facto wife's lover. So I wonder if on this day she was taunted by other children about how she was the daughter of a crazy murderer. Because in time, they did get told this and more. Kendall was quiet, withdrawn, and polite. She was naturally shy and insulated, but she could be friendly and social, and soon she learnt that she also had a spirit stronger than anyone around her.

On the day of his burial, Phillip was still lying at the city mortuary in Melbourne. That morning, he was not ready to be put in the ground, but the employees at the morgue had been notified that a body was required for a date with dirt, and they moved swiftly to organize his release.

He was actually being cut up and peered into as his postmortem was carried out December 5, 1960, and as the report tells us, Phillip had his head opened and brain cut to recover the .22 caliber bullet from his right occipital bone. We are told that Phillip's brain was moderately hemorrhagic.

The rest of Phillip was opened, his ribs partially removed to allow access to his organs. His heart, lungs, liver, and other vital organs were snipped from their connecting tissue and examined, weighed—all were within normal limits. They were returned to the body, but not sewn into place. The incision from clavicle to pelvis was stitched up, then his entire body examined for signs of struggle and bruising. There was none. He was ready to be 'tagged and bagged', as they say. He was cocooned in plastic and transported to a funeral parlor for a grieving family and widow to say their final goodbye.

The funeral service was deliberately late in the day to ensure Phillip's body was at his own farewell. The funeral parlor administrators had been waiting at the city morgue to take possession of his body once he was legally released by the governing department. When this was done, the funeral parlor employees organized the body and the coffin. Phillip was now in place for the service to begin. A man can't be late for his own burial.

This was no simple effort, as he needed to be placed in suitable clothes and made presentable for death, which included all the tactics funeral administrators are apt at doing, should a viewing be requested by the family. They also transported the body from Melbourne to Frankston.

At the church, the entire Harper family stood together and was offered the respect the distraught family deserved. Their son and brother had just been taken by the actions of another, and his loss was sudden and unnecessary. This was a situation no one had anticipated, and the shock was still with them. In fact, they'd only had the weekend to adjust, and that's not enough time to process what's happened, let alone grieve. All was happening at such a fast pace—everything appeared instant. Instant death. Instant burial. What was next?

The church filled with the heaviness the occasion brings. They were gathering together to show their support for a murdered man. Not a death by natural causes or accident. This added more weight to the grieving pain and anger.

The church walls bore much weight. No one in the room could have commenced processing how they felt yet. I suspect they were all on automatic pilot. Sorrow, pain, and rage for their loss was a natural composition of their disposition.

It was said Agnes Harper handled the situation very well. It seemed to Lilly she had to, to keep the family together. "She was aching all right, but she had a son to honor and therefore she stood up," Lilly told me. Her husband, three other sons, and three daughters were by her side, as were their spouses and friends. The Harpers saw that they were well-supported and represented. Rightly so.

Pearl was there, and she was being consoled and supported for her loss by friends and some of the Harpers. Her sorrow was one of the heaviest in the room. Everyone who knew Phillip had lost something. But there was no one else in the room that had lost a man who held them at night. Who said, "I love you" and meant it, as Phillip had done when he spoke to his wife. What they had gone through to be together was something only they understood, and now Pearl only had herself to share that with. Her loss was not the sort you ever recover from; she was gone from that day forward.

With the Catholic service telling the gathering how much of a family man Phillip was to his wife and stepdaughters, and how much his biological family loved him and the tragic nature of his death, and that he was with the Lord now, he was taken to the local cemetery where he was placed to rest. A hole had been dug for his coffin and was waiting for his arrival. He was covered with soil and the loved ones said their goodbyes through tears and heartache.

It took the action of one second to hurt many people. The psychological states of three families were drawn and would hurt forever. Phillip was buried; his existence was covered in earth and sealed in its place.

The sadness of the occasion lingered about the cemetery for some time, and it followed Pearl and the Harpers when they returned for the wake, and continued long after the guests left. Time kept moving forward at its regular pace, though; and life for those who still breathed went in different directions.

That evening Pearl spoke with the Harper family and they stated that she was to arrange to pay for the funeral of her husband—the onus fell on her. She was not in a position to pay for this; Phillip was still owed money by many clients who had yet to pay their construction accounts. They had no savings. It was decided that she would have to sell Phillip's belongings to pay for his funeral. She also needed to pay their debts and organize the settlement of the block of land they owned.

The only thing she didn't know yet was that all that was left of any worth was his car—his utility. Pearl had to think fast while under pressure. She had financial obligations and responsibilities, and she had a life to continue. She also had to do everything on her own now, and she was the sole provider with four mouths to feed.

Selling the car was done quickly, and from this sale she paid out the costs of the funeral and the small debts they had. She also purchased a suitable and elaborate gravesite tribute—a well-inscripted headstone, that was accompanied by a slab grave marker with engraved columns that covered it entirely. Atop this grave cover was a cross, representing his religion. The surface of his grave was filled with small white pebbles, and at the base was a stainless-steel flower grate. For its time, this was a monument of significance. Pearl had the final say for Phillips gravesite, and the woman who loved this man didn't hold back. His head stone reads:

In Loving Memory of
Phillip Patrick Harper
Died 2-12-1960 aged 31 years
Loved husband of PEARL
R.I.P

Pearl's name is in capital letters, and this gravesite and what is written on the headstone is a tribute to him and their love.
All done.

People returned as much as possible to the lives they had before their world had been shattered.

I would assume the emotions that were present at the funeral service and burial were still living on in many. Of course they were; it had only been four days from beating heart to down in the earth. Pearl was sickened by her loss and she was also wracked with a guilt she would not let anyone see. She knew she had played a role in Phillip's death, and although she would crucify Harrison every way she could, she would never admit her part. That went in the ground with Phillip.

But that didn't save her. Her own demons circled her mind, chanting her guilt at her. She was no innocent in this scenario, and she knew it. Guilt was veiled behind her pain, but it was visible in the lines on her face, her drawn-down mouth.

She was also furious that the one good thing she had to hold onto had been taken from her, and not by her choice. Why did life take her love? Why take the reason she smiled? Why was the man, who would have been a great father to her daughters, so brutally taken? Why take away the giver of a clear vision of a safe and happy future? Why, damn you, why? This was her rage.

The Harper family both secretly and openly loathed Pearl; they blamed her. He wouldn't be dead if she hadn't had the baggage. She brought the vile man who killed Phillip, into their lives. He was an associate of hers, even though it was Phillip and Harrison that worked closely together on the lights. They never understood why Phillip took on Pearl and four daughters that weren't his to begin with, and now he was dead because of this. They could only place their anger and disgust with her. She was alive. Phillip was not. If Harrison had still been alive, the anger would have been directed at him, but Pearl would not have escaped their wrath.

Yes, they despised Harrison Bennet and would refer to him as "that man" from here on out, which is understandable. He had taken what wasn't his to take. But there were a number of sides to the story, and "that man" had a family, and that family was in pain, too. They were also putting a brother they loved to rest; one they said had a very different story than what Pearl or the papers would tell you.

On the same day Phillip was subject to his postmortem and burial, so was Harrison.

For men who tore each other apart, they spent a lot of time together after death. Harrison, too, was lying with Phillip at the city mortuary in Melbourne and was cut open for examination.

On Monday, December 5, 1960, a senior government pathologist and legally-qualified medical practitioner worked over the forty-two-year-old Harrison. They found that Harrison was well-built, with a bullet hole in the center of his forehead, just above the roof of his nose—exactly the way Harrison planned it. The bullet had shattered his skull and ripped through his brain, ending up just below the surface of the upper part of the back of his head.

The same as Phillip, Harrison had all his organs cut away from his body, weighed and examined, then returned to their positions. Harrison's heart had signs of fatty deposits, and parts of his arteries—including his aorta—had degenerated.

His lungs had an accumulation of blood in them, and there was no fluid in his stomach, just a fair quantity of well-digested food. No alcohol was mentioned, nor was his cancer.

He was looked over, turned this way and that, and given the all-clear to be stitched back up from sternum to pelvis. I am not sure if he was redressed in the clothes he arrived in, or whether he remained naked when put in a bag, zipped up and ready for collection. No one would be viewing this corpse. For Harrison's death, the measures and care were least of all. He was possibly collected that day, as was Phillip, only Harrison travelled in unmarked transport and was driven straight to the hole that was waiting for him. No church, no sacred meeting place, just a hole with a man and his shovel.

Possibly over the weekend or even on the Monday, April, Thomas, and Cameron gathered at the Richmond home to discuss and organize Harrison's burial. They also had to organize to pay for it. The least onerous option would be done with their brother Jason, who was long cold in the ground. No one really wanted to use their own money to pay for a funeral or burial, and Harrison had no money of his own. He was broke, and had left nothing of value his family could use. I assume it was unanimous that no funeral was needed; just a burial, and the grave available to them at the least expense.

The cemetery authorities were asked to open the burial site of Jason Bennet. The plan was to place Harrison on top of his brother. It is known that Jason's grave was in the same cemetery as Harrison and Jason's mother and father—Frances and Jake—and their resting sites were not a stone's throw away from each other. The difference was that Frances and Jake had a headstone and grave cover; Jason's site was bare soil. No headstone, no marking, not so much as a twig stuck in the ground. Just flat earth.

With such stigma involved since Harrison was a murderer, he was not afforded a send-off. In fact, what he was given was quick and without fanfare. This way everything Harrison brought with him was buried.

The opening of Jason's grave was approved, and with that, a man and his shovel dug out the hole until he reached the vicinity of Jason's decayed skeleton in its wooden tomb and put Harrison on top. All was done, and it was just a matter of refilling the hole; no emotion or sequence of grace or Lord's Prayer. Not even a farewell.

I am unclear on whether Harrison was in a coffin or just wrapped in cloth and put in the hole. He was simply covered with the dirt that had been twice moved now. Was it stomped on to compress it? Some might suggest it be good thing if it was.

April and Cameron walked away from the torment of all things Harrison. The bad penny was gone. An unmarked grave was only considered a grave because it was situated in a cemetery.

Was it all this simple and comprehensible? I am not so accepting of that. A man died at his own hands, and he took another man with him. He was every bit a murderer. Nothing can take away his demonic action, but this action, whilst it was his most heinous, did not define him entirely. But there are no voices of an alternate opinion right now, and his silence was his sentence—he was demonized for decades.

Until now, no one has clearly said there is more to this person than that day.

There is insight into this from the truth of two individuals.

After his death, April fell seriously ill and took three months to recover from her heartache. Her sorrow took the form of psychological debilitation, but it was her physical body that held her captive, bedridden. Cameron was not greatly affected, and moved on without much care or burden.

Kendall's words explained how Pearl and his daughters must have felt.

After she took a deep breath, she said to me with a deep heaviness, "Do you know what it's like to have to live under constant fear, to be in fear all the time?"

She meant it, and I was shocked to hear this was how she lived—in constant fear. Kendall had the utmost clarity of how bad Harrison was. She said his "violence was crueler than cruel." His taking of Phillip's life was the ultimate cruelty, and to them he was pure evil.

In adulthood The Four Ks had much anger and disdain for Harrison as they talked of him. They did not call him 'Dad.' If they referred to him at all, it was as Bennet. They only referred to him very briefly, and with little detail or expression. He was removed, made a stranger—but then again, a stranger rarely has the power and effect over you that Harrison did over the years his daughters lived. The anger was visible, and you could see that they had trouble speaking of him. There were a lot of trapped and unexpressed feelings throughout the years. To me, it is more evident now than it has ever been.

Not at any stage have the Four Ks been able to acknowledge how they were hurt, too. This wasn't their choice. Pearl made the decisions for them. She created much of their continued pain, but they would never lay down the swords with which they protected their mother.

I have considered that they may not remember many of the incidents from 1960 and before. I have also questioned what they did legitimately remember. Is part of what they were told done so with vested interests? Yes, absolutely. I have been able to tell Kendall truths about the story she did not know. Hidden truths that would never have surfaced had I not gone searching. The other aspect to consider is which part of their childhood memories have restored true, and which have been warped by false memory syndrome. You can be assured numerous memories were naturally forgotten.

One aspect that is real and true yet not accepted by the Four Ks is that part of their sadness as they kept Harrison at a distance was that they lost a father and lived without a true male loving figure. Perhaps some of their bitterness and sadness was based on this, as was their anger and guilt. To them, it seemed he did all the wrongdoing and at no stage was he worthy of any love or worth in their lives. Not then.

But that's not completely true. Fair enough it may be, but it is not fairly delivered.

I am in a difficult position here. As I listened to the words my dear Aunt Kendall spoke, I heard her voice and believed what she told me. Yet I also heard and listened to members of Pearl's family, and they said not one negative word about Harrison, nor did the members of the lighthouse community. I encountered many different depictions of one man. I also identified several honorable behaviors of his, and his profile was not as clear as Kendall described. I believe he was a man of both menace and charm.

I drew my own conclusions and reminded myself of the times I spent with a school friend throughout our secondary education. She and I were great friends and our times together spanned years. These years were spread through weekends, school hours, evenings and, most memorably, holiday breaks. Her father was a man to stay away from. He was a habitual drinker and had a menacing composure. He was a hard worker of sorts, yet the family lived on little.

He and his second wife brought together children of their own; all now under the one roof. My friend was a smart girl, and she and her sister shared a room. A lot was happening in this house. Like the patriarch of the home, the stepmatriarch was never too far from a glass of casket wine. The man could laugh and make you laugh; he could be friendly and yet quiet. I watched him yell and explode when he disciplined the house.

My clearest memory is of when we were many miles away from home camping in a caravan park. For some reason, he exploded with uncontrollable rage. My friend was in the small two-man tent we shared for our holiday. The man took to this tent as if it was a paper bag and thrashed at it while my friend was inside. She was crying and screaming while he beat her about. I remember watching in horror because I loved my friend, and I knew what was happening was wrong. He stopped stomping and tearing the tent apart and my friend was able to find the zip exit and got out. She then ran to the toilet block, where I joined her. I'll never forget crying with her in the public toilet block. We were angry too; we were strong teenagers.

We hated his guts. "The sick prick," we called him. But he scared us. By the time we returned, he'd realized he was out of control and disappeared for several days. He took off with the only car we all had, leaving us stranded. But we were glad he was gone.

After the days had passed and our holiday had come to an end, he returned. The most noticeable thing, other than his unremorseful pathetic head, was that the front windscreen on the car was broken. He'd smashed it up and didn't care to have it fixed. We all travelled back to the city in a car without a windscreen. We all pretended we were okay, but none of us were.

He continued to be a violent man with an explosive temper. He eventually killed himself by his own reckless actions of suicidal intent. At his funeral, a lot of people congregated in support of him as we heard how outstanding a man he was. But this was not the case, and it was the first funeral experience where I realized a lot of garbage is said of a person at their death ceremony. Would anyone have believed the truth? I know for a fact there were people in that room who didn't like him. He wasn't such a good man, yet he wasn't such a bad man either.

He had many similarities to Harrison, and yet I will tell you straight I didn't like this man and it felt safer when he wasn't around. Yet when he was around, you pretended that being in his company was okay, and you could clearly see that he didn't have a clue how much he was feared or loathed. He possibly wouldn't have cared anyway. I can still see him, hear him, and hate him. But that entire aside, the point is this: it is the experience the person gives to you and your life that matters. It does not matter what others say of him or her. They have imprinted on you, and you view them through your lens.

Harrison inflicted blow after blow to Kendall and her family, and even if he had another side, ultimately, he hurt them. To them, he will forever—appropriately—wear the bastard tag.

Do not ever dismiss an individual's experience of another. Don't cover it up, put icing on a cake that's burnt, or use any dismissive tactics to remove the voice of a survivor.

I question whether I would be able to rest at ease with him in my life. Would I trust him around me and my children? I am not convinced I would, and I couldn't say to you honestly that I would welcome Harrison into my life. I believe I would be on edge, but I would want to give him a chance. But giving Harrison 'a chance' infers that I have concerns about his behavior in the first place, and those will be ever-present. In my life, I am protected by a set of boundaries; you cannot breach those boundaries if I can't trust you. And even though I love the part I have found in my grandfather, he has not entirely passed my boundaries.

Therefore, I would always have one hand clenched, and that's no way to live.

So, no, I don't think I would let Harrison in.

GO ON: IT DOES

With the bodies buried, that part of the Four Ks history ceases. Pearl also ceases. It was a cheerless life for them for a long, long time. It was more than cheerless, it was dreadfully sad.

It's not just the killings; it was the young girls witnessing the goings-on, it's Pearl's screaming pain, the suffocating fear, the irreversible outcomes. It's the rage of being powerless to save a loved one, the fury at a previous loved one being the one who inflicted this pain. It's the gutted spirit in silence as the bodies were removed, and the vacancy of the family home.

Staring at your husband's clothes that will no longer be worn, and the utility car and carpenter's tools that will no longer build the family home. His shaving gear is no longer required.

It was now time to face raising four daughters who hurt as much as you do. It was the absence of everyone once life went back to 'normal.' Emptiness everywhere: the bed, the kitchen table, the sink, the discussion, and the silence in your head.

Reading my Nana's statement makes me feel sorry for her and sad for her ill-treated life. When you looked at her life, you could see her sadness, and as I read her words, I could feel her sorrow. As much as I tried at this point, I am wondering how any positive outcomes came of this day, and I cannot see or contemplate any. The only point I could make is that Harrison was now out of his own misery, but at what cost?

How do you process the pain, the loss, the trauma? Where does it go? Does it have a name? Was anyone explaining it to anyone? Did any of the girls talk to each other? Did they sleep well anymore? Did they pick up habits of self-destruction as per their survival mechanisms? Pearl took to drinking, but what do you do as a ten year old, an eight year old, a six year old, and a four year old? Did they ask Mum for a cuddle or did they withdraw so deeply that they existed in a shell?

Do you ever recover from an event like this?

By Tuesday, December 6, 1960, Beatrice, Morris, and Tony were continuing the clean-up. The paint was drying on the walls, and the smell of death was lifting. The home was nearly ready to be occupied again, and those occupants were nearing their return.

Five days had passed since the gunshots; Pearl was undoubtedly in survival mode and although she hadn't spent a day without a tear, she wanted her independence back. She made arrangements to return to the only place she knew to be home. As horrendous as it sounds, she and the Four Ks had nowhere else to go. They all returned to the scene of the crime.

That afternoon, Pearl returned with Kendall and Kylie, and the three of them spent their first night back in the hell hole. There was communication with Beatrice and the Harper family, and it was agreed that Pearl and the Four Ks would continue to live at the prudent dwelling. Even though they were related by marriage, Beatrice didn't do Pearl any favors; the rent was still due at the end of each month.

Kristen and Kate would return in a week or so to be with their mum again. It must have caused them quite some internal anxiety when they were taken from her, and although they were sent to their grandparents' home, with whom they were familiar, they had been removed from their mum at a time when all they wanted was her.

They knew their dad was dead, and they knew their stepdad was dead; the brutal experience stayed with them all those waves away. The silence and unknowing led to abandonment issues within the two young girls. Here, though, the two of them forged a connection. Of all the Four Ks, Kristen and Kate were the closest for the longest period, but that wasn't an everlasting period. One of them ended up being less forgiving than the other.

How did Pearl cope with her first night back? She was an astute woman, and she would have noticed missing items and tools no longer about. It is not clear whether she mentioned this, but she would have seen it with clarity.

Those first steps she took through the entrance at the rear door and into the kitchen, how terrible that must have been. Did she stop and stare at the place her husband fell? Despair her companion. Did she walk in as if there was no change and wear her matter-of-fact appearance?

I am not sold on this. With so much love in her heart, she couldn't be so bold. Yet I have not heard a story of this moment, so I cannot distill in your senses if Pearl's eyes were wet or stone cold. I can only assume that her sorrow hadn't left her.

She may have slept in the same bed as she had Thursday night, or gone into the other room with Kendall and Kylie. Company, even that of a ten and four year old, was comfort she needed, what they all needed.

She wasn't in fear of an unannounced attack; the only person she knew capable of that was now buried. It was Phillip and his loss that consumed her thoughts, which had her at night, toss.

But this moment wasn't her rude awakening—that was coming. What was nearing on New Year's Day was about to come at her door with a knock. This was a man who was in fact a cop. Could they handle anymore proceedings dealing in rip your throat out shock?

The new day started as all other days. The back door was opened, and the parade of little and big feet went to and from the outhouse to the kitchen. This was the first time Pearl had stepped outside since the barrel of a gun was in her face. This moment, then, was when she would again be answerable. Did she second-guess herself? Have a flashback? Or, did she not see the connection and just walk past those areas as if nothing had happened?

Kendall went to school again. Eventually, Kristen and Kate returned to their mum where they were reintroduced to their home. I wonder how it felt for them to return, and how it felt for their young souls to not have a father around anymore.

How did they sleep that night, and what did they think about? They returned to school with Kendall and the three of them saw the year out. The Harper men, Tony and Morris, were around helping out as best they could. They saw that Pearl was alone and in need of help and they offered their hands. Morris was a provider right to the end; he made sure there was wood for the fire, and every now and then he would drop off some vegetables he had sourced from market gardens in the area.

This was both a blessing and a curse, as with Morris around to help, so too were his mates. In time, one of these friends was going to be a menace and make Harrison look like a mere apprentice.

Morris was always up for a good time. He was a friendly fellow who loved a drink followed by a nod and a wink. "Everything is going to be all right, Pearl," he would say while they sat at the pub together. Pearl had found her old friend again, the taste of beer and the local pub was always in her sights.

The Ks returned to their old routine, even if it was missing a link. No negotiation, what was there to negotiate? Nothing, they just had to get over it and get on without.

Upon their return to Seaford State Primary School, they had to endure being taunted and harassed by the other school kids. It was quite severe; they got teased and called names, one being 'the murderer's daughter.' Whatever they were taunted with, it was about the murders. That alone was a lot to take on as innocent children who also carried the pain of loss. No one involved in this situation switched off. Even though they were pulled aside and told by Pearl what she wanted them to know, the clause for silence on all things was all that mattered.

At school, facing the other students and their taunts only increased their anger, and one or two of the school bullies copped a whack back when Kendall stood up for herself and her sisters.

The year was winding down and Christmas was nearing. In a time when it was going to be the hardest, Pearl packed them all up and they took to Tasmania to spend it with the Joyces. Pearl returned home where she could be amongst her own and be supported.

Before they left for Tasmania, Agnes Harper, who was by now very fond of the Four Ks and was to them Nana Harper, made the effort to give them presents. Since meeting them, she was ready to accept and embrace them. She loved them and insisted that she be called Nana Harper—not Mrs. Harper—when they digressed from calling her Nana. She had her heart broken at the start of the month but by the end, she had given her heart to Kendall.

She was the only person in Kendall's life to acknowledge her birthday—the 25th of December. She had knitted a pink bag and bought a framed picture of Jesus and wrapped it in birthday paper and then in brown paper with a home-made fruit cake placed on top of the package. She made sure Kendall received it.

The fruit cake is gone, but the pink bag and the framed Jesus still have pride of place with Kendall. The frame is displayed itself on a shelf, and the pink bag is only a drawer away.

Agnes cared when no one else did, and this is another part of Agnes she has with her today. Her birthday wasn't much to celebrate, and for years she hated that it fell on the same day as the Christmas celebrations. This year her birthday was not acknowledged by her mum or sisters, and it wasn't the last time that would happen.

Kendall once recalled that she had not been wished happy birthday, and she sat silently all this birthday watching the Christmas day cheer. At around 10p.m., she took herself outside and began skipping around the shack, singing, "Happy birthday to me, happy birthday to me.".

At about the tenth lap, Pearl came out and said, "What are you doing?" Kendall told her mum that she was singing Happy Birthday to herself.

Pearl looked back at her and bluntly said, "Yeah, that's right, it's your birthday. Happy birthday then."

With that, she turned and walked inside without another word or pleasure. Just bitterness and self-esteem-destroying neglect. Kendall continued to run around singing, but the damage was done. She went to hate both Christmas and her birthday for decades. She said she didn't care, but inside she did. We all want to be seen by someone, and Kendall was about to lose herself without so much as a choice.

The New Year was celebrated, and 1961 began. They were to live in the Seaford shack from 1960 to 1967, and a lot happened in those years. There were new situations, and with that, behaviors which all led to further damage and destruction, and more of the making of who these women were to become.

NEW YEAR CARRYING COLD DEATHS AND OLD HABITS

By early January, Pearl and the Four Ks had come back to Victoria. It was not unfamiliar to them; they had spent the rest of December in the shack. There was ill feeling, but it was not a disastrous situation on the surface. But what was coming into their lives was.

Once more, it was out of their control. Their mum was about to have it happen to her again. She was to face the music, and the orchestra wasn't playing a tune Pearl was anticipating. She was about to be the recipient of unsuspecting guests, and for Pearl they had come to arrest.

The police arrived, parked where Phillip's utility used to be, got out and gave a holler.

Pearl came to the door and greeted the men, and they said these words: "Pearl Harper, we are arresting you for your involvement in the murders of Phillip Harper and Harrison Bennet."

She was in complete shock and dismay. "What a stupid thing to say," she told them, followed by, "How dare you say such a thing."

The police didn't so much care for anything this woman had to say. To them, she had much blame to hold and they believed she knew a lot more than she had let on. She was taken to the police station and they charged her with murder. They held her at the cells and took her statement. She was advised that her fingerprints were found on the barrel of the rifle, and that she was involved in the shootings. She was in serious trouble; the police firmly believed she had been more involved than she'd let on.

The Four Ks were in disarray as their mum had been taken from them. They knew she was in treacherous trouble. She admitted to touching the gun, but it was to push it away from her face, not to point it at anyone's head. After some grilling and banter, the police put Pearl through the ringer. They also let her know in no uncertain terms that the letter in Harrison's suit jacket was a disgrace, and she was as much to blame as Harrison himself. They told her she delivered the "death notice."

They were not at all happy with Pearl, and she was informed of this. She was released from the cells and the charges were withdrawn. But she was warned it was only going to get worse.

She returned home flustered and disturbed, shocked and angry at what she had gone through. She "didn't need it or deserve it." She had been crying for hours, and when she had a shower, she couldn't scrub away the guilt and disdain she had for herself. She was a mess.

She had just been torn to pieces for something she did not do. Pearl didn't pull the trigger; she had nothing to do with the shootings in that sense. The police didn't see it that way, and she was just dragged through the mud, and that stuck for some time.

At this time, it was already tough going. The Salvation Army was assisting Pearl and the Four Ks. They helped with cleaning up around and they also helped with food and clothing. Pearl was dirt poor, and she relied on the widow's pension to survive, which was twenty-seven pounds a fortnight. This was to cover the rent of three pounds per week, which was expected without concern every month.

All the food, utility bills, and numerous medications she and the young Ks were on for the various anxieties they had developed from living on the lighthouses and since the shootings she had to purchase. Clothes and shoes were often secondhand or donated. Pearl also had to pay for the occasional outings plus her beer.

The outings for the Four Ks were few and far between. They were taken to the pictures twice a year, which consisted of a trip into the city. They were also taken to the zoo and The Royal Melbourne Show every now and then.

Kendall stated that the police had blinders on and came after her mother. Pearl spent another night isolated in the shack, and she took to beer to help her sleep.

In the next couple of days, she was given notice about the inquisition. Here, she was further taken to task about her part in the triangle, and dragged about, to see if any accountability could be laid upon her. It was, as Kendall described, when "all hell broke loose." She shuddered as she recalled those times.

It wasn't just Pearl's rude awakening on January 24, 1961. When the inquisition commenced before the coroner's court in Melbourne, the Four Ks copped a sentence they never expected or deserved—they were all forcibly removed from their mother's care and placed in the care of the state. The sisters were placed in a foster home for three to four weeks. If the Four Ks didn't have abandonment issues bubbling before, they certainly did now.

This also provides insight into how the Four Ks like to have control in their lives, because up until then, they had none. They were taken on a roller-coaster of emotional experience that wasn't even slightly pleasant: pain, rejection, loss, fear, uncertainty, absence. All because they were in an environment that was unsafe because of others' behavior, not theirs. They were innocents in this. They were on a course directed by someone else. No wonder they all had control issues in their lives.

The start of 1961 was the sequel to a little girl's nightmare. All four had similar but different horror themes. February was torture, and they didn't see their mum or know how she was. They just knew she was at court. Pearl stood up for herself as best she could, and was adamant she loved her husband. She didn't go into too much detail where she didn't have to.

Pearl was acquitted of any wrongdoing and released without any legal repercussions. She walked away unscathed, but her state of mind was nothing but wobbly.

Once the proceedings were complete, there was concern for the well-being of the Four Ks from a governmental department, but Pearl showed testaments of her character, and her daughters were returned. She won, and they came back to her.

They lived in that shack a further six years.

When the school year started, all the girls returned to the school they had previously attended and tried to live as normal a life as possible, but they were taunted and teased and put down by the school kids.

They tried to stick up for themselves, but they copped a serve for their dad's actions. They were embarrassed and angry, so some kids got away with the taunts while others took a whack by the three eldest Ks.

Kendall attended as much school as she could, and during that time she met a boy who stayed around—even to this day. Michael was in Kendall's class, and years later she would add brother-in-law to the title when referring to him. Michael was like a little brother to her—they were good mates. This was another part of her life she remembered well and held dear to her.

Kendall suffered relentless bullying and was kept down a grade because of all the factors she endured. She told Pearl one day of the bullying. Now Pearl was capable of being quite a fierce character. She took herself to the primary school and word was out she was there to take on the school's principal. The person who offered me this memory was a pupil at the school at the time and recalled how Pearl was at the school to punch the principal's head in. All the kids at the school were terrified of Pearl and thought she was a witch. It reminded me of a time when my mother took to the school to confront my grade three teacher who was bullying me; I now see where she modeled her behavior. As a mother, I would do the same thing and I'm no witch, not even slightly. Nor was my mum or Pearl. The matter was heard just as mine was; at the time I too endured prejudice from ignorance.

Life continued as best as it could.

Because Pearl didn't drive, they took trains, taxis, and buses whenever they needed to travel. Pearl did not have a license, and she never learnt to drive. The train line from Frankston to Seaford was a regular route they took, or they walked. Walked to school, walked to the beach, walked to the local milk bar, and anywhere else they needed to go.

As you might understand, Pearl's ability to function took a dive, but before she was rendered unable, she did one thing that would warp the girls' sense of identity and confuse the rest of us when we came along. She changed their surname from Bennet to Harper by deed poll. And they took on that ownership. They all say they are Harpers, even now some of them will tell you they are Harpers. But they are not. They are Bennet and Joyces, not Harpers.

It was Kendall who told me how life progressed for the remainder of 1961 and onward. "Mum was so bad that she couldn't do anything." Pearl was quickly developing a severe drinking addiction, and very soon she would have nothing to offer anyone in her untenable state.

When this happened, it was Kendall who stepped up and took over the running of the house. She was ten years old—going to be eleven soon—and she became mother to all. She was removed from school and never returned. Imagine that one day you are a pupil at school, and the next you're removed permanently. I look at my own daughter, who is also young, and I think of how such innocence would be ripped from her soul if she was to relive Kendall's existence. This breaks my heart, but I also see how amazing my aunty is. What a woman.

Pearl was about most of the time, but she wasn't too useful, she was almost a burden. She stayed at home in the shack for a year or so; she was capable but not overly so, and gave some support to Kendall. This lessened as Pearl's drinking grew. What Pearl needed most of all was beer, friendly company, and to just simply lose it, drop her bundle.

She did.

Kendall didn't.

She stood by the family; her and, more often than not, her alone.

You'll quickly hear her say, "But Mum didn't give us up, she didn't walk out."

My answer to that is, "No, she didn't, but you are the one who stood up. That's stronger than not walking away."

Any dreams or expectations Kendall had for her life was extinguished. Part of her life had been abducted. No longer did Kendall, the child, have a childhood. Instead, she carried Pearl, Kristen, Kate, and Kylie aboard her shoulders and forged on.

Pearl's decline was part of her grief; the loss crippled her. On top of that was her guilt, self-loathing, and pain, which gutted her. From this shell, she took to a substance to survive. This wasn't a stretch, as she had a well-established palate for consuming beer. Her drinking increased to such proportions that she instilled this memory in others. It took years for her to dwindle away in her own self-loathing, and for every year spent spiraling down, Kendall spent keeping everyone afloat.

Kendall's job became full-time carer, and she was responsible for everything—absolutely everything.

She organized the cooking of meals, yet she wasn't an established cook. She had the experiences of island living, and in part she was already the little helper and knew a lot more than ordinary young girls. That is the key to this story. Kendall was never ordinary, she was never untalented or incapable, quite the opposite. She was extraordinary. She was every bit capable and talented.

She didn't come equipped with a filo-fax of recipes from previous cooking classes, but she did know how to read, and even though she didn't have the money to buy the magazines or papers, she was able to get her hands on them from time to time. She learnt how to cook various dishes by reading the *Herald Sun* recipes at the local milk bar. She would take in every detail she could, then she would go home and try it out. Kendall was the one who did all the grocery shopping. Pearl would make her a list and Kendall would add whatever else the house needed. As there was little money in her hand, she had to stick to the items as much as possible, but when she could she got something new or extra.

As she was telling me the story, she was distracted by another memory. She pondered her ability to read. She sat before me and joked at the minimal level of schooling she had. She said she wouldn't call the homeschooling on the islands a proper education. "It's not what I would call it. But at least the old dear [meaning her mother] taught us how to read. She did that much."

Kendall didn't like reading, but that is the one skill that got her by.

As I am experiencing her memory, I too digress. I am still at a loss to understand how a child becomes 'Mum' when she had her own life to live. I mentioned this to her, and she said quite directly that she had to.

"No one else was going to do it, and Mum was that much of a mess that I didn't have a choice in the matter." She quickly added, "I cooked, cooked all the meals, breakfast, lunch and tea. I cleaned everything. The house, the garden, the works. I washed all their clothes, all the linen and towels. Every morning made the beds, put the lunches in their bags for them, paid the rent and any bill that I retrieved out of the mailbox I went to everyday. I bought the groceries, walking to the shops and back every time. I picked up the medications from the chemist that we were on and we were on a few, believe me. After what we went through, we needed them, I can assure you. I took the dog Buster for a walk, fed Daffy the duck. I chopped the wood and stacked it all up. If there was ever a mess I cleaned it up and at times I had to go looking for her, Mum. If it was up to being done, it was me that saw to it."

There you go. An expression of existence straight from the mouth that lived it. That's some clarity right there.

What she also did was provide the home with hot water in an inventive way. There was no hot water service at the shack. You either had to boil the kettle, or for bigger needs such as the bath, Kendall used the washing machine and turn the hot water cycle on so that the hot water was generated through the old washer.

There it all is. Kendall saved all, and in return surrendered herself. She never returned to school. Ever. And she stayed in the shack looking after everyone from 1961 to 1967.

Then Kendall said, "And that wasn't the only shit I had to put up with."

I looked at her and thought, *oh my god, what else could be added to such an exhaustive list?*

I was told that in this time, there was much to see and fear especially when there were certain activities going on in the shack. Kendall knew not to be around at those times.

I looked at her quizzically.

She saw this and added: "Overall, if anything needed to be done, it was me who did it and I assure you, I noticed everything. If it was going on I knew about it. You see, the lot of them thought I was stupid but I wasn't bloody stupid. I knew, believe me I knew," she said, with a defiant nod.

I think I got what she was saying, and I believed her. I took this opportunity to share with her something I discovered about Pearl during my research, but I hadn't broached it with her yet for confirmation.

We were sitting at her dining table when I said to her, "I don't know how to tell you what I found out because I don't want it to hurt you. I wasn't going to tell you this time, but since you said that nothing got past you, I think it's my call. Besides, I can't hide anything from you."

I continued hesitantly. "So, you know how we know Nana had loose morals. Well, I kind of found out she went a bit further with that... and she used to get paid to have loose morals," I said, and sat there waiting for Kendall's response.

"I thought so," she said straight away. "That answers that." Another nod.

"No, you can't do that to me. I'm hanging here. What answers what?"

We laughed. It turned out that Pearl had the company of men in Eden Road after Phillip and Harrison were dead, and that Kendall saw men coming and going and this would always follow with them having extra bread and milk money. Kendall knew what was going on, and she thanked me for giving her confirmation and answers to her thoughts and observations as a young child. Nana was good at keeping men happy, and yes, she was in the business of prostitution at different times of her life.

My god, what a conversation we had! What a moment from niece to aunty, and how well we dealt with one's findings and one's memory. It really was gorgeous. We laughed and talked more, and I jokingly said, "Great, so now I know my grandfather was a murderer and my nana a prostitute. Beauty!"

"How do you think that makes me feel?" Kendall said. "That's my mum and dad. Good combination those two. Bloody hell."

We laughed more.

So my nana did entertain men in a way for a personal and profitable transaction again. She did what she did, and was what she was. I have no judgment upon her for this. One of the oldest professions in history and she did it to survive. It doesn't detract from my opinion of her.

What I found astonishing was that, as I knew her, she had no sexualized energy about her at all. In fact, although she had loved and care for me, in all those years not once did I see the appearance of sexual energy about her. She was so closed and drawn that there was not the slightest hint of her being able to accord herself that way. Prostitute? No way! Are you serious?

When Kendall acknowledged this, too, I was just gob smacked, and I laughed because it was so not what I ever thought I would come across. I have said, "That's my nana, you're talking about. My *nana*. The straight up-and-down woman who didn't like to smile. We're talking about the same woman, yes?" That was my response. Astonishment, acceptance, understanding, and well... I didn't know her back then, so rumor has it the beer and bread were bought from behavior in the bed.

She didn't partake in this activity daily. She did it, but not all the time. Kendall couldn't tell you how often and who it was with, but she did see men come and go. end of story.

Having enjoyed the distraction, we returned to the original conversation, and Kendall said, "Now, where were we? That's right, the bloody capsicum." She shook her head. "Do you know all I had to cook on was an electric fry pan?

That's all I had to cook meals with. That was it. No oven or stovetop, and certainly no microwave."

I sat there in stunned silence; she was great to listen to. She had all the passion, anger, and even freedom in her voice as she told her story.

She recalled that she was always asked to make stew. "This bloody, boring, bland, yuck stew."

At this time, the recipe for stew consisted of meat, carrot, and potato, which she clearly thought was bland and distasteful. A short time before she was asked to make the stew, she remembered reading a new recipe and wanted to give it a go. She went to the store and bought the new ingredient. It was a green capsicum, and into the stew it went without her telling anyone.

The meal was served up and Pearl sat at the table sifting through her plate and she angrily asked Kendall, "What's that green thing?"

"It is a capsicum, Mum."

"It's what? What is it doing in my stew? I don't want this."

"Well, you can at least try it. I read it in the *Woman's Day* recipe section and decided to give it a go."

The Four Ks and Pearl ate the stew. After the meal was cooked, eaten, and agreed to be delicious, Pearl told Kendall, "You can put that green stuff in the stew again when you make it next." Not a word of thanks or support or a pat on the back, just an accepting snide remark.

Kendall went on to cook for the family only out of an electric frying pan, and as the years passed, so did her ability as a cook grow. She added extra spices and herbs and all sorts of stuff. Most of the time Pearl and the Four Ks had no idea what they were eating because it was better if she labeled whatever it was as a basic food stock.

Then Kendall's face lit up when she remembered how she found new spices and would sprinkle them in the pan when no one was looking, and they would eat her food and tell her how delicious it was and not have a clue what she had put in it. "I got good at cooking," she said triumphantly, and today it must be said that Kendall is one of the best cooks around.

We took a minute to picture the psychology of the Four Ks after the shootings. She agreed they were told to be silent, to not say a thing to anyone about anything. They obeyed. They didn't even speak amongst themselves, let alone anyone else. It was bottled inside their bodies, and it affected their minds. They were all traumatized, and they couldn't express their emotions. They hadn't been taught or ever encouraged to.

She said it was at least about six weeks before any of them cried after the shootings and funeral. "We were all just numb and shut down." She said that she used to wet the bed, and they all had nightmares and would yell and scream in the night. They also had their own episodes of screaming and yelling through tears that were not comforted or shown purposeful care by either Pearl or each other. They were in part left to their own devices, and with that, bad communication habits and lack of emotional regard established themselves.

I heard the words, "We were happy with Phillip. We genuinely were. We laughed, and had a good man caring about us. That went when he did." I asked her if that happiness ever came back. She told me she doesn't think so. But I see it now. The thing is, it took decades to reclaim.

She told me Kylie couldn't sleep by herself, and she used to sleep next to Kendall. For Kylie, Kendall was her teddy bear and they cuddled each other to sleep.

If a picture forming is of quite a hostile environment to grow up in, you are seeing it for what it was. All of them attacked Kendall psychologically most of the time. She was told she was stupid nearly every day. "Hey stupid", was an accepted comment, as was, "You're a dummy." She was even told by Pearl more times than she should have ever had to hear was that she was "useless." According to Pearl, Kendall was "good for nothing."

The ridiculousness of this is that the taunts they served at her—and these taunts were served with poisonous intent—were hypocritical, as it was they who were all surviving because of her.

To my lateral way of thinking, it was the person who was calling her that who was the stupid one. When a child who has had to become a woman overnight is the one who cares for you because you are incapacitated, and who cooks for you, cleans your home, pays your bills and runs your life smoothly... what are you doing relying on someone who is supposedly stupid? That would only make you stupid.

But it's not the truth. Kendall was clever. She was so clever, and she never turned around and left. She never told her mum or sisters that they were stupid; and she never hit her mum over the head with a piece of wood.

In her grave, I believe Pearl owes Kendall an apology followed by a thank you.

Every rent day, Pearl fell ill, and Kendall had to walk up to the Harper's house and pay her aunty the rent money. She told me, "Beatrice was a hard, old bitch." She didn't do her or her sisters any favors, and she gave them nothing.

One day, Kendall was on a tram and as Beatrice was a tram conductor, she happened to be on the same tram this day. As Beatrice came through the carriage, she noticed Kendall and stood before her demanding payment for her carriage, even though they were related. She did so with coldness and not a hint of regard for Kendall.

She said it again, "She was a rude bitch." And when Kendall was given her chance, she let Beatrice know. This came after they eventually moved on from Eden Road. Some years on, when she was walking back from the shops with groceries in hand, she walked past the Harper's house and

Beatrice and Morris were out the front gardening. They weren't going to look at her, but she stopped and deliberately said, "Hello, Beatrice." Beatrice looked up and looked straight through her. Kendall said, "Do you know who I am?" Beatrice kept staring and Kendall said, "Thought so. I'm your niece." She walked off. Beatrice or Morris didn't so much as try to stop her or run after to her to ask her how she was; they just returned to their garden. The Harpers abandoned Pearl and the Four Ks after Agnes died, and that is another sad affair in the succession of events of this life.

Now it's for the broken Agnes Harper to secretly fight for survival.

Her son's murder took its toll on her. She suffered immeasurably, and she would die not long after she buried him. It could be said that she died when Phillip did.

Some say it's possible to die of a broken heart, and it was said this was what took Agnes. It was June 24, 1961 when she passed. Not a year had circled, and the Harpers had lain to rest two members of their family. The matriarch and the fair son both gone, and those who were left had to soldier on. They did so without Pearl and the Four Ks.

As Kendall said, they lost a good friend the day Agnes left, and they in turn lost any support or affiliation they had with the family whose name they went on to keep. This brings up the question, given the Four Ks spent the rest of their unmarried lives as Harpers, and went on to refer to themselves as such; did that add to the unconscious sense of abandonment in them? The Harpers never truly embraced Pearl and the Four Ks, yet they saw themselves as Harpers. It was a family heritage created of fantasy.

It's an awful misconstrued world, too. Who do they belong to? Where is it they come from? Do they know? Or has their mum's insistence on them adopting a family's surname severed all ties to belonging?

For the remaining part of 1961 to 1965, life was quite mundane. There were not a lot of incidences to report, but that doesn't mean things weren't happening. The three girls continued to attend state primary school, and established quite a tough exterior. They weren't to be messed with, and if you took on one, you had three to answer to. Kendall was a protector even when she wasn't a pupil. When the summer months came, the local school kids from along the stretch of the bay would congregate at the Seaford pier, and it was here that a lot of friends were made.

Unfortunately, one more character was to arrive—the menace I briefly introduced earlier.

Not long after two bullets were fired, a man began lurking in the shadows. This man was one of Morris's drinking mates. His name was Hadley, and according to Lilly he was always around—part of the drinking scene. He and Pearl began drinking together almost instantly upon meeting.

He didn't have an instant place in Pearl's heart, as that was still black and dead yet beating. He would sleep outside under a pergola area for some time before he eventually made his way into her bed. The Four Ks welcomed their new father figure, but it wasn't a discussion had with them, it was more: this is your new stepdad, deal with it.

He was a man with as much baggage as Pearl, and concealment was his game.

DIRTY MAN STALKING

Pearl took a position at the Phillip Morris Cigarette Company. She got her smokes for free, and they were encouraged to smoke along the belt line they worked during eight-hour shifts.

Dissent remained in the shack. Kendall was still the provider—or the slave, depending on how you saw it.

Hadley made his intentions known to Pearl. He fancied her. She didn't return the offering, but she couldn't be rid of him either. She told him if he wanted to be around, then he could sleep outside under the pergola area; no dispute, no negotiation. He took his conditions and made a bed out of it—and a position in their lives. Not a good one. Like I said, there was no consultation with her daughters.

Kendall was being savaged in a way that hell wasn't an accurate description. She endured torture in a suffocating cocoon glazed with death threats and evilness. This beautiful girl had her life taken. She still bore the scars of her treatment by her father on the lighthouse islands, had carried the pain of the shootings, and possibly hadn't had time to mourn the loss of herself.

And now she was being brutally assaulted.

Hadley was molesting Kendall on a regular basis. He did so for years. He got away with it because he told Kendall to shut her mouth or she'd be dead. To Kendall's way of thinking, if it was happening to her, it wasn't happening to her sisters. She made a conscious decision to put up with it and remain silent because she would rather it happened to her than her sisters. This fills me with rage I cannot contain.

There is dispute over whether Hadley was molesting the other Ks. Kristen, Kate, and Kylie deny any such abuse, but some of them went on to display overt sexual behaviors consistent with molestation in childhood. In fact, one of them entertained men herself for a living for a short while.

Kendall was assaulted in silence.

The older Ks were about to start high school at Longreach High.

By 1965, Pearl had a family duty to attend to. Her father was dying, and she was summoned back to Tasmania. It was care she was supposed to deliver at his bedside, but it was loathing she spat as she encouraged his entry to the grave. Pearl had elsewhere to be.

As we know, Pearl did not accord herself with decorum or affiliation

Instead she was bitter with her words and strident of her selfish needs.

Her father died, she attended his burial, then made her way straight from Beaconsfield Cemetery to book a return passage to Victoria.

With Christmas celebrations soon to arrive, Pearl took up making her acquaintance with her new neighbors. A young family had moved next door—Arnold and Veronia, with two children were a welcome diversion for her. Veronia and Pearl developed a deeply connected relationship based on their own losses and misgivings. They both had disturbingly in-depth problems, which they would discuss for hours and hours while drinking and smoking together. Women united by chronic alcoholism—liquid amber and companionable intoxication.

Veronia told Pearl she was adopted out as a baby to a loving woman called Ruby. Who was kind and gentle with the devotion it took to raise a young girl by yourself in the 1940s. Ruby was a hardworking woman, and had to leave young Veronia alone for long periods so she could provide for the two of them. Veronia never knew her biological dad, but her adoptive father was a man Ruby cherished, who would die on the Burma Railway during World War I. Both pined for him forever.

Veronia had much to contend with by the time she arrived at Eden Road— abandonment issues, the isolation of being an only child, the death of her mum not long after the murder of her own young son. So, when she met Pearl, they formed an instant bond, yet they had many differences in their values.

Both caused concern to their families.

One particular day when Kendall had been sent on errands, she returned unable to find Pearl. She was not at work, and had not left a note or any sign of where she could be. Kendall crossed the yard and knocked on Veronia's door, but neither Pearl or Veronia was there.

"They're at the pub," Kendall said.

She caught a train down to the next suburb at Frankston, and then walked through the town to the pub—the same pub she, her sisters, Phillip and Pearl had stayed in when they'd first fled Tasman Island. Here she was again, only this time with much more baggage than she had in 1959.

She ascended the pub stairs timidly, and entered. She located her mother and Veronia with Hadley. The three of them were highly intoxicated, and unable to make sense or be sensible. It was not a pleasant atmosphere Kendall found herself in. Men made references to her, and she was uncomfortable with not only the burden of having two women to get out of a pub, but also the embarrassment and repercussions she would cop from the evil drunk tongues of the very ones she was trying to help.

Kendall asked them to leave, and a bit of nonsense went on with the women not too willing to be told. Both were capable of harshness, and could snap at you quicker than a rubber band flicks back.

Seeing the situation, the publican had a word, and the women walked out with the young, humiliated girl. They caught a cab home in silence before heading to their respective homes. Behind closed doors, their lives continued, but an argument erupted over how Veronia got to the pub. Veronia was definitely an alcoholic, but she drank behind closed doors; she never went to the pub. Pearl almost lived at the pub.

Kendall was told to never show her mother or Veronia up again. Kendall's response was she was just trying to help them.

She couldn't; Pearl and Veronia were friends who continued drinking together, heavily. They were the best drinking buddies you could find. No one was going to stop them; they both wore their victim-of-circumstance boldly— it protected their addiction.

While, I concur they had right to feel incapacitated due to the tragic loss both endured, they did not have the right to completely wreck the lives of others, especially when they were responsible for the lives of others. That was an act of selfishness and betrayal. The biggest act of betrayal, however, was yet to come.

For someone who never let anyone talk about her when she was alive, in death, Pearl's life is worth discussing. Tragedy followed her relentlessly, and Eden Road was the scene of one major event after another.

On Monday, May 1, 1967, Kendall had some big news to share with her mum. Kendall had missed a cycle in her menstruation. She did not have a boyfriend. She had a monster, and Kendall was both terrified and horrified. She gathered all the courage from her ravaged spirit, sat with her mum, and broke her silence. Kendall had never so much as looked at a boy her own age, let alone had sexual relations with them.

She chose her moment with Pearl and spoke softly and timidly because she was terrified of how her mum would react. She told Pearl that she had missed her period, and Pearl wanted to know how that could be. Kendall explained that Hadley had been abusing her for years, and the situation was due to his abuse.

Pearl went berserk. When Hadley returned to the shack from his drinking session she told him in no uncertain terms that he was disgusting, and he was to leave her life immediately. She called him a perverted pig that should never have been let anywhere near her or her daughters—to get the hell away from them.

She then rallied her daughters and they had another "them only" meeting. Pearl wanted to know if the filthy bastard had got to the others. Silence filled the room. None of the other Ks raised their hands or voices. No one confessed to being abused by Hadley except for Kendall. Pearl said this wasn't to be spoken of again. He was going; she had told him to leave. It was a very tense situation and yet again it was Pearl's life choices that were ripping into the innocent hearts of girls who were not so innocent anymore.

She was crushed. She heard, "Mum, I've been attacked by your boyfriend for years, please don't hate me." It was the most awful conversation to have had in an environment where care didn't exist. Survival care was present, but not protective care. Every goddamned second you protect your offspring. You say you didn't know. Your job as a mother is to always know, to always protect, to forever love them.

There was no way these girls had a chance to live anything but a complicated life. Their psychological and emotional trauma was so great; they may not ever be able to work through these experiences. They were not shown the skills to deal with such trauma at the time. They were taught to shut up about it; to be silent. So they buried it deep, suffocated those memories. Their minds acted as guardians, sentinels against the awful truth of it until they reached a point where "that didn't happen". But it did. And truth fights for its freedom against the guardians. They may cling to righteousness, and vehemently deny all parts of their past, but that doesn't free them. They may think they are in control, but it is the past that dictates, controls them. They haven't moved on, they've just gotten older.

It was a tragic day that leaned into a tragic night. Pearl continued her "don't tell no one nothing" tale, and she made it clear that the matter would be taken care of. They began to smell smoke and heard the crackling of a fire's growth. The acrid scent of petrol rose, and smoke began to appear before them. The shack was on fire.

They bolted outside.

While all of this was unfolding, Veronia was staring out her kitchen window, unaware of what was about to happen right before her own eyes. She first saw a figure with a can, shaking its contents around the base of the shack her drinking pal and daughters lived in. She wondered what was happening at Pearl's, and continued to watch this man circumnavigate the premises shaking this can about until it was empty. She thought it was Hadley, but wasn't too clear on this. Veronia kept watching, confused, until she saw the man take something from his pocket then strike a match and light the flammable liquid. Her confusion ceased.

As the home caught fire, Veronia picked up the phone and called the fire brigade, explaining what she had seen. She said the fire took off very quickly—with a swoosh—and before she knew it, the place was ablaze.

She hung up then ran back to her observation point.

The fire truck arrived in time to extinguish the fire, but not soon enough to save the home.

The police arrived in quick succession and arrested the perpetrator who was still in the driveway watching his pathetic doings. Hadley. He was immediately handcuffed and escorted away.

The fire brigade made sure the fire was well and truly out, then searched inside the dwelling. While it was cleared of structural damage, it was deemed unsafe and declared condemned.

Pearl and the Four Ks had just lost their home.

Standing out the front was one Beatrice Harper, and she was furious. She'd had enough of Pearl and her lot. She wanted them long gone, and she had no reason to be keeping up appearances from here on out. They were nothing but trash to Beatrice. She was glad the house was condemned so that lot could move on and cause grief in someone else's life. They never saw the Harpers again, and no one cared to keep in contact. The families split, but the Ks kept their surname. Why?

The pitiful act that just rendered the family homeless wasn't the first time Hadley had attempted to burn it down. Pearl had caught him in the act once before but managed to stop him. It also wasn't the first time Hadley had decided to cause harm to those he supposedly cared about either. He was a man of violence. He had punched and shoved Pearl about a number of times prior to the arson attack.

"He used to push and hit mum around a bit," Kendall said to me one day. "This one day, Mum was copping a hiding from Hadley, and all of sudden she fought back and hit him with whatever she could find. She gave it to him good and proper. She belted him that day. He stopped hitting her from then. He never so much as raised a finger after that, he knew."

Several serious issues were facing the Four Ks, Pearl, and Hadley. The putrid pig was in custody. Kendall had disclosed her hell, Pearl had gone flat-out riotous, they had all just survived an arson attempt... and they were now homeless.

Did they tell the police that Hadley was rightly accused of sexually assaulting Kendall? The molestation or sexual assault details were not in the criminal documents; therefore, it was a crime for which he never did prison time.

Pearl and her "say nothing about nothing" tactic had just let Hadley off the hook, and he was unaccountable for his rancid behavior. He at least pleaded guilty to the arson charges.

The details provided were found in the *Victoria Police Gazette*, February 15, 1968, edition and it tells us that:

McDonald Hadley: case number 61/254; was tried at Melbourne General Sessions 1st May 1967 for attempted arson and was sentenced to one-year hard labor. He was also tried at the Cowes Petty Sessions on the 1st June 1967 for the crime of having an ineffective silencer, and was given a penalty of $10 or two days' incarceration. A warrant was executed on the 30th of August, 1967, for his arrest, but presumably he was already in prison for the arson conviction.

He also had two previous convictions, was five feet and eleven inches tall, and had brown hair, hazel eyes, a fresh complexion and a medium build. He held a Victorian driver's license. He was released from the Barwon Prison in Geelong on the 30th of January, 1968. The last address he was known to reside at Eden Road Seaford, and the arresting officer was First Constable Potter 13344.

I do not know what his previous convictions were, but I discovered he had a long past, as well as a wife and children. When he arrived on the scene in 1961, he was thirty years old and had a record for not paying maintenance for his three children. He was a long-haul truck driver and boozer; they were the words I most heard repeated. I wonder if he did the hard labor for which he was sentenced.

Pearl did not attend Hadley's court case or sentencing, but she did know he was going to jail and was fine with that. She saw to it they got a new home as soon as possible, and they moved into a house in Carrum, not far from Seaford. They lived there from 1967 to 1969, and the three Ks attended Longreach High.

Kendall was starting to flap her wings to work toward flying out of her own suburban prison and being free. She had commenced full-time work in South Melbourne at Sunray Lingerie Company as a sales assistant, and she was beginning to develop her own sense of worth away from the ties of her ungrateful sisters and belittling mum. She was earning her own money, and her self-esteem was no longer tied to the home or her duties for the survival of her sisters and mum.

The year 1968 turned out to be a year of the height of Pearl's betrayal. Over all the years Pearl had dictated this story, I attributed this one to be her worst. This I don't forgive her for; I don't have to. She needs to be held to account.

She was set to do the unthinkable, and Veronia's husband, Arnold, and son, Michael, were a part of that. On January 30, 1968, Hadley was being released from Barwon Prison and it was Arnold and Michael that drove to bring him back to the Carrum home. Pearl took back the man who molested her daughter. Does it get any lower than that? Seriously, does it? What a confronting scenario for Kendall. What confusion for the remaining Ks. Would Pearl go on to do any good in her life?

Hadley didn't apologize or repent his wrongdoings. The pair of them—Pearl and Rapist—simply shacked up and drank some more while the Four Ks scrambled to forge their own lives and get out of there.

Hadley had attacked one, if not more of her daughters, beat up on Pearl, burned their house down, and here she was kissing him hello after the stint in jail. Does it get any more warped than that? I don't understand how she resolved to having this man in her life again.

Did she ever stop to consider the very daughter who had saved her since Phillip's murder? Did she ever stop to consider that this same girl gave up her own life to give one to her? Did she ever stop to consider that she was the reason why her daughter would suffer with a molested child's memory? No, Pearl thought of only herself.

On this ultimate act of betrayal, I will stand by my claim and say, "Now get out of your grave and come and say sorry. Sorry to Kendall first and foremost, and then sorry to the rest of us who have to carry the generational burden of being part of you."

That's what I would sternly demand of her today.

Back to reality.

Kendall had to cop it, nothing was said, nothing was discussed, the molestation never happened. In fact, no one went on to talk about Kendall's enduring suffering at all. Ever. Until now. I'll talk about it with her. Silence is like a cancer—it destroys your inner self.

She lived a life of harbored cruelty and deceit; was molested, bashed, vindictively put down, her life unacknowledged. All this and her problems taped to her forehead by her own mother.

ESCAPE THAT, HER LIFE

By the end of 1968, love was blossoming for some of the Ks.

Kristen, had been developing a relationship with the boy next door, Michael, Veronia's son, and they both were looking to complete high school. Kendall had taken herself to a dance at the Mechanics Institute Hall in Frankston and met a young man she considered favorably. He in turn considered her the same, and they agreed to meet again. She had kept her employment and made a connection with a man who suited her soul.

Kate was searching for answers and would soon seek them afar, and Kylie was about to simply vanish. Pearl spent more time at the pub with Hadley these days than she did drinking with Veronia. But Veronia continued to drink her beer at home in her chair listening to the horse races on the radio, with a turf cigarette in hand. The two once-best-friends didn't see each other so much anymore. Arnold was heading toward success as a pathologist and was a hardworking provider for his family.

The final year to end this decade of catastrophe had begun, and 1969 saw all Four Ks ready to leave their nest. Pearl, too, was readying to fly from her own coop. They all headed in opposite directions, but one returned to where it all started.

1970 arrived.

Kendall had begun saying no to her mum and sisters. She no longer wanted to cook for them and repair their socks, bleach their shirts or fill their baths with hot water. She had seen them through puberty; they could now take care of themselves. Kendall wanted to be left alone.

The man she locked eyes with had asked her to marry him, and it was easy to say yes. He was a country boy who was polite and gentle in his manner, and he loved Kendall for all that she was. They had blossomed together, and they gave each other their first taste of freedom and love. Ray was the support by Kendall's side from when they first met in 1966. He saw that she was the servant and helped her pack her self-esteem and individual aspiration to get away from it all.

On December 19, 1969, Kendall and Ray said "I do" to each other and their love was stamped with approval at the church in St. Kilda. Kylie stood beside her as her bridesmaid. Kendall's freedom from their immediate demands had been set. It was not total freedom, but it was a start. The happy pair moved in with Ray's family, and Kendall was wrapped in love.

In the meantime, her sister Kristen was well-involved with Michael, and by early 1970, they were actively involved in creating a reason to marry. I was on my way, and by October I was ready to be part of this world. Kristen and Michael married September 12, 1970, and Melissa—'The Sparkling Kid'—the first grandchild, was born in October 1970.

Kate was having less luck attracting love. She had been living with the label 'the chubby one' for as long as she could remember. She was just about ready to vanish like her youngest sister, Kylie, but Kate would keep in contact with her family.

Kate took a train across the Nullabor and lived in Western Australia, where she finally met the man who would become her husband. They had two children together, but Kate's past continued to nip at her heels, and her marriage did not last. Nor did her persistent past leave her. She is still greatly affected by it today.

Kylie, with her beautiful, flowing blonde hair, became involved with a man named Ben. He was a most untenable human being who used her and removed her from her family for nearly the next decade. She was present for Kendall's wedding, but from there she simply vanished and did not contact her family at all. This period she spent in isolation and away from her family lasted for approximately ten years. No one knew where she was. Pearl and the Ks presumed she'd died in the 1970 Cyclone Tracy disaster in Darwin.

It was time for Pearl and Hadley to feed into their own darkness, away from everyone and everything. Pearl returned to Tasmania, and for some reason they chose the remote town of Derby to begin a new life together. This situation was ironic, as there was conjecture that Harrison took to lighthouse keeping to remove Pearl from others, I can't help but sense it was Pearl who took Hadley away from him harming others on this occasion. For her own reasons, she stayed with Hadley. She said she loved him, and both wanted to escape the view of others. Pearl left her daughters behind. They had all gone their separate ways.

She hid somewhat in a house overlooking a town nestled in the side of a small mountain. She and Hadley got married; this was her fourth husband, with only one not being legally represented. Her home was situated not fifty meters from a family she knew and that liked her. Yet she did not make contact with them, nor acknowledge they were there, even though she walked past them daily.

I discovered this when I spoke to the children of this family—the Jackons—who are now quite elderly but still manage to retrieve their memories well. The Jackson family were on Tasman Island when Pearl escaped with Phillip in 1959—the ones who loved Harrison and Pearl.

That's right. Pearl fled an island where she lived near the Jackson family, only to ten years later flee again and live right next to a Jackson family member. Still on an island, just a bigger one.

I was told by the sisters that their father, Bill Jackson, went on to be the head keeper at Bruny Island from 1963 to 1967. It was their mum, Mabel, who thought of Pearl as a best friend. They told me she was hurt when Pearl returned but didn't say hello. Her daughters asked me why Pearl didn't say hello to them, and I told them I didn't know she hadn't, but would ask Kendall to see what she thought of it.

The Jackson women went on to tell me that before they realized Gwen lived below Pearl, their mum had heard on the grapevine that she was back in Tasmania. They were excited when they knew she was only a house away, but then shocked and disappointed when they realized she would never say hello. I told them Pearl didn't even tell her family, the Joyces, she was in Tasmania. In fact, she told no one.

As Kendall and Kylie have told me, Pearl didn't want anyone knowing she was there; she wanted to be left alone and she was embarrassed and on guard because of her past; she wanted to leave it behind. She felt guilt and shame and wanted it all to go away and did her part to hide. But as I've stated over and again, nothing ever goes away—you cannot hide from who you are.

She never spoke to any of the Jackson family, even though they would have welcomed her with open arms. She literally wanted to shut down and be shut away.

I guess if you don't want your past coming with you, you shouldn't go back to where it started, especially if it was such a small place. If you really want to run, run farther. But then that shows the modus operandi of a human's nature: we go back to what we know. Pearl's entire family was only an hour's drive away, and most of them were still alive, but she steered clear and no one heard from her.

Hadley became a manager at the tin mine, and he and Pearl established a modest yet isolated life. They did not want for much and were happy to retreat into each other. He didn't hit her anymore; she'd put a stop to that, but they continued with their heavy drinking.

One night, when they were returning to Derby after being out socially, Hadley had drunk way more than he should to be competent behind the wheel of a fast-moving car, and as he took the bends of the isolated country road, he ploughed straight into the Black Creek Bridge.

The car was a wreck, and so was Pearl. Parts of the car and the bridge pierced into her body. She was severely injured in this collision and taken to Launceston hospital where she endured life-saving surgery. By operation's end she only had a quarter of her stomach left and even less of her bowel. So severe were her injuries, the surgeons had to remove what organs couldn't be saved so they could save her.

It wasn't Harrison that was going to nearly kill her—it was Hadley. Did she ever get handed a break in life?

With a hysterectomy and the removal of most of her stomach and her bowel, there wasn't much left of Pearl and she spent quite some years recovering slowly. She and Hadley remained at the Derby house.

As a direct result of Pearl's injuries, she was no longer physiologically able to drink alcohol. She could hardly eat, but her drinking days stopped. She went on to be a tea drinker. Pearl didn't smoke or swallow pills; the only vice that continued to grip her was sadness, and she took that with her into the afterlife.

For now, she was about to be buoyed by the return of someone she thought she had lost forever.

Kylie walked in and said, "Hi, I'm alive. I left you, Mum, because all we did was fight and I'd had enough, so I left. But right now, I need my mum."

The past years in another state with a controlling, volatile man hadn't been generous to her. Kylie came home to recover. She endured the sexual advances of Hadley, but told him to "fuck off", and he didn't make any further snake-riddled moves.

Hadley was a repulsive man who went on to introduce Kylie to her future husband, as they both worked at the tin mine. From here, she and Adam went on to be in a domestically violent coupling that would incur her spirit further misrepresentation. She was a good person, Kylie; that isn't to be mistaken.

All four individuals eventually left Derby and moved to the suburb of Ringarooma, still a small, quiet country town. Kylie and her husband stayed to raise their family.

Pearl and Hadley returned to Melbourne, where they lived in a caravan in the paddock next to Kristen and Michael's house for some time. Eventually, they took up permanency at the Hastings caravan park, and it was there that Pearl lived until her death.

The cancer finally got her.

Goodbye, may peace have hold of your hand.

The End.

Of a generation.

TO SUMMON ON THE STRONGEST NOTE

Her name is Kendall, and she's the one who spoke. That's why this chapter is here to finish.

She is the woman you passed and didn't account for at all that was her past. She was kind, but that wouldn't enter your mind. She was strong, but don't get it wrong, it wasn't given to her. She earned it because yes, she had been worked to the bone. She had a dynamic heart, which is the reason any of us should have 'belief' as our mantra of "where do we start?" One of the first things she will tell you is, "Don't ever feel like you are alone, because you're not. I'm here to tell you, you're not."

She is the courage of the story. She was the light that took out the fight.

This is her account of what she saw; these are her words from a voice that kept silence in chords before a niece asked her to speak. Two years after I asked, she agreed to their release. I haven't taken this lightly. You can't when you're responsible for the enormity of someone's life.

She was the eldest. The one who remembered most, who saw more, heard more, and watched it all. That makes her the one who bore more than the others, and all this happened in her formative years. Did she ever have a chance? What occurred to her started long before she, her sisters, and Mum left Tasman Island in July 1959, without their Dad. It was the start of life, an isolating one of being a keeper's kid, and she was learning a most desperate view.

Though she had some fun, and she'll show you laughter with several of her memories, most of what she recalls is horror and destruction that thrashed down upon her bitterly. It may be conceived that the winds that lashed the islands were an exact match to the temperaments of the adult occupants. Blasting winds that nailed pain into everything they sailed past. Whoosh! Get hit with that for nine years and see if you can stand clearly, or if you are brought to your knees. This woman met her hard hitters head on with significant strength.

Kendall was no quitter.

First, she wants you to know her 'Dad Harrison' was a strong man, fit and able. He took to her as company; she was his offsider. Where she could go with him, he wanted her along. She was his little mate, and he taught her what he knew. That included everything he could share, including guns, animal slaughtering, watch fixing, and hard working. He was tough. He taught her much and he did love her, but he also hurt her. He had his own demons, but he also had purpose: to provide for his family and be a friend to someone, and have someone be a friend to him. Kendall was the friend claimed, and friends and foes they became.

She remembers he was very familiar with firearms, particularly rifles. They were a way of life and survival to him. They were ever-so present again on an isolated land where you had to slaughter your food stock to eat, to kill vermin, and even perhaps for protection from the arrival of strangers, which was not so unlikely given they were living in an isolated way.

He would spend hours with Kendall teaching her to aim a rifle and shoot a target. This exercise was a bonding experience for Harrison, and from the age of five, he regularly taught Kendall the skill of target shooting. She still has faith in her shooting ability today. Kendall thinks she was the son Harrison left behind, and that is something she would have felt at the time.

It wasn't just rifle shooting he taught her. He also taught her what it was like as a child to be beaten. Harrison knew all about this. Just like his dad, Harrison, too, possibly had delusions of grandeur and authority. When he was thrashing his loved ones with his hands, it was the rifle he used as a means of abuse. He continued the cycle.

He most unfortunately taught Kendall what it was like to be savaged as a child. There was no way of escaping her destiny; she was born into life to a man and woman whose troubles ruled them. By the time she arrived, her dad was a wretched man and her mother no match to conquer that. So many times did Pearl and Harrison hit Kendall about her head, her vision was altered. She would be smacked over the back of the head with either a fist or the butt of a gun; her ear would be twisted, and sometimes her throat grabbed. And she definitely knew what it felt like to be slapped.

Kendall said that Harrison used the .22 rifle as a control threat. As you'd expect, she hadn't much warmth in her voice when she told me of the times he raised his gun at her. He would gesture at her with it to manipulate her. Fear was the trigger, and any minute it could be pulled, but always that feeling would linger. In turn, he would get his family to do what he told them.

As I was sitting with Kendall, listening to words I had never heard before, I was blanketed with shock. She stated clearly, "He was cruel beyond cruel."

Kendall continued, "I will never forget the day I looked down the barrel of the .22 rifle when he had it pointed at my head and told me, 'go and shut that baby up or I will shoot you.'"

He was referring to the crying Kylie, who was only a baby, and at the time was ill. In utter terror Kendall went and hushed her sister.

I was still in shock, trying to grapple with how a child copes with such a life. What I find remarkable about my aunty is not only did she endure such horror, such terror, but that she went on to protect life as much as she could while on the islands.

One day she was told to hide all the knives and weapons in the shed. "God, I'll never forget that day," she said. I had read it in Pearl's witness statement, but I had not known how or why it came about, or its authenticity.

Kendall said, "It was true that you had to hide the knives and guns and axes from him because he was a pure nut case. He was born an alcoholic and he was ruled by his addiction." She stated this calmly, but also with all the pain of that knowledge. And as I look at my aunt, I wonder how she has such a soft face and soul. She explained there were slaughter knives on the island as each keeper had their own livestock on which they survived. Killing sheep was the reason such weaponry was available, but Harrison threatened to use them to hurt his family. The family's way of thinking was that if you hid the blade, you saved your throat.

All right, I just need to stop here. Imagine living in that environment. You never know whether you are safe, or when—and if—you can ever let your guard down. There's no time for innocence.

Our conversation was open and honest. We agreed that it was not a very courageous way to behave, given a gun was going to win against a defenseless child and woman anytime. What a gutless coward Harrison was. How dare he. How dare his weakness inflict such hurt on those he was supposed to love, to protect.

As I was watching this innocent woman relay her memories, part of me wished Harrison was alive so I could let him know how powerful a woman can be in our society today—gun or no gun. There would be nowhere for him to hide from me—not today, not tomorrow. And in the present, he is unable to hide his yesterdays from me. For I know how he lived.

For as long as Kendall could recall, she was given orders and chores to do. She was the go-getter, the fetcher, the calmer, and the nurse. Her love was in the care and service of others. Her identity and the concept of love was entwined in caring for them. If she was giving, she was receiving love. She was pleasing those who expected her to carry out her duties, and they were showing her—both directly and indirectly—approval for her doing so. It was engagement, the interaction when they openly showed her gratitude by thanking her or smiling at her or even the rare occasion of being praised, which encouraged her to care through chores.

She was granted approval if she wasn't chastised or beaten, so even in their silence, in being left alone, she was told she was doing the right thing. The message in the silence was, 'You are doing a good job, and we have nothing to be on your case about.' She was being groomed to care for others, and learning to be loved for it.

The lists of chores were similar on all the islands. It was just the scenery of isolation that changed. The inside duties included cleaning and washing furniture and all homewares. Mainly, though, it was all cooking and food preparation. She can still smell the fresh bread baking in the oven she cooked daily. She made beds, cleaned sheets, hung out washing and brought it in and folded it. This may sound menial, but when you are a child and you're facing gale-force winds, it's a perilous job.

There were times when the linen would be put on the line and within an hour it had vanished. Literally swept away by the sheer force of nature. The winds on these islands were unbearable, and you could forget about brushing your hair, because once you stood outside, your hair was at its mercy. There were calm days, but those were rare. That's the reality of it. Unless you have stepped on an island within the sea, you could not possibly envisage how intoxicatingly suffocating living in such conditions would be. Even the sound of the winds would have torturous effects. Given their playtime had a near-to-constant repeat of this sound, it wouldn't have been too inviting to participate, but what choice did they have?

Even with this, Kendall did everything she could as her mum's helper. Kendall's role extended to being big sister to her sisters, and entertaining them. They made everything they ate, and if something broke, they had to fix it however they could. Pearl was a lousy sewer, but she had to darn socks and re-pin buttons on coats and the like. Where she lacked ability, Kendall held the needle and fixed broken dolls' limbs, repaired dress straps, and all things haberdashery.

Her mum "wasn't the best chef." She laughed about the island's culinary collection, but she did make excellent jams, which Pearl can claim. She would stir the ladle through the fruit they had ordered from the supply ship. The bread they made daily was baked in ovens heated by briquettes; those, too, were brought in from the supply ship. There was no gas supply to the islands, and fresh water was collected from rainfall and stored in tanks. It rained substantially, so there was no concern of waterless living.

She thinks it was from the kitchens of the Eddystone, Maatsuyker and Tasman Islands that Kendall began learning to cook. I would guess that between then and now, she has set thousands of tables in preparation for her meals.

For as much she was the beaver inside, she was even more so outside with her dad. Because whilst he had the capacity to be a "nut case," as she described him, she was still her dad's helper. She fed the chickens and all the other animals, including the livestock, which consisted of horses, cattle, goats, and sheep. She would bring in wood for the fires, rake debris, sweep and clean anything that needed neatening up. She would do all the chores in the morning, and by mid-morning she began her homeschooling with Pearl.

The government sent the education curriculum to the families, and the parents were responsible for the homeschooling. She scoffed and laughed at Pearl's homeschooling abilities, and said, "Well, at least the old duck taught us how to read. She did that much. Wouldn't credit her for anything else, but she did that."

After the school tasks were completed, the children were free to play.

Kendall sees that she was fortunate in many ways, as she had an entire island as her very own playground. She took advantage of the skills and mannerisms Harrison had been teaching and became the adventurer. She knew the layout of the islands and sought her own expeditions. It was also a way of getting away from everyone; her time for herself.

Throughout her childhood, she had three islands to search and explore, and in doing so she developed her love of all things green. The islands were full of untamed foliage, and covered in natural formations such as crevices, slopes, dips, and grand expanses of bushlands—all for her to inspect. Kendall knew all the hiding spots and loved looking at the trees and grasses. At each new lighthouse posting, she established vegetable gardens, and was at each island long enough to see the fruits of her labor. There was joy at harvesting crops on numerous occasions. It's the simplest things in life that give joy, and Kendall had it.

She and Kristen used to have lengthy arguments about whether the world had more green or blue in it. Kendall was in the all-things-green corner, and Kristen was in the all-things-blue corner. Kristen's point was that the sky was bigger than the grass and trees. Even today the disagreement stands. Kendall's love of nature has never stopped. She says she would be very comfortable talking to a tree or plant.

The following says it all.

I asked Kendall if she knew she was about to leave the island when they escaped off Tasman, and she said, "No. If I had, I would have grabbed my garden seeds." She had received garden seeds as a gift for her Christmas present that year, and of all her belongings, she treasured this small bag of garden seeds the most.

Kendall does not remember much of the other families with whom they shared the island. Whilst each family worked together, they also kept to themselves. She remembers families and other children, but not their names or situation.

As the mood shifted throughout our discussion, I asked her if there were any happy times on the islands. She instantly said there was, but seemed startled at linking happiness and childhood together. "Happy times?" she stated, gazing heavenward.

Yes, there were thankfully, and it was a relief to hear about those times amidst the fear and abuse and isolation.

The happy times were when the supply ship would arrive, and the keeper's families would cart the goods to their various intended locations. The men would be working, and thus Kendall and her sisters knew their father was not around.

There is sadness in this dynamic. You're happy because your dad will be occupied and won't be able to inflict harm. When Harrison was busy, happiness returned to Kendall and her sisters. Scarred by the hurt, but this absence was innately a breath of fresh air, and they breathe that happiness in deep.

These girls were born happy, normal, living creatures; capable of appreciating what was before them. They could read situations where they were safe, and sadly that means they knew what it felt like to not be safe.

As the ship docked off the island, it brought excitement because supplies were coming in, and it brought a form of contact from the outside world, which was supported by the buzz of the island working to unload the supplies. Taking them to various homes, unpacking the goods, seeing the new items, and being ecstatic about what they were receiving was a thrill.

Good often brings upon good. Even waving goodbye to the supply ship played its role in the happiness of the island's atmosphere. It was like, "We are happy to wave goodbye to you in thanks for our goods, but also because your visit means we haven't been forgotten." It is the human-to-human aspect of interaction. "We have a relationship with you because you will return, and you bring us goods that make us happy, so we are happy about you."

They were also pleased about one particular item. Amongst the supplies was a tin of boiled lollies. Every time the supplies arrived, what the Four Ks did was sift through the tin to be the one to find the prize. Every tin had one special particular lollie in it. There was only one that had a beetle imprint on it. It was like a version of lucky dip, but lighthouse rules of first to find wins. Simple things, smile to it brings.

There were the times when they could watch the whales swim past their home and follow dolphins playing in the ocean. They watched the Sydney to Hobart yacht race to their final destination every year, and everything else that swam past or amongst the island's shores and edges. When the weather allowed, they would be taken to the jetty to swim in the safe waters. Here they could play in the rock pools and forage for crabs, starfish, and any other living sea inhabitant they could find.

Kendall recalled being taken camping on a number of occasions. These trips occurred on and off the islands. She remembered staying on Maatsuyker Island. They had set up the tent and made camp when unbeknownst to them, as they were in the tent giggling, the horse spotted their activity and decided to join in. He came over and put his head in the tent and pulled the tent down on the girls.

This had Kendall laughing as if it happened yesterday. She told me through her laughter, "The bloody thing just came over and thought I'll have a look at what's going on here and sticks its head in, looks at us. This big head is just staring at us and we all started squealing and laughing. And it thinks, I've had enough of this, and yanks its stupid bloody head out and in doing so pulls the tent down."

She was still laughing, and it was lovely to watch. "Never forget it," she said. "Bloody stupid horse." The horse was there to pull the cart up and down the island. He was an old, docile friendly sort of giant, and was liked by Kendall.

I wondered if there were toys to play with as I was aware of the stark living conditions they had grown up in. She told me there were. Not a lot, but they did have toys and they had school books—again not a lot, just whatever the authorities supplied them with.

But it was their imagination that helped create their fun. On one of the islands they played with a sled, riding it downhill and ploughing into the hay bales they had stacked one on top of the other. They thoroughly loved this, and it created loads of fun for them until the hay bales were removed and the sled put away. Perhaps the children had forgotten about the perils of living on islands with cliff faces that would frequently take sheep to their death upon slipping and falling into the abyss.

Kendall also recalled a time when the Four Ks and some other children were chased by a mad bull. She started laughing again. She legitimately couldn't believe someone wasn't hurt. "It was a large beast, and it moved fast." They were possibly harassing it and caught its attention and aggravation.

The bull charged.

They bolted.

But you can only run so far on an island before you reach an edge. They quickly reached that edge and with nowhere else to go, they climbed up a tree. All the children were hanging onto this tree for dear life as the angry bull was intent on getting to the screaming kids. The children's screams were heard by the adults, and the men came to the rescue of the hung-out juniors.

Unfortunately, the bull was eventually put down. It was considered a menace, and the island community shared the meat. The children continued living on an island where they had free range to make their own fun, and with full bellies for weeks. And not a hint of sadness about the bull's outcome. That's not what life was about, what island survival was about.

Kendall was on a roll now, and she was remembering more and more happy times. Kate had a habit of sleepwalking. One evening she disappeared. Alerted to her disappearing act, it was Kendall and her mum who were ordered by an angry Harrison to find Kate. By the middle of the night, in blowing gales of freezing wind, Pearl and Kendall held tight to their flashlights as they searched for the young Kate. They couldn't find her, and in their distress, they looked down some of the cliff faces just in case she had taken herself off one of the edges. They even searched inside the other homes, but to no avail, she couldn't be found.

It wasn't until a crying Pearl, who was sitting on the sofa in her lounge room, looked up and saw a small piece of white cloth in the chimney of the fireplace that they had a clue. Upon closer inspection, it was Kate's nightie with a sleeping Kate comfortably snuggled in the fireplace's chimney. She was retrieved and put to bed. The fireplace was covered over the next day.

I asked Kendall what she loved about being an 'island kid.'

She replied so enthusiastically, it was fantastic. I got to enjoy and experience seeing her come alive while she recounted the times she watched the sheep being dipped. She said, "I know I'm mad, and it's a weird thing to love, but I did, I loved watching the sheep getting dipped." She would watch the process on all the islands she lived, and loved the fact they would come out of the dipping clean, like they were being bathed. After this she would walk around in her jodhpurs and gum boots and be one with nature—sheep and all.

Before we knew it, there were numerous reasons to remember fun in her childhood. She told me of the times they would buy new shoes and coats on their holidays, and how they always had what they needed.

We were nearing the end of Kendall's happy memories, and I began to think of questions that were coming to me as a result of the information I had been loaded up with. My first was why the isolation? And then how did he get away with the beatings?

I was churning about the wider picture of this information, and Kendall could see that I had stopped to consider. She was agreeable with my thought pattern, and we entered longer discussions. We wanted to identify why we thought Harrison and Pearl deliberately chose to take to a life of isolation. Kendall agreed that she, too, thinks both Harrison and Pearl had been hurt by others in their lives and wanted to run away from the pain.

I told her I could account for who hurt Harrison, but not Pearl just yet, but I would find out if it was there to be found. I had tracked Pearl's lineal genetic heritage and haven't yet uncovered explanations to cause and effect. Either nothing was there, or it was instantly buried and never aired.

Kendall said that she thinks her mother was a loner, that she just wanted to be left alone. She remembered her mum "didn't really like people, so being on an island would have suited that aspect of her needs. She just chose the wrong man to seek that with."

I agree with Kendall's assessment, but my thoughts shifted again to why she was attracted to the wrong men. Neither of us know.

I couldn't fathom taking myself or my children onto an island. I asked Kendall if she would, and she nailed it in her response: "What do you think I am? Mad or something? No thanks, I like people, not a lot, but more than none."

Oh, how we laughed. It takes a certain character to choose to go to an isolated position to live. They chose to run away from certain aspects of their lives, but the cost they paid was more damaging than the initial reason, especially in this case.

Along with the isolation, I had difficulty coming to terms with the level of violence Pearl and Kendall described that Harrison inflicted upon them. I believed their accounts, but my scrutiny did not balance with several presenting facets of the knowledge I had gained from the accounts of others. There were two starkly different portraits of Harrison, and that depended on who you spoke with.

I can believe people's accounts, but they need to be backed by evidence. There were three other families, and governing bodies present on the islands. *People* were present. This population was smaller than a country town. The lighthouse community per island could be counted on two hands. What did and did not go on in the presence of others in such a small space? How can there be such differing accounts considering the size of the community? Did no one speak of what they saw or heard? How exactly can a man get away with such brutality? How? Especially when I have heard from other sources that lived on the islands that Harrison was not a man of menace.

The families moved from island to island, and people within the island community knew of each other. This was especially true of those who were there in the network for long periods of time. People talk. People gossip, and if there is a reason for a person to rid themselves of another they don't like, then they will use that person's behavior to do so. What better way to get rid of Harrison than 'the man is a cruel nutcase who bashes his family?' Once that was said to the authorities, would the appropriate action have been taken? Not necessarily is a reality facing.

But...

Self-policing was taken seriously by the island community, and the logbooks were, more often than not, kept to absolute detail. There were no charges brought against Harrison, no reports, and this is from a community where a child from another family was reported for taking a biscuit. I just didn't get it, and part of me began to consider whether Harrison was truly bad, or if he was painted as such to suit the lies of another. It is a question worth asking and investigating.

I asked Kendall how bad the beatings were, and she said, "They were bad." She said they mostly took place in the house, and it was Pearl who bore the brunt of them. When asked, Kendall told me there were physical signs of the beatings: black eyes, fat lips, and bloodied noses were visible. "If they were looking, that was."

I asked Kendall how no one said anything or reported Harrison, and she said, "Because they turned a blind eye and looked the other way. It was none of their business, and they liked to keep it that way."

This meant they kept to themselves. Just because they were on an island together, didn't mean they were friends or that they even liked each other. There was another aspect that contributed to men getting away with questionable behavior from Kendall's perspective, and that was that women and children were deemed possessions and not much more. She, too, didn't understand how it went unreported, and added, "You would have to be deaf to not hear his yelling, and hear the screams." That sends shivers down my spine.

In my understanding of lighthouse family dynamics, it is true to say that they were the staunch, stereotypical 'men are men and women belong in the kitchen' ideals. The men, as per their essential duties, tended to the work of the lights, and when their shifts were over, they came down from the towers to a warm meal and bed to sleep in.

There were no female lighthouse keepers, no women who knew the craft of keeping the ships safe by working the beacons. Because to not have the knowledge was to keep the status quo and restrict the abilities of women on the ground, while the men took to the high status of the island's keeping.

In my need to understand the circumstances of living on lighthouse islands, I ordered a book, and as I was showing Kendall the pages of island history, upon seeing a photo I didn't think twice about, she stopped and pointed. "Yuck," she said with distaste. "I remember having to eat these stupid birds, there were stacks of them. Yuck, hated the bloody things. Awful they were." They would catch Mutton birds on the island, pluck their feathers, gut them, and then boil them. I agree with Kendall, yuck. My goodness did we laugh and gag.

I asked Kendall if Harrison spoke kindly to them, as the picture I was seeing only involved violence and yelling. Whilst I have heard people tell me he was incredibly charming, and I have seen the smiling face he had, I am unable to see Harrison as a regular human being. I have read the war transcripts, have seen that he was able to respect fellow human beings and authority, and that in the case of his two court martials, it is clear he was able to establish the difference between right and wrong. He served in the military for over six years; held employment in various capacities.

He was able to speak for himself before the magistrate at his attempted suicide hearing, but nowhere was it reported that he spoke to his family.

She responded by telling me that yes, he did, and he would say to them "come and give your dad a kiss." And then she told me of the times he taught her how to shoot, explaining the mechanics and skill involved, and how they would go swimming together and there would be laughter. I finally heard it. He communicated with them, and he also made them laugh. She then moved to something else she wanted me to know, telling me that Harrison himself was not foreign to deceitful behavior.

She recalled a time where he deliberately cut himself, slicing his hand so that he could get off the island to be with a woman he was having an affair with in Tasmania. I have located this documented entry in the official logbooks. He cuts his hand as he was butchering the sheep, but there was no mention of him taking leave. That doesn't mean he was not involved in an affair. He was a charming man and he did like women, but I can find no evidence to support this.

However, I wasn't there; Kendall was.

She told me of the times the family went on holidays to the beaches of Tasmania. They would also go fishing, and one time they found a snake and Harrison went off at them because "he wasn't too fond of snakes and didn't handle it well." She laughed. I guess she found humor in seeing her father scared by something.

Even though what I have been told is unproven, could be categorized as anecdotal, hearsay that has no supporting evidence, it is worth taking seriously. Based on the knowledge his daughter shared with me, it is my opinion that what Harrison Bennet inflicted upon his family would have him incarcerated for many years by current standards. He would be identified as not only a physical abuser, but also a psychological perpetrator.

On this I was told, "It was better when he was drunk because he would pass out," and then the girls and Pearl had some room to move. It's a pity this man was not taken to task for his child abuse by the other island employees.

Kendall remembered meeting Phillip for the first time when he came to Maatsuyker Island. She didn't remember when, and the logbooks cannot support her memory of the Bennet family and Harper being on Maatsuyker together, but that doesn't necessarily mean it didn't occur. Kendall believed he walked onto Maatsuyker as a relief keeper, saw his wife-to-be, and decided in his mind that he would marry this Pearl Joyce.

Kendall remembered the islands being a lot better off after Phillip found his way to them. He was easygoing and pleasant to be around. He treated them well, and he treated their mother with respect.

I asked if it was an obvious development. She didn't really remember anything obvious about what her mum and Phillip were up to, but she definitely remembered the day they left the island.

Her body shifted, as did her tone. "I'll never forget that day," she said. "It's the reason I freak out about being left behind. I hate the idea of being left out of anything since that day. It scares the hell out of me."

She recalled that her mum and Phillip "were taking a long time making the tea that morning." She noticed that they were fiddling around a lot, but she didn't think anything of it, and left to tend to her chores, which most certainly included feeding either the goats or chickens. Having done so, she made her way back to the house. It was here she realized for the first time they were about to get off the island.

She says as she entered, she was shaken by the fluster that was before her. She had never seen her mum or Phillip act like this ever, and she was yelled at to get a move on. There was no time to ask questions or grab anything—not even her garden seed. No time to think clearly. She didn't really know what was going on. It was a mass of panic and confusion.

Stunned, she ran to the front door where her family was about to leave without her. Had she not walked in the back door at that exact moment, she would have been left behind. She raced away from the house with nothing but her coat on.

Unbeknownst to her, Harrison had been drugged and was in the house unconscious. Although she didn't see him in any such position, she did suggest that he had been drugged. He had to have been. And she added there must have been a lot of planning done prior to this moment. She did not remember Harrison being locked up in any rooms. She didn't hear a sound from him either, not one. No muffles, no kicking or banging, no evidence to suggest anything other than he was incapacitated. She said, "The run down the island was full on, and there was no looking back."

Kendall says when they were leaving, they weren't sad; they were relieved and calm once they realized what they were doing. She says it was more of a relief to leave than a concern. "We wanted to escape him, and leaving the island life was a good idea, too." But the initial 'getting away' part was a frightening race.

All that Kendall could surmise from that time is that when they flew out of Tasmania, they were relieved, and they didn't really look back. She has a clear memory of how she felt at that time, and for the next eighteen months, she was happy as. "We were glad to get away from him," she said. "We had a new life, a better life."

I heard all of this, and I agree wholeheartedly. Removing themselves from Harrison was a good idea, and it was done the only way it could be

However, accepting of this, I did question that as a young girl, Kendall had bonded to Harrison. She called him 'Dad.'

For nine years he had been around. Then one day it was decided he wouldn't be. He was not there anymore, and no goodbyes were said.

I can't help but wonder how realistic that is. How does a child forget their dad? This dad was good to his daughters, too. They had love and care shown to them, and he provided for them. He wasn't always bad, and for a child, this can be forgivable. How the children of this man have been able to disengage any care, thought, or affiliation with him is questionable to me. I can hear them say, "We didn't look back. It was good that we got away." But I watch their inner turmoil and self-destructive processes, and I see unresolved issues that have come along with them from their past.

I care for my aunty and her sisters greatly, and most certainly my own mother too. For me, watching their pain is directly related to much more than the loathing they have for their father, which I see as the front of the mountain they really feel. All the rest is hidden inside, visible in their eyes, yet resting in their minds.

It has occurred to me they could have warped ownership of what happened to their father subconsciously. Was there any internal guilt they took on because they left their dad too? Do they feel any guilt or responsibility for their perceived part in how much destruction was in their lives? What did they do? They may reject this and not be aware of such feelings within them, but I cannot see how they have not associated themselves with some of the occurrences and choices they made. They were right in amongst it. It happened to them, and therefore part of that lives inside them.

I asked Kendall why she loved Phillip so much.

"Because he showed us love," she said. "Every Friday night he would bring home two bottles of beer and four bags of lollies for us. He gave us a happy life, a good life. He was a good man."

She told me that what we didn't see was that Phillip would come into the girl's room at night and kiss them in a loving, fatherly way. Every night, she says. He was to these girls the first experience of love. He showed them tenderness and kindness, and not once did he raise a hand to hurt them. It was clear from listening to Kendall that Phillip loved them unconditionally, and you can begin to see and appreciate why they saw him as their father and took his name.

He loved them, and they loved him. This isn't to be discredited, ever. It was possibly the only pure truism in her young years.

I then ask about his death, and as we have established a safe and calm space, she is able to do so.

She says it was the shouting she heard first, the pleading of a man whose voice she loved seeking to be spared from certain death. Harrison arrived in the morning's first light and served his last stand. He located the man he would blame in the mix of his own shame, and he would take out that name and its meaning.

Kendall says she watched this.

She saw Harrison, as cold as he was.

She is able to replay it and see it as if it was yesterday. She still has vivid and terrifying nightmares. She still wakes screaming, and she has had trouble sleeping her whole life. She carries these memories, and just like when they were on an island with nowhere to go, her memories also have nowhere to go. They become part of our character map, and there is always a tie between them and who we are today, who we are in our future.

So Harrison got his way. He's always with them.

At this point, I wonder why Harrison decided to kill himself where he did. He could have gone anywhere: his car, another location within walking distance, or he could have driven to another place. Perhaps he chose to die as soon as possible. A short walk to some bushes with no one around was the easiest and quickest choice. Or perhaps he wanted to be found; knew that he would be seen shooting himself and thus found to be taken away.

Or perhaps he wanted to hurt Pearl as much as possible and killing himself in her home, albeit outside, would never leave her or his daughters. If his memory of dying was as close to her as being on her property, then he would haunt her forever. Every time Pearl or the girls walked past where he killed himself, they had him with them.

Perhaps he didn't think this through and he just wanted it over with quickly.

Whatever the case, those who act with such evil intent, are not then held accountable. So even in death Harrison was a coward. He never answered for his crimes.

Kendall says he robbed everyone of everything that day, and she carries a lot of passion in her beliefs that suicide is one of the most selfish actions a person can take. And there are many people who would agree with her, especially in these circumstances.

In that moment, her pain was a devastation unfelt by many people in our world, and yet there were many who would know what it felt like for her. Her youthful soul was shattered. Her loss was immeasurable, and her life from there on was wrecked. She was thrown into a pit of hell topped over by barbed wire, and there was no escaping for decades.

Kendall and I sat and considered Pearl. Because what Kendall really needed at that time was nurture from her mum, especially when her dads were dead.

We agreed Pearl may have not been as spirited in her capacity to live since her time with Harrison. We wondered who she was prior to living on the island. How she grew up and how she saw life and who she saw herself as. We know she was never a hugging style of mum. She was not forthcoming with affection, and this transferred to other parenting methods. She was protective to a point, but she didn't embrace the outward showing of affection. With all that in mind, it is not a stretch of truth to suggest that after 1960, she never recovered from her personal devastation. We are of the mind that might have been enough for any person to render them lifeless but still of the breathing—a walking dead.

On that we agree; Pearl never came back to the joy she felt when with Phillip. In that sense, Harrison won the game of life. He check-mated her and wiped the board clear. This ripple affected the life of his eldest daughter, as it was she who had to fill the void that was left in her family. Kendall didn't get the love, didn't get the care. She was stuck in the pit, covered and alone.

It was up to her to learn that vital lesson in life: you're the only one who can save you. That's the stamp of this story. That's the line I really want you to read.

Life really is survival of the fittest.

There is a component of dog-eat-dog amongst family members that suffer from sibling rivalry. There is, of course, another side of this—of family members protecting one another.

Kendall's life had all of this. She had her sisters competing against her, often taking things from her and putting her down. The mental badgering was incessant from her sisters. Her mother was not innocent in this either. Pearl compared Kendall to her sisters, and would tell her to a fault how inferior she was in comparison. And yet, Pearl would speak to them in terms of sticking together and looking out for each other. This mixed messaging and insistent demands on Kendall pushed her to the point where she put herself in harm's way to save her sisters time and again. In her words: "it was better me than them."

When Kendall needed the protection only a mother could give, it is with sadness I write that it wasn't forthcoming. Pearl failed Kendall several times in the most appalling of ways.

Pearl's parenting style is conflicting. She generally did not hit the children, but there were a number of occasions where she did "go over the top", as told by Kendall. Kendall says Pearl was "very cranky a lot of the time", and "don't you worry, she could give you a whack as good as any."

So where does that leave perception? Not a lot of self-esteem, victim of beatings who also gave them to her daughters and wasn't happy a lot of the time.

I stand by what I have said; Pearl failed her daughter in a most inexplicable way during her life as a teenager, and I am not sure this sort of betrayal is ever repaired. Kendall and I agreed that when trust between two people is broken, it is broken forever. You may still see and speak to that person who has hurt you, but inside the trust is gone.

Imagine living with a woman you cannot trust, and that woman is your mum.

This dynamic gives you an insight into why the Four Ks do not necessarily have trusting relationships with each other today. They still bicker, they still fight, and some still put each other down. Trust has rotted away. It would explain why not all family members retain contact with each other, or either of the Bennet or Harper families.

Damage done is damage carried, and although three of the sisters see each other today, there is one who is estranged. And it boils down to bitterness and trust. A situation that is not unique but cannot be repaired.

Kendall and I discussed at length how it came to be that no one stayed around at all.

It wasn't that the girls or Pearl did not want to see the rest of the family. To Kendall, it felt like the Bennet and Harper families didn't want to see them. That they were abandoned by everyone.

"It was like we were just left there, and no one made a genuine effort to help us."

This may be attributed to several factors. In such a tragic set of circumstances, the devastation was so powerful that all the remaining family members could do was survive for themselves. Any association in a deep and meaningful sense may have been just too hard because of the pain on all sides.

From Pearl's point of view, and based on feelings amongst the girls, all they had left was each other, and with that they stuck together in treachery, not trust.

The reality is the women were raised from shattered trust, their role model was alive but realistically she was lost. There could possibly be an argument she struggled with this all along in her life as she "didn't really love herself," Kendall acknowledged. She "wasn't the sort that could be by herself, she had to have a man around." That is what Pearl directly and indirectly passed on to her own daughters. That was their teaching, the model to which to aspire. So, when they were at an age to be free, they were all partly broken before they were released. How do you trust yourself when you're modeled on a need to be with another when that other is criminally inclined?

Well, instinctively that's how.

All of them wanted to be loved, and they also wanted to escape. This may have been one of the reasons—among many others—why all of them searched for husbands as soon as they could. Albeit from a model on dependency, they were also, in part, their own saviors. It must be acknowledged that each of the Ks are fierce survivors, yet still soft enough to want to be loved.

They have all learnt what it means to get to the next day, and they all have enough spirit to want to live and strive for a life of happiness.

When Kendall and her first and only husband Ray met, she was a worker, a well-versed homemaker. He, too, was of hard work. As chemistry will have it, they matched, and thus she and her loving man set up a life and began building their future together. They wanted the lot, just as most do: the home, children, pets, and love.

Ray was a man of military enlistment and he was called to the National Services during the Vietnam War. He answered his country's call, and Kendall patiently waited for him. Upon his return, Ray and Kendall wanted to start a family. They also became part of the army life and community. The saddest and happiest part of what Kendall and Ray were going through at this time was that it was difficult for her to conceive. Her reproductive organs had been so damaged by her molester that it affected her right to bear her own child.

Never ones to give up, Ray and Kendall tried and tried and tried again, and through miscarriage after miscarriage their hope was kept alive, and finally her body held onto the life of her firstborn. She arrived in their world in March 1974. For the first time in her life, Kendall held her own kind and she fell in love with her daughter, Maddison.

Kendall took to mothering naturally, and she loved her first child enough that they decided she needed a sister or brother. They knew what lay ahead, but this time she didn't miscarry, and they called the pregnancy a miracle. In July 1976, Maddison was joined by her sister, who was lovingly known as Dakota. The family was now complete.

They moved about Australia as per Ray's postings for his military employment. They lived in the army communities of Puckapunyal, Sydney, Perth, and Townsville before returning to Carrum after Ray's retirement from service.

There was a large part of life where Kendall did not see her sisters and mother, and her family did not see her or Ray. The army life was theirs to live, and it took them away from constant physical contact as they moved regularly. Phone contact though was a regularity, but they just couldn't see what was going on behind closed doors.

During this time, it was to be expected that Kendall struggled and fought with her pain from her past; fought with her innate self-identity, her mind that had been poisoned by others' cruelty. It was a fierce battle.

She didn't come out of that pristine. That blood doesn't easily wash off. But she was able to collapse because she'd found her safety net. A man who loved her, and so to her knees she could fall because his love protected her.

Kendall suffered terribly from nightmares and bouts of a need for a solitary existence. She wasn't a diagnosed sufferer of depression, but she did have times where she shut down and stayed in her bedroom with the door closed. She would come out and be part of her life when she was ready, and she wasn't ever too long away, but she did become rendered into silence when this occurred.

Her daughters possibly didn't understand too well what their mum was experiencing when those situations arose, but they accepted it was part of who their mum was. She continued to cook, clean, and create a well-fed and cared-for home. They went on family outings and celebrated birthdays; they had existing friends and made new ones whenever they moved. What she did very well was that she stood up for herself and her family any time she had to. Being part of the small military communities, she was called upon to be the biggest lion in her savannah on numerous occasions.

She didn't seek counseling. She sought herself. As she battled, she learnt, and as she learnt, she grew. She kept employment in kitchens at hospitals and ran these kitchens perfectly. She, too, was very good at her job, just like her dad.

Kendall had friends, and those friends liked who she was. With this, she continued to grow. Yes, she made mistakes, and she got worse before she got better, but this woman and her fighting spirit weren't about to lose to her past. Her family grew up and her life changed with the decades, and she went with its style.

She loved her daughters better than she was loved, but they did feel her past. Nonetheless, they stuck together because the core of her love was her strongest teaching. She would always love them, and they would always love her even when angry with her. That alone was a triumph.

The daughters reached an age where it was time to leave her nest and pursue their own careers, but they kept closely in touch. Kendall had succeeded. Her daughters were well-balanced and healthy participants in our community, and they smiled just as beautifully as their mother.

This left her in her own peace and quiet. She and Ray had by now moved to the country and established a comfortable home-life. She still had daily contact with her daughters, and thus a source of love was ever-present. They went on to include her in their lives, and part of that were grandchildren of both the human and pet variety.

Here she established her haven, her own safe space and her own call to comfort her and her needs. Her final destination was built of genuine love. In this space, she would heal thoroughly. She was the reason she fought so hard, because she had always known wrong from right, good from bad, and now she had her own grace. Her mind began the best work yet on healing her past.

How Kendall overcame the psychological torment is an accomplishment grander than its feat. She had her father telling her she was no good, and not a kind word came her way even after he died. Her mother and sisters took on similar roles. She was so belittled that she can still tell you, "Have you ever been told that you are useless, stupid and no good to the point that you believe it?"

"Yes," I replied, "but I never believed it."

We come from the same blood line.

I know where she has been.

She was not useless at all.

Knowing what Kendall did for her sisters and mother, you

also know she was the sort of person who is a genuine success story. She was the hero of this story. She may not be famous, and to look at her you cannot grasp the enormity of her struggle. But if you knew, you could only admire her. She has found that life is about choices, decisions, nature, and seeing love blossom through self-nurturing. True, she never went to school past primary grades, but she is world-experienced and has a home most people strive for. She made it. She and Ray made it.

Kendall says we all have choices. "Choices to be better, choices to not hurt, choices to leave situations and choices to work, it's all a choice today."

More to the point, she was the chosen one in this family.

There is a passion to her other than being kind to others, and that is all things knitting. Pearl was a good knitter and always had a knitting bag by her lounge seat. It has been interesting to watch how all four of the Ks are avid knitters. There have been numerous attempts to instill this skill on the daughters of the daughters, but I think it is safe to say all five of us run a mile when we see the knitting needles and wool, and hear the words: "here, I'll show you."

Kendall knits every day, and she makes jumpers and scarves and booties, and all manner of things, which she sends to the needy. She is also well-known for driving to her favorite wool shop some eight hundred kilometers away. But she enjoys the travel and her freedom. She has also visited wool stores in various shops all over the world. You can't help but love the fact that she has found comfort in her thing, even if it is knitting.

I believe Kendall has the last word of all of us.

In 2009, we had been speaking for six months or so, and on this occasion, she was sound asleep in the space she had made her loving comfortable home. She was awoken and sat bolt upright and saw Harrison in the corner of her bedroom. She said she could see him standing there, wearing his bow tie as he stared back at her.

She said aloud to him, "I told you to leave me alone and go away." But Harrison stayed. So, she said, "Okay, Harry, I forgive you." But Harrison had no intention of leaving.

Kendall sensed this and said to him, "That's not what you want to hear, is it?" Harrison kept looking at her, so she sat there for a short while with him then said, "Dad, I forgive you. Dad, I forgive you." She then wished him well and told him to go to the light and be at peace.

He left, and she went back to sleep. What courage, what a connection, and what a brilliant way to say all is done, and all that awaits is ours to live.

All her life, Kendall had been unable to sleep well, but from that moment, she was able to finally be at peace.

This occurred in July 2009.

She called him "Dad" for the first time in fifty years. She said, "I forgive you."

He has left her, and Kendall said her words had lifted a holy great burden from her shoulders, and she has slept blissfully since.

There are women like her all over our world that we share our lives with; it just takes a moment of consideration to see them.

Kendall, I will always see you and I hope others do too.

A PARTING SHARE

The final word is to you, dear reader. If you have life situations that are part of your family's past or present, and you would like to know their factual basis, let no one stop you from finding it. Find the truth, be persistent for yourself in the body and mind you live in. Rely on yourself to be the one you can trust. I encourage it; I support such actions even in the face of repercussions, angst, and alienation.

No one has the right to lie to you, just as you do not have the right to lie to others. This work has been as much about truth-seeking as it has been about generational healing. I am not living with these characters' pain, and I would suggest to you that you do what's possible to not live with anyone else's pain either.

I am free, I have the truth, and that is the most courageous key I'll always use.

You, too.

All the best.

In strength,

Melissa

ACKNOWLEGMENTS

Suzan Trajanovksi
Jacky Claxton
Jasmine and Caleb
Violet Armstrong
Lyn Baker
John Cook
Karen Lee
Linda Atkinson
Editha Barnes (dec.)
Val, Tom and Max Lowe
Rhonda Peck
Judith Parish
Ray Clark (dec.)
Leslie, Gwen, and Sally Nichols
Maureen and Derwent Ogilvie (dec.)
Ray Claxton
Leola Lowe
Eileen West
Kevin and Dianne Dungey
Shirley Britter
Lorraine Yates
Graham and Karen Redfern
Helen Yates
Joan Primrose
Anthony Tregenza
John Tregenza
Robin Bowles
Catherine Deveny
Julie Postance
Amanda J Spedding
Stephanie Kakris
Nelly Murariu

ABOUT THE AUTHOR

Melissa Pearson grew up in Victoria, Australia. She's Australian-born but feels as though, she is made by the world. She esteems pure satisfactions in learning about all peoples of our earth. She has degrees in Community and Sport Psychology, and worked as an adviser in sport/business performance, court evidence testimony, and cognitive comprehension management.

An avid pursuant in matters of knowledge, she self-educates in principle, every day. Learning is a proponent that keeps her mind calm. She is home to a hyper-vigilant brain that is ever-searching and persistently occupied in reaching. She positions off the standard introvert scale and is better placed in obscurity, as most introverted intuitive empaths are.

She has two children, which she interprets as challenging natural love. She would list trust, truth, respect, and unassuming as the categories she sees best in herself and others.

She'll openly admit to having met death once, when it gurgled, hovering over her beaten head. Offering to which, you wouldn't want to hear that sound often. Then quickly apprising it, as one of the reasons she will never give up, and if you met her she wouldn't let you down.

www.ingramcontent.com/pod-product-compliance
Lightning Source LLC
Chambersburg PA
CBHW032024290426
44110CB00012B/664